IMAGES
of America

MINERAL WELLS

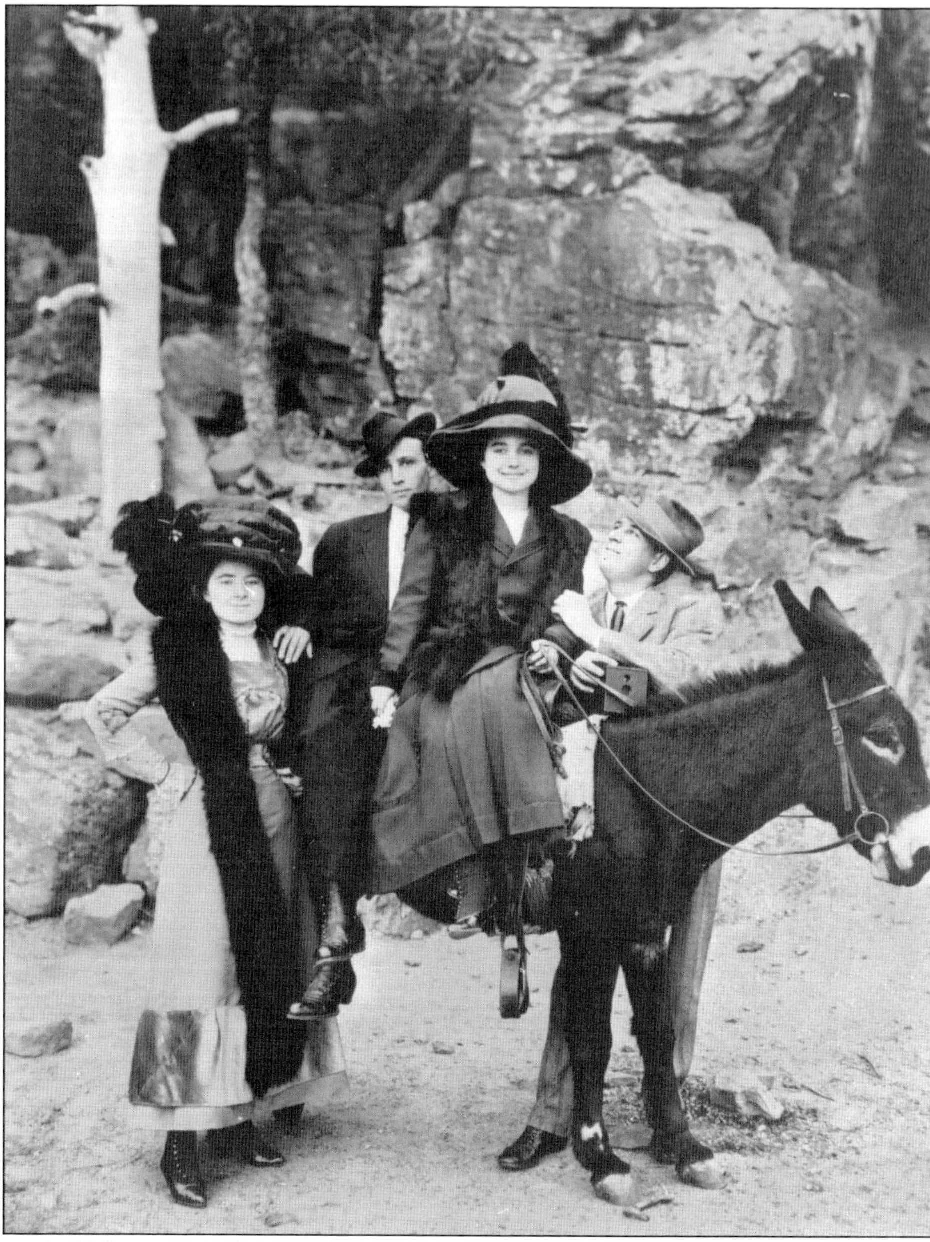

This early-20th-century photograph was taken on one of the donkey paths on East Mountain. J. C. McClure, an early photographer, first owned these donkeys but was killed while riding a wild stallion on Oak Avenue. J. L. Young and his wife then took over the donkeys and built a rock house on the trail as a backdrop for souvenir pictures. (Courtesy of Boyce Ditto Library, Weaver Collection.)

On the Cover: This 1910 fountain, located near the Famous Water Company, was one of several places in Mineral Wells serving free water to health-seekers looking for the elusive "Fountain of Youth." On the left is Ellie Landry of Dallas, and second from right is Mrs. William Whitehead Gardner of Lawrence, Texas. (Courtesy of Boyce Ditto Library, Weaver Collection.)

IMAGES
of America

MINERAL WELLS

Sue Seibert

ARCADIA
PUBLISHING

ISBN 978-0-7385-7985-6

Published by Arcadia Publishing
Charleston, South Carolina

Printed in the United States of America

Library of Congress Control Number: 2010940820

For all general information, please contact Arcadia Publishing:
Telephone 843-853-2070
Fax 843-853-0044
E-mail sales@arcadiapublishing.com
For customer service and orders:
Toll-Free 1-888-313-2665

Visit us on the Internet at www.arcadiapublishing.com

This book is dedicated to my husband, Raf Seibert, without whose help it would have been impossible.

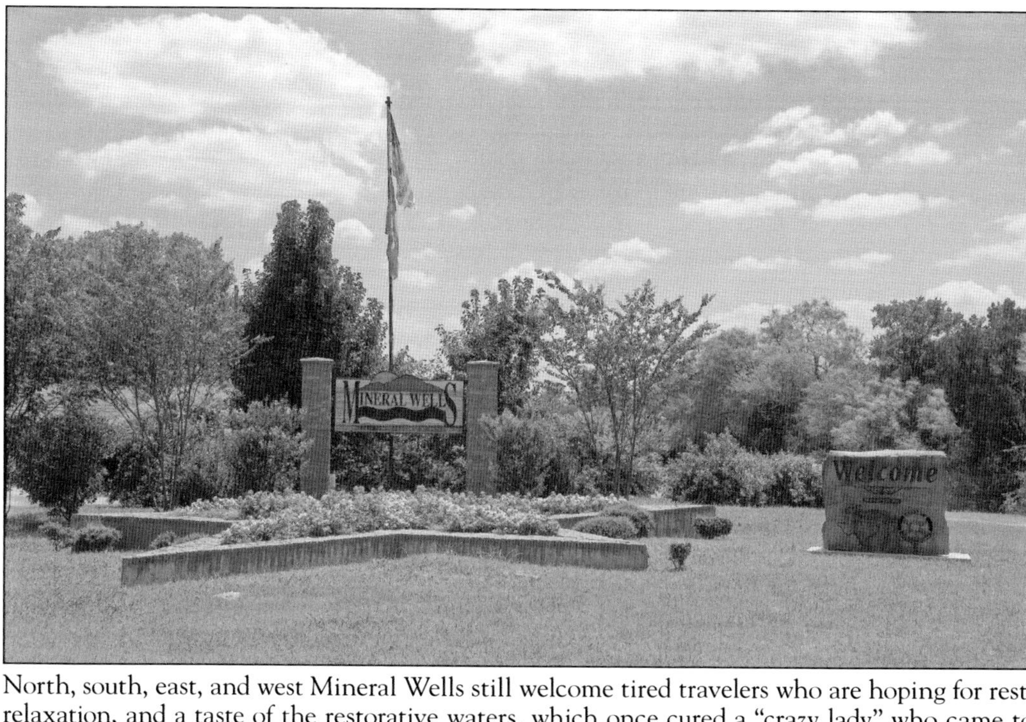

North, south, east, and west Mineral Wells still welcome tired travelers who are hoping for rest, relaxation, and a taste of the restorative waters, which once cured a "crazy lady" who came to Mineral Wells seeking to alleviate her madness, as they learn the colorful history of the place and perhaps chase a Baker Hotel ghost. (Photograph by Raf Seibert.)

Contents

Acknowledgments		6
Introduction		7
1.	The Earliest Days: Prehistory	9
2.	County and Town Frontier Settlement: 1830s–1900	15
3.	A Spa Town Is Born: 1900–1960s	39
4.	Petroleum, Brick, and the Economy: 1910–Present	85
5.	Military Presence: Indian Wars–Present	101
6.	The Fall and Rise of Mineral Wells: 1973–Present	119

ACKNOWLEDGMENTS

Mineral Wells is an area rich in history. Its history is not necessarily that of the Wild West—as is Palo Pinto County's—but the history of industries and businesses making a town grow in the midst of the Pinto Hills, a town that would be a beacon of rejuvenation and health for many people around the world.

Many people in Mineral Wells and the surrounding area have assisted with information and photographs for this book, and they have been happy to do so. They are acknowledged after each photograph.

Those who were particularly instrumental in helping this book come to life were Lou Hayes Warren, whose grandparents were early settlers; Doris Perry McConnell, whose great-grandfather Cicero Smith was one of the early entrepreneurs to market the waters and grow the town; Joyce Ann Murray Watson, whose grandfather built a café atop East Mountain to refresh the tourists after their donkey rides; Jim and Louise Dillard; Judith Richards Shubert, whose family pioneered the area; Lottie Williams Eubanks, owner of Century Flight Systems; Bob Kimbrough, whose great-grandfather Pat Gallagher built many area buildings; Doyle Marshall, author of *A Cry Unheard*; Sheila Brock Eggleston; and the Boyce Ditto Library, which provided photographs from the Col. Willie Casper and A. F. Weaver Collections.

Raf Seibert, my husband, provided most of the present-day photographs, listened to my thoughts, read my text, and gave me many ideas to enhance this book.

For more information about Mineral Wells history, please contact the following:

Mineral Wells Heritage Association/
Little Rock Schoolhouse Museum
P. O. Box 846
105 Northwest Fifth Avenue
Mineral Wells, TX 76068
Phone: 940-325-2726

Mineral Wells High School 50 Year Club
602 West Hubbard Street
Mineral Wells, TX 76067
Phone: 940-325-5600
50year08@att.net
www.50yearclub.org

Mineral Wells Area Chamber of Commerce
511 East Hubbard Street
P. O. Box 1408
Mineral Wells, TX 76067
Phone: 940-325-2557
info@mineralwellstx.com
www.mineralwellstx.com

Boyce Ditto Public Library
2300 Southeast Martin Luther King Jr. Street
Mineral Wells, TX 76067
Phone: 940-328-7880
library@mineralwellstx.gov
http://boycedittopubliclibrary.org/

INTRODUCTION

Mineral Wells is often described as "the town built on water," and certainly, water is what brought people, both Indians and white settlers, to the area. But what brought the water?

The Pennsylvanian Period was also called the Carboniferous Period because of the abundant coal deposits formed during this time. It was in this period that the land Mineral Wells sits upon was made. Thus "the town built on water" was first built on the sandstone, limestone, and shales of an earlier age.

In recorded history, William Alexander Anderson "Bigfoot" Wallace, a soldier and Texas Ranger, surveyed the frontier in 1837 and was probably the first white man to set foot in what is now Palo Pinto County. Before the Civil War, settlers began moving into the region, including Oliver Loving, Charles Goodnight, and Reuben Vaughan, all of whom established cattle ranches here in the 1850s.

In 1856, the Texas Legislature established Palo Pinto County from lands formerly assigned to Bosque and Navarro Counties.

There were strained relations between the settlers and the Indians who had roamed these beautiful hills for so many years. In 1854, the government set up the Brazos Indian Reservation northwest of Mineral Wells for bands from several tribes, such as the Delaware, Shawnee, Tonkawa, Wichita, and Caddo. There were many Native American depredations in the early settlement days, and whether they were caused by free-roaming Comanches or Kiowas passing through or by reservation Indians from Indian Territory (Oklahoma), most were attributed to those in the Brazos Reservation.

Over the years, several settlers were kidnapped by Comanches. The most locally significant was Sam Savage, who, at age 5 in 1866, was kidnapped from a ranch near present-day Cool, Texas, and taken to Indian Territory, where he was ransomed later the same year. As an adult and until his death, Savage lived in Mineral Wells.

Eleven years after Savage's abduction, the family of Judge James Alvis Lynch, age 50, moved from Denison, Texas, heading west to find a drier climate that would help his malaria. He and his wife, Armanda, also suffered from rheumatism.

As James and Armanda Lynch traveled, they heard of the terrifying attacks of the Comanches on white settlers farther west, so on Christmas Eve 1877 they decided to settle in beautiful Millsap Valley in the Pinto Hills, where Lynch purchased 80 acres for the price of $240.

James hauled water from the Brazos River for 4 miles to his land until well driller Johnny Adams dug a well for him. The water tasted strongly of minerals, and at first only the livestock drank it. But the family decided it was better to have water on their property than to haul it, and it seemed to have no harmful effects on the animals, so they began to drink the well water. As they drank the water, James and Armanda began to feel better. Eventually their arthritis was cured, and James became healthy and strong, taking on weight lost during his illness. By 1881, people were flocking to the Lynches' well, so James laid out the town, and the first stagecoach arrived the next year.

The town boomed as a health resort after 1885, when the Crazy Well was dug by "Uncle" Billy Wiggins. Crazy Water containing lithium, which is said to have cured a "crazy lady," was bottled and shipped throughout the country. People rushed to Mineral Wells to drink it and bathe in specially constructed bathhouses. J. C. Son, founder of the *Palo Pinto Star*, wrote articles extolling the virtues of the water in exchange for one of Judge James A. Lynch's town lots. The railroad reached Mineral Wells in 1891, and the first of several resort hotels, the Hexagon House, was opened in 1897.

Thus the story of healing mineral water in Mineral Wells was born. Hotels, spa resorts, and casinos sprang up around the town, and celebrities and just plain folk from across the country traveled to Mineral Wells to drink the waters and be cured of their ailments. At the same time, tourists and adventure-seekers came to view the spectacular beauty of the area. As people came to be entertained, businesspeople saw a market for donkey rides through the rocks and up the mountains to view the Brazos Valley below. They also opened souvenir shops, restaurants, water pavilions, and more hotels, most notably the Crazy Water Hotel and the Baker Hotel, built in 1929.

In the early 1900s, the Pennsylvanian Period once again affected the Mineral Wells area as oil and gas were discovered. Today Barnett Shale gas fields are still being drilled in the area. The geology of the area also helped the economy, as plants were built to produce brick and ceramics.

During the Indian Wars, Texas Rangers and U.S. cavalry patrolled the area. Then in 1923, Troop F, 124th Cavalry, was reorganized by the 112th Cavalry Regiment as a U.S. National Guard unit. Troop F was stationed in Mineral Wells along with the regimental band and was activated and sent to Fort Bliss from Mineral Wells in 1940.

In 1941, Mineral Wells' Camp Wolters became the largest infantry replacement center for the U.S. Army in World War II. From 1951 to 1956, Wolters became an air force base, and then it was transferred back to the army as Fort Wolters and became the primary helicopter training school during the Vietnam War. In 1973, Fort Wolters closed.

By 1920, the town had 400 mineral wells and was billed as "the South's greatest health resort." Many visitors were attracted each June to the Texas Health Festival. The population was 577 in 1890, and in 2000, it was 16,946.

In 1952, Mineral Wells was the host of the Republican State Convention in which delegates had the chance to vote for Dwight D. Eisenhower, a native Texan, and Robert A. Taft. The convention voted 33-5 in favor of Eisenhower.

Mineral Wells was the birthplace of Chester R. Upham. He was chairman of the Texas Republican Party from 1979 to 1983 and founder of Upham Oil and Gas Company in Mineral Wells and the Loveland Ski Area in Colorado. Other well-known people such as heart specialist Dr. O. H. "Bud" Frasier, astronaut Millie Hughes-Fulford, Texas senator Tom Creighton, and baseball player Aubrey Huff were raised in Mineral Wells.

Mineral Wells is on the rise again, as tourists from all over the country visit the area to partake of the waters, ride their motorcycles and bicycles through the hills, water-ski and fish, listen to music of local entertainers, and explore the natural beauty at Lake Mineral Wells State Park and Clark Gardens. They visit Mineral Wells Fossil Park and the historically significant Vietnam War Museum.

Although the town has remained a center for recreation, health, and retirement, it also has a healthy industrial base in the manufacturing of clay pipe, aircraft systems, plastics, electronic products, bricks, feeds, clothing, and other products. An extension of Weatherford College is also located in Mineral Wells.

One

The Earliest Days

Prehistory

Mineral Wells is a town built on mineral-rich water, and like the oil, gas, and clay in the area, all are the result of what happened here eons before man set foot in this section of the world. If it were not for these prehistoric events, Mineral Wells might very well have never existed at all.

During the Pennsylvanian Period, the Ouachita highlands bordered the eastern margin of several inland marine subbasins, including the area in which Mineral Wells is located. The Pennsylvanian and Mississippian sandstones and the Strawn, Marble Falls, and Ellenburger formations from that period have led to the production of oil and gas wells in the area as well as the healing minerals in the sediments, which were laid down in this period and deposited in the curative waters of Mineral Wells. The clay for local bricks comes from the prevalent shale in the area. The sediments created in the Pennsylvanian Period have enriched the area and given it an abundance of resources not found in other areas of Texas. Recently the Barnett Shale has been explored and developed, and more natural gas has been discovered in the area. The Barnett Shale is a geological formation located in the Ben Arch–Fort Worth Basin. It underlies the city of Fort Worth for at least 5,000 square miles.

Most of the rocks in the area are limestones, sandstones, or shales. The shales provide the clay minerals to make brick and ceramics. The sandstones and limestones provide the reservoir of water and hydrocarbons that have been so valuable to the region.

The water minerals include calcium, magnesium, potassium, bicarbonate, chloride, sulfate, fluoride, manganese, zinc, silica, and lithium. All these minerals are part of those sediments provided for today in that long-ago age.

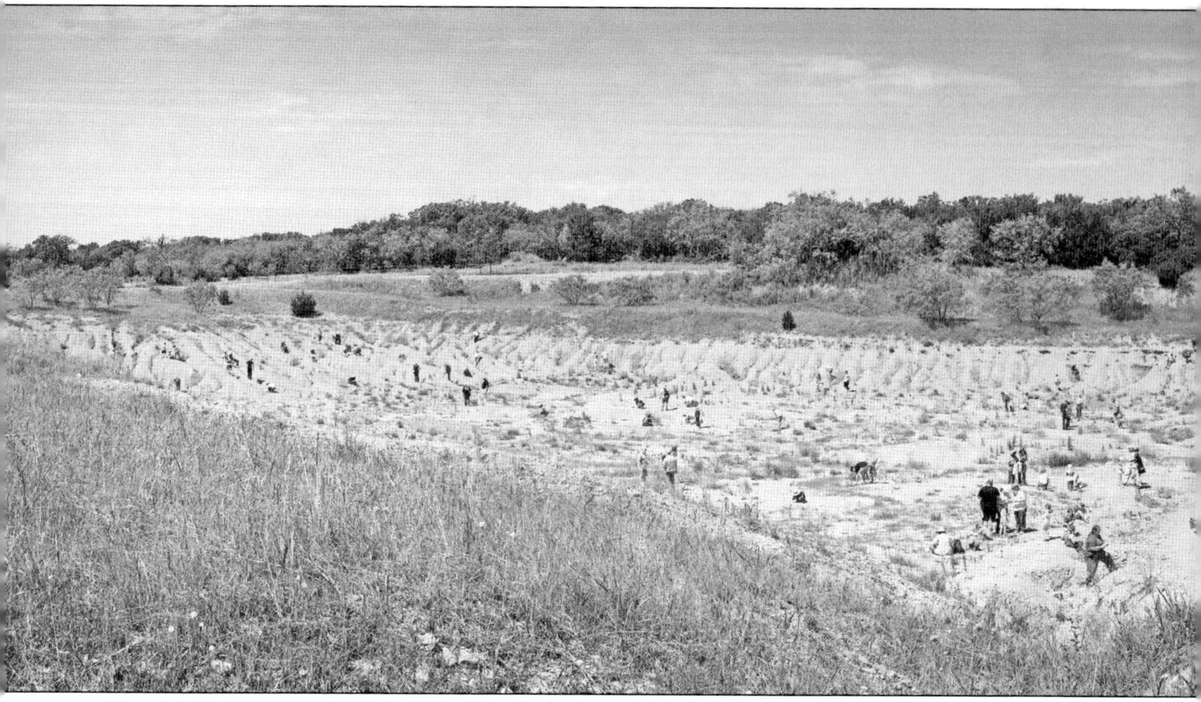

Due to these formations, the Dallas Paleontological Society, along with the City of Mineral Wells, has developed and opened Mineral Wells Fossil Park, which provides the fossil enthusiast, paleontologist, and student an excellent opportunity to see and collect well-preserved Pennsylvanian Period fossils with ease and abundance. These fossils have been dated to be just over 300 million years old, and one may collect and take the fossils out of the park for personal use. The park, as it

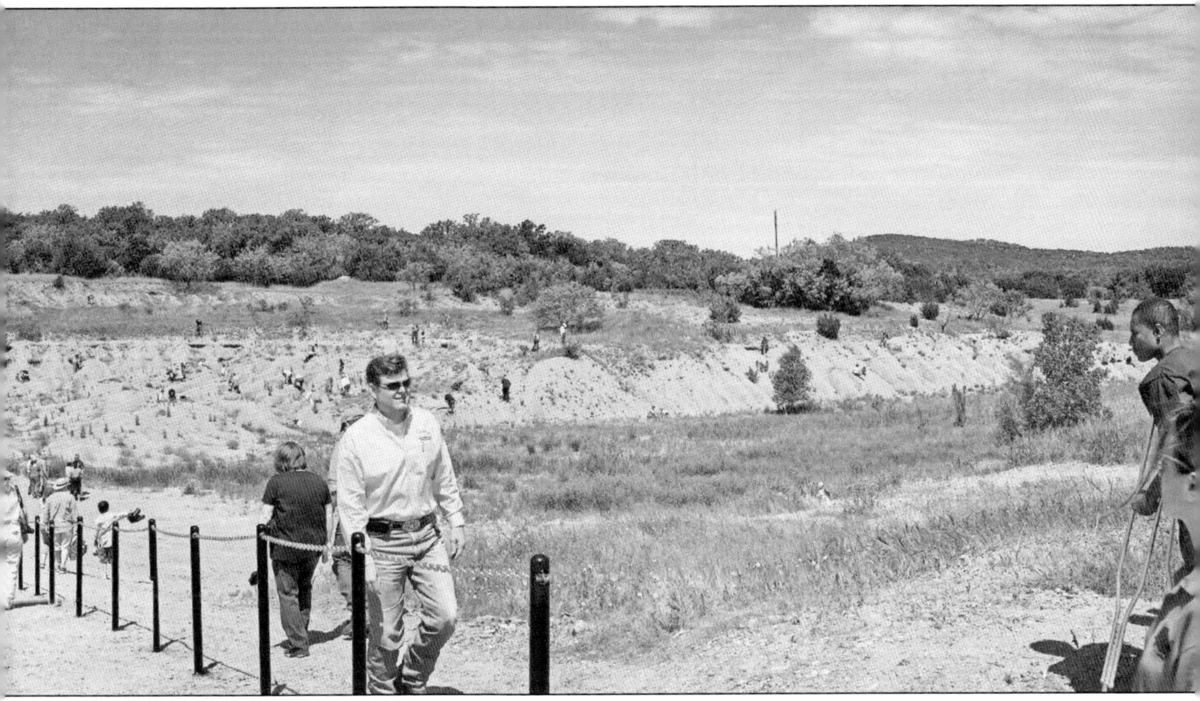

exists today, is the result of 20 years of erosion to the old City of Mineral Wells' landfill's borrow pit just west of town, which closed in the early 1990s. The erosion of the borrow pit has revealed fossils documenting ancient sea species of crinoids (sea lilies), echinoids (urchins), brachiopods, pelecypods (clams and oysters), bryozoans, corals, trilobites (arthropods), plants, and even primitive sharks. (Photograph by Raf Seibert.)

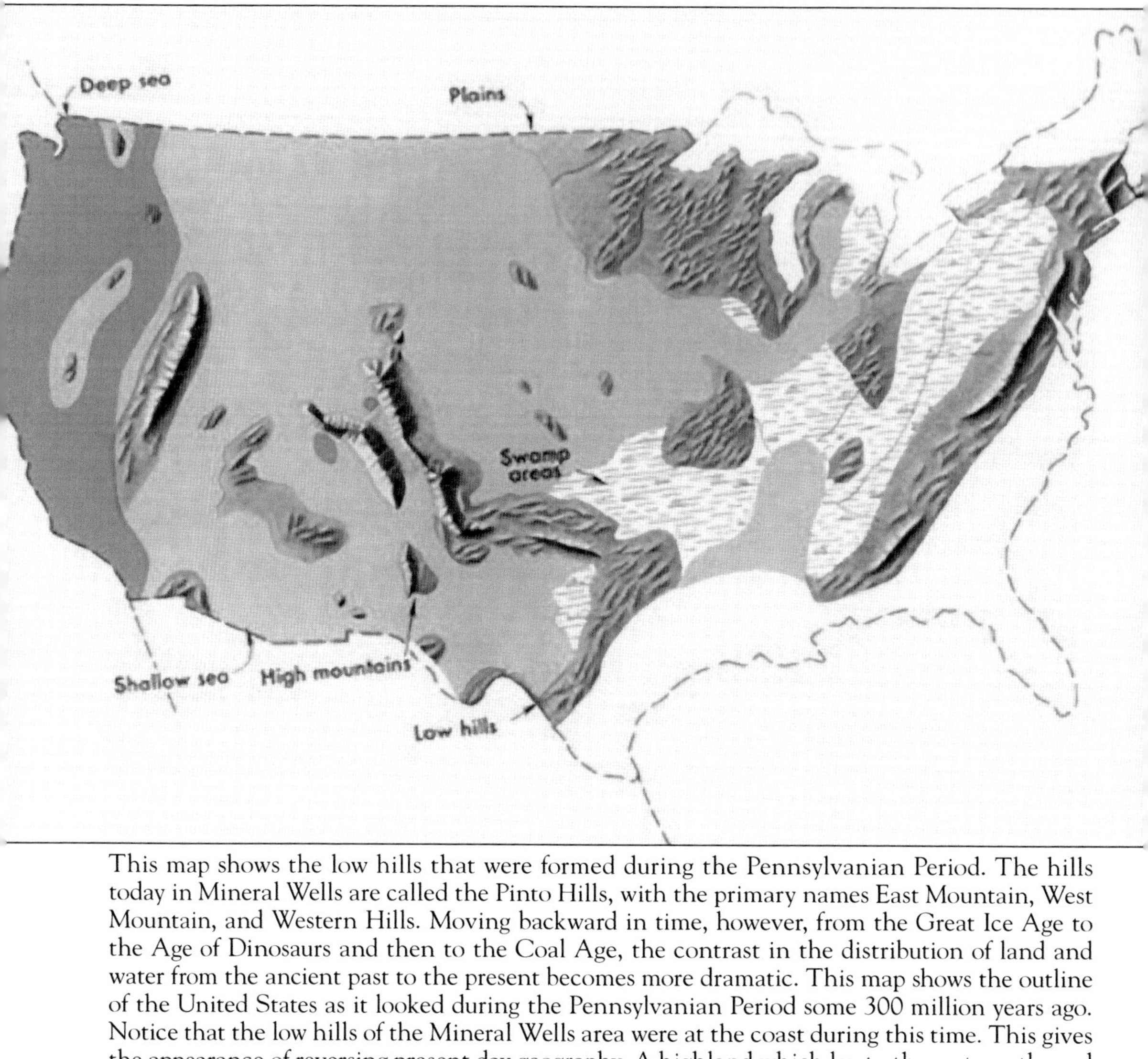

This map shows the low hills that were formed during the Pennsylvanian Period. The hills today in Mineral Wells are called the Pinto Hills, with the primary names East Mountain, West Mountain, and Western Hills. Moving backward in time, however, from the Great Ice Age to the Age of Dinosaurs and then to the Coal Age, the contrast in the distribution of land and water from the ancient past to the present becomes more dramatic. This map shows the outline of the United States as it looked during the Pennsylvanian Period some 300 million years ago. Notice that the low hills of the Mineral Wells area were at the coast during this time. This gives the appearance of reversing present-day geography. A highland which lay to the east, south, and north supplied much of the sedimentary debris that was spread over the Midwestern part of the United States. The Midwest was mainly a low swampy area in which scouring rushes and fern trees grew in profusion. Sediment was carried into the region from deltas to the east. (Courtesy of the U.S. Geological Survey.)

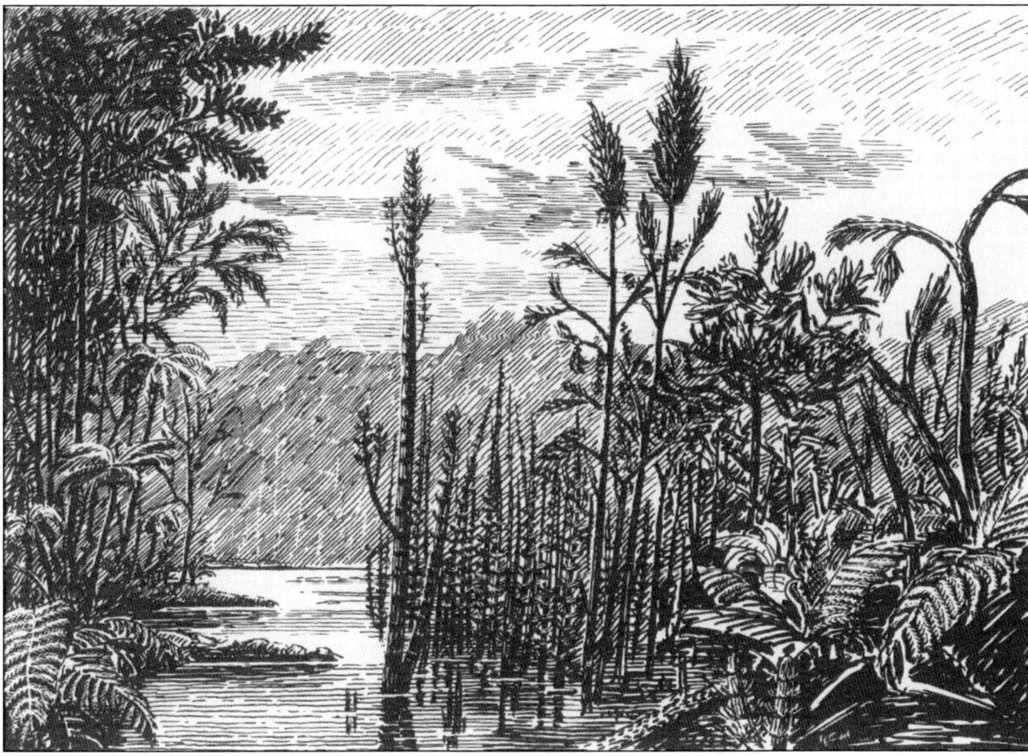

Raymond Cecil Moore of the Kansas Geological Survey devoted 57 years to the study of the Pennsylvanian Period geology. He rendered this depiction of a Pennsylvanian Period coal swap that would have been in the Mineral Wells area. (Courtesy of Kansas Geological Survey.)

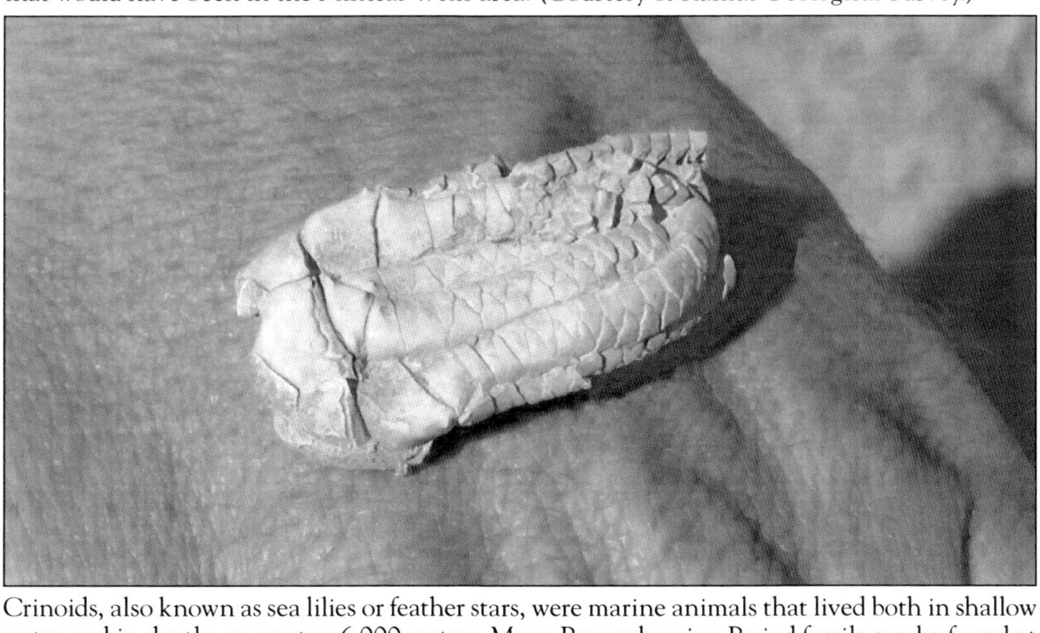

Crinoids, also known as sea lilies or feather stars, were marine animals that lived both in shallow water and in depths as great as 6,000 meters. Many Pennsylvanian Period fossils can be found at the Mineral Wells Fossil Park. The Dallas Paleontological Society works closely with locals to provide a scientific experience to all who visit. (Photograph by Lance Hall.)

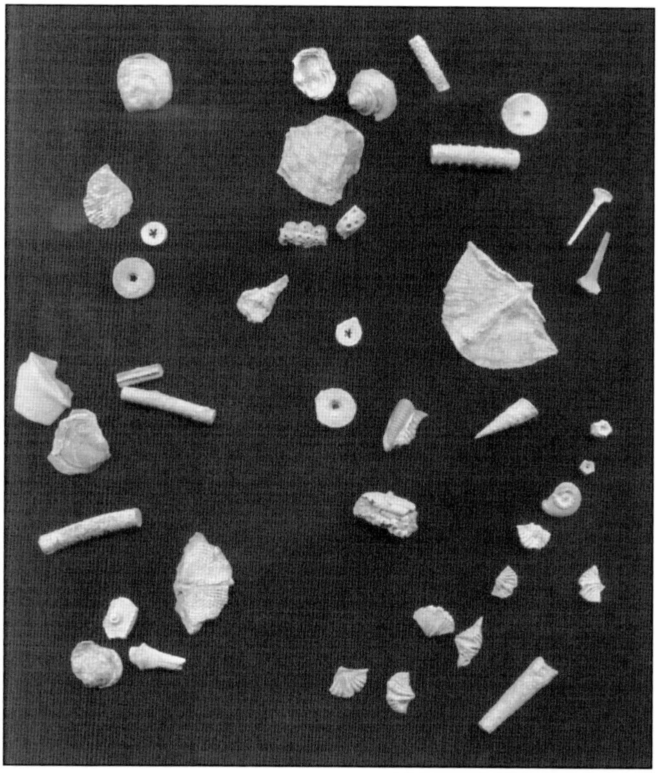

Local historian and fossil hunter Jim Dillard often goes to the Mineral Wells Fossil Park on hunting expeditions. Some of his most recent and interesting finds include several bits of marine animals, crinoids, and brachiopods. (Courtesy of Jim Dillard; photograph by Raf Seibert.)

Tourists from around the area hunt at the fossil park in Mineral Wells while enjoying the stark beauty of the West Texas landscape at the western edge of the Cross Timbers. (Photograph by Lance Hall.)

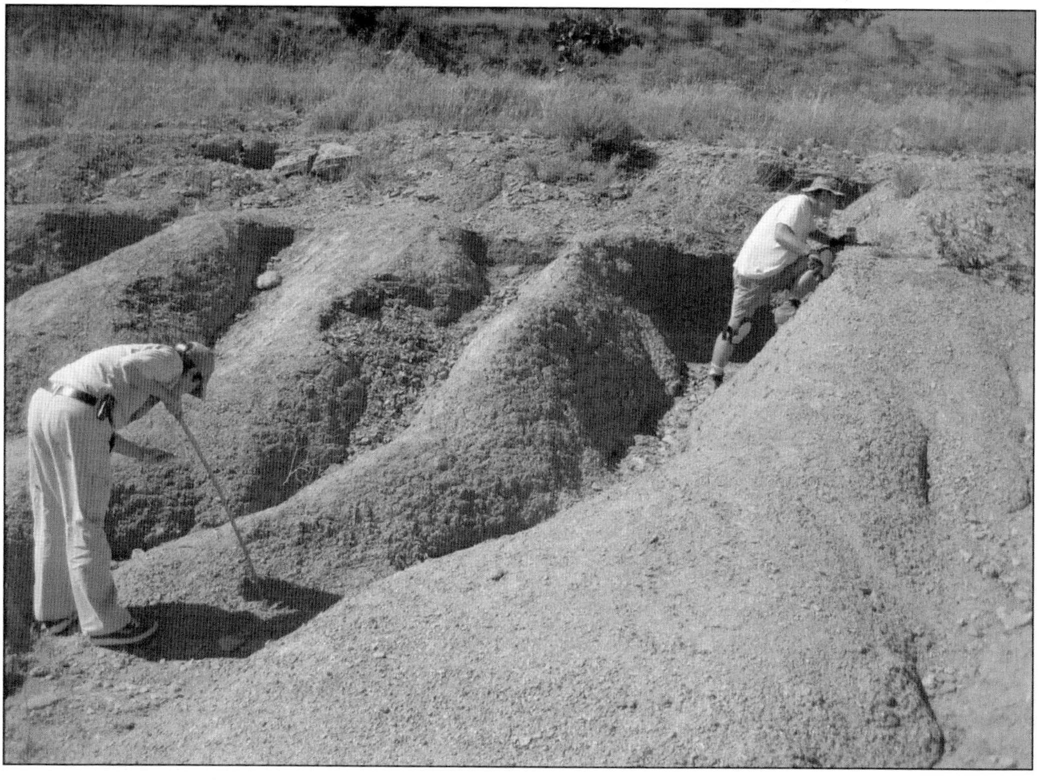

Two

County and Town Frontier Settlement 1830s–1900

The first people in the Mineral Wells area were Indians. There were several tribes in the territory, including the Delawares, Shawnees, Tonkawas, Wichitas, Caddoes, Keechis, Kiowas, and, of course, the Comanches. These peoples roamed free of fences and foreigners for hundreds of years. Then the settlers came.

The first white man in the area was probably William A. A. "Bigfoot" Wallace, who came to the Mineral Wells vicinity in 1837 to survey the frontier. The ranchers who came next included Oliver Loving, Charles Goodnight, and Reuben Vaughn, but they are part of the Palo Pinto County story, not the Mineral Wells story.

There were many Native American depredations in the middle of the 19th century. One of local significance was the Comanche raid on March 2, 1866, of the Bolin Savage and James Savage ranches about 6 miles east of Mineral Wells. Both Bolin and James were killed. Sam Savage (age 5), his brother, and two cousins were captured by the Indians and taken to Oklahoma, only to be ransomed a few months later for $414. When the Comanches captured Savage, they traveled to Oklahoma up what is now Northeast Sixth Avenue in Mineral Wells, a former major route for the Indians.

In 1877, Judge James A. Lynch and his wife, Armanda, left the town of Denison, Texas, with their 9 children and 50 head of livestock. The Lynches were searching for a drier climate because their family had been in poor health. James and Armanda both suffered from rheumatism, and James had malaria as well. They were stopped in their travels by news of Comanche attacks farther west, and on Christmas Eve 1877, one of their oxen collapsed and died after crossing the Brazos River, and another was struck by lightning. Thus they turned back 4 miles east of the river and settled in Millsap Valley, tucked into the beautiful Pinto Hills in what is now downtown Mineral Wells. There they dug a well and built a tent city, and then local tourism began. Thirteen years later, the town numbered 577 permanent inhabitants.

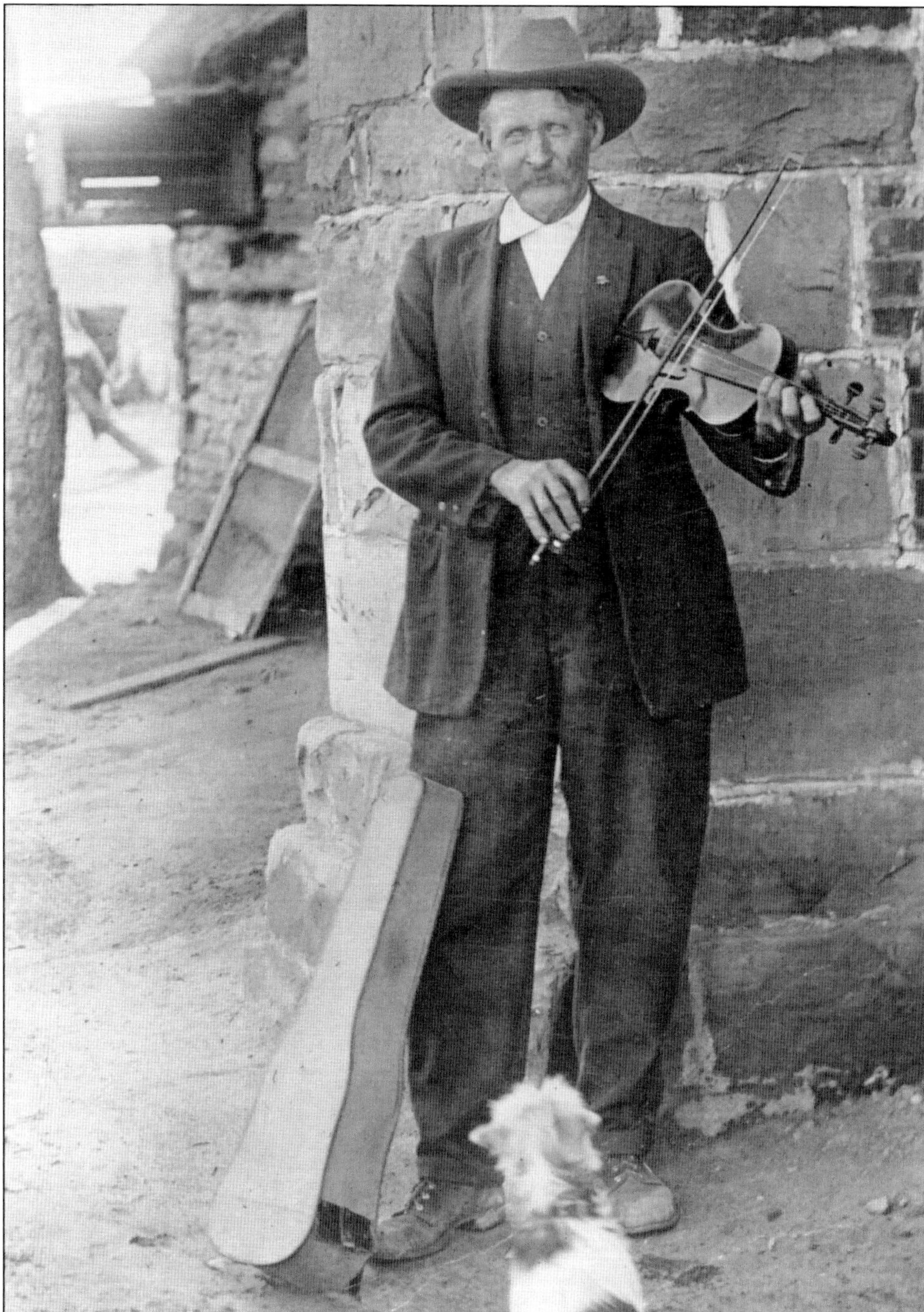

When he was five years old, Sam Savage was captured by Comanches on March 2, 1866. He was taken from the home of his father, Bolin Savage, on Sanchez Creek in Parker County. Bolin was killed, and Sam's brother Marion was shot in the shoulder but survived. Another brother, Jim, was also captured along with two cousins, Jennie and Jim. Jim was abandoned by the Indians and was later recovered by a posse pursuing them. The three other captives were ransomed several months later in Indian Territory by a white trader. (Courtesy of Doyle Marshall.)

In 1881, Sam Savage married Arizona Pierce, who, with her brother, had settled west of Mineral Wells in 1876. Sam and Arizona were married by Judge James A. Lynch, the founder of Mineral Wells. The Savages settled on Kent Mountain, located northwest of Mineral Wells, and lived there until they were elderly. They then moved into the cove that butts up against East Mountain on the east side, close to Northeast Sixth Avenue, which used to be a Comanche route from south to north. Sam became an acclaimed breakdown fiddler. They had five children—Sally, Martha, Bessie, Thomas, and Arthur C. Sam loved to hang out at the fire station or on his front porch, and he captivated people, even World War II soldiers, with the true story of his capture by the Comanches. He died at the age of 90 in 1951. (Both, courtesy of Doyle Marshall.)

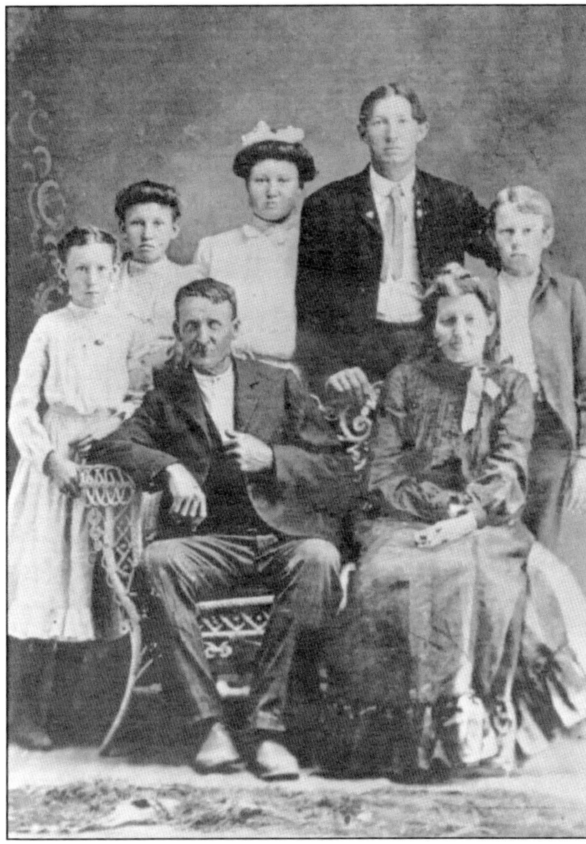

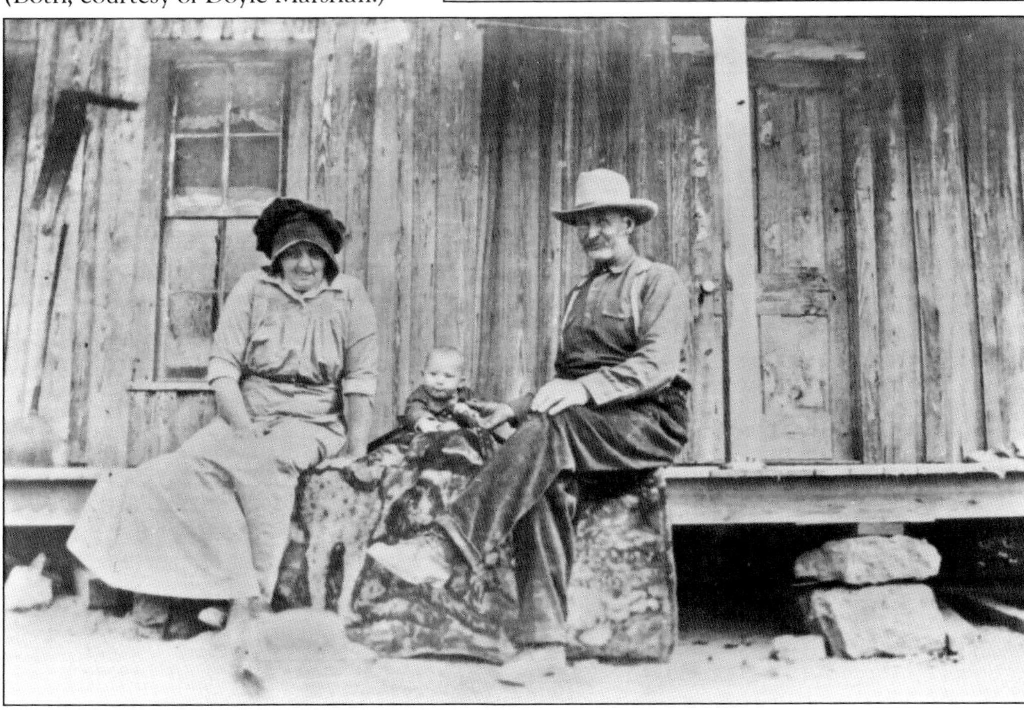

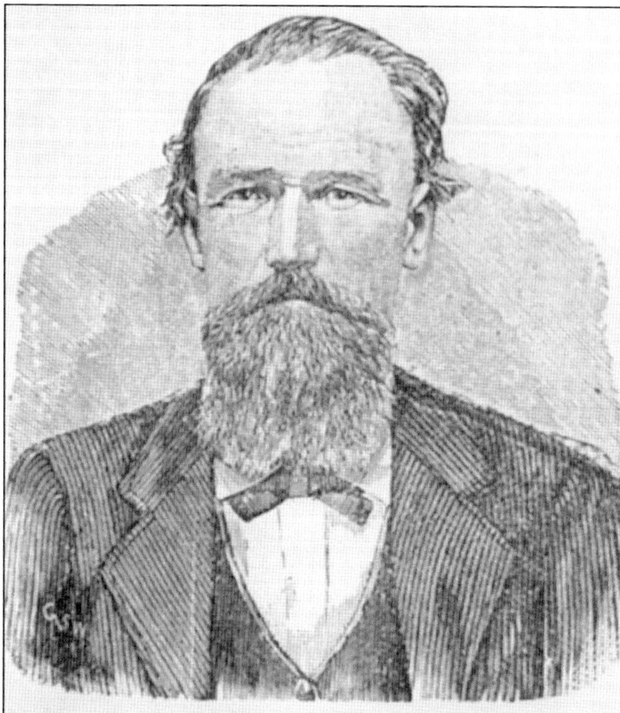
JUDGE J. A. LYNCH.

Judge James A. Lynch was the founder of Mineral Wells, Texas. This portrait by Thomas Beauregard shows Lynch as a young man. He was born on April 28, 1827, in Lexington, Missouri. In 1849, he married Armanda Swenny in Arkansas, and in 1861, he moved with his family to Texas—a wild, new country. During the Civil War he served the South and his adopted state in the Confederate Army. Below, James and Armanda Lynch pose in a family photograph in their later years. (Both, courtesy of Boyce Ditto Library, Weaver Collection.)

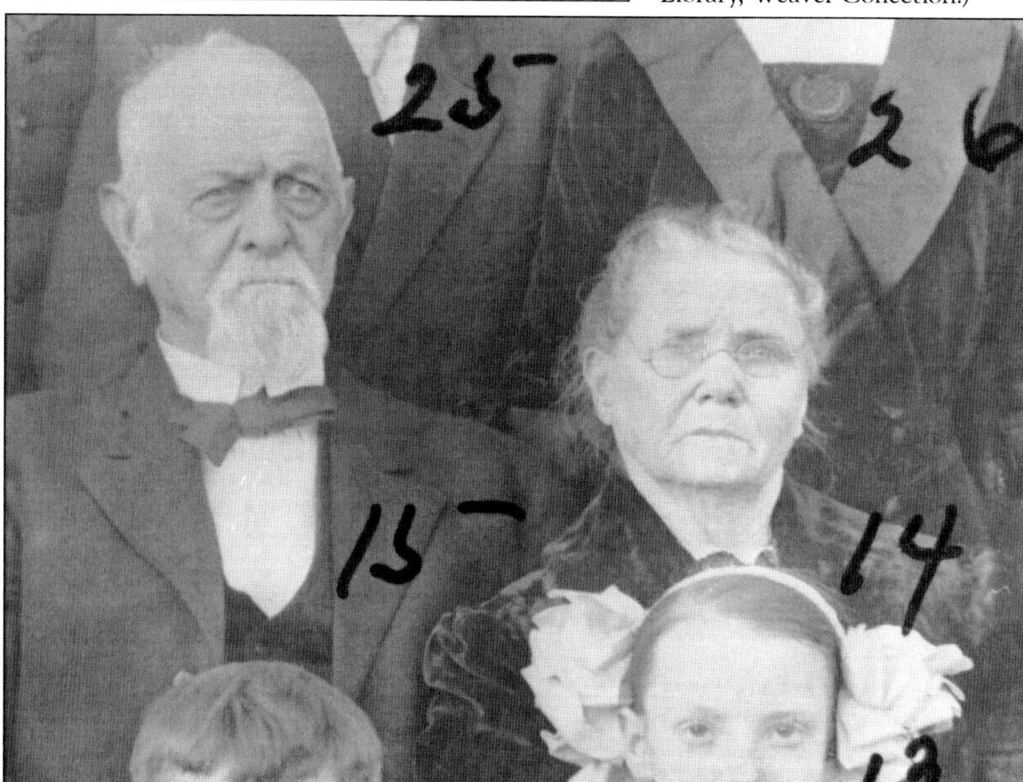

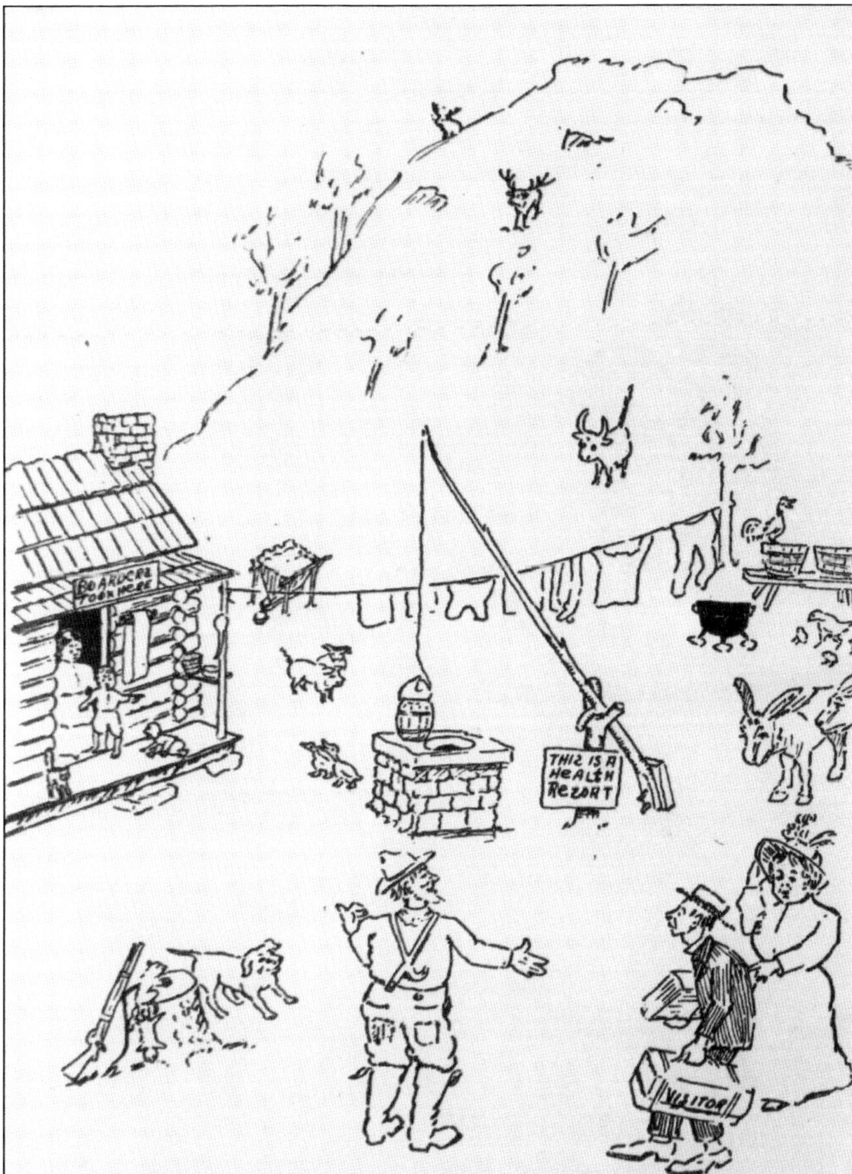

OPENING OF THE FIRST SEASON AT MINERAL WELLS

The Lynch family settled in Millsap Valley, 4 miles east of the Brazos River, in 1877. For three years, the Lynches hauled water from the salty Brazos River. In the summer of 1880, well driller Johnny Adams happened upon the Lynch ranch and agreed to drill a well on the property in exchange for a yoke of oxen. At first the Lynches were hesitant to drink the water because of its odd taste, but hauling water for 4 miles was hard work, so they began drinking the well water. Then a funny thing happened—James and Armanda's rheumatism was cured, and James, once frail and gaunt, began putting on weight. News spread fast. Neighbors began trying the water, and within a month strangers were coming to the Lynch ranch inquiring about the water. Lynch began selling the water for 5¢ a quart. The water grew in popularity very quickly, and by the end of the year 3,000 people at a time were camping on the Lynch property. (Courtesy of Boyce Ditto Library, Weaver Collection.)

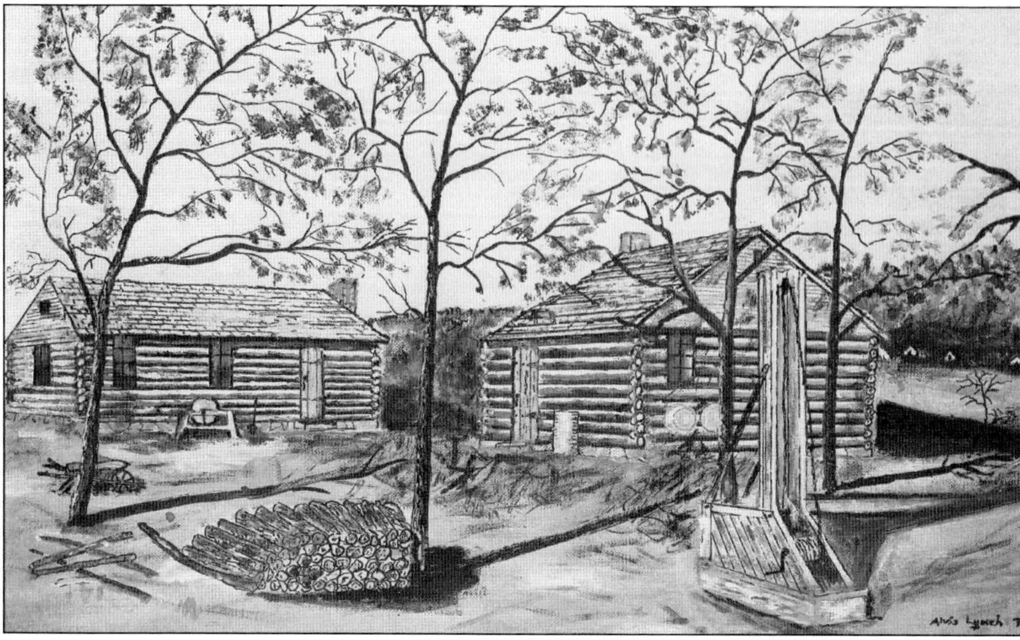

This drawing of the Lynches' cabins was done by Jarmon Alvis Lynch, grandson of James Alvis Lynch. The original mineral water discovery well, with a windlass for drawing water, is seen in the right foreground. Note the tents in the background at right. H. M. Berry, Mineral Wells' first teacher, noted in an article he wrote that when the reputation for the curative powers of the water spread, the area looked like "an army on the move" with health-seekers temporarily camping in tents until housing could be built for them. (Courtesy of Boyce Ditto Library, Weaver Collection.)

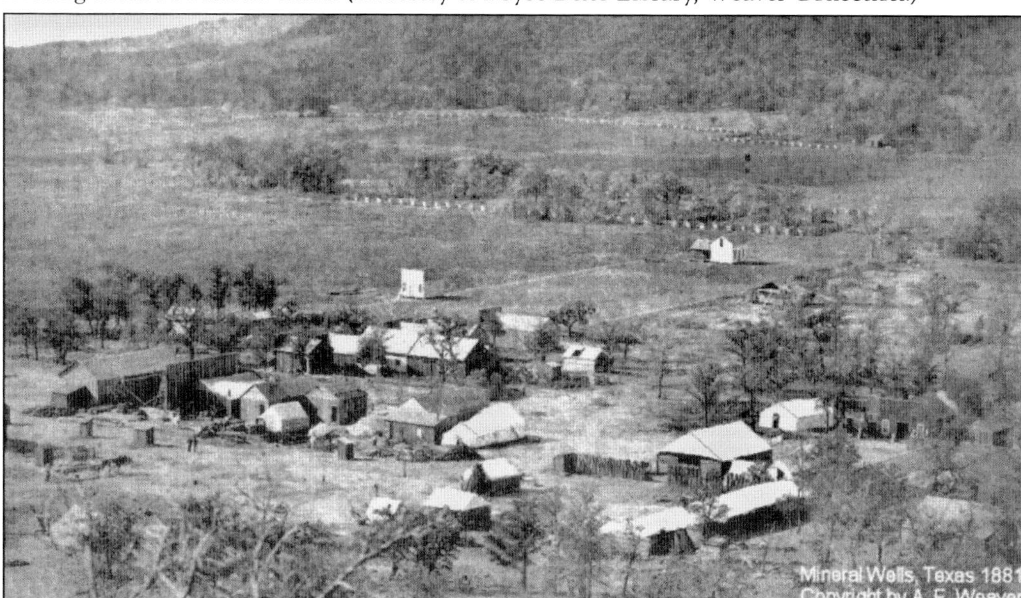

Taken in 1881, this is the earliest picture of Mineral Wells available. James A. Lynch laid out the city of Mineral Wells on his 80-acre farm in 1881. The white objects that dot the background are tents. H. M. Berry wrote in 1921, "By the first of October [1881] it looked like a small army was camped here, tents were everywhere." (Courtesy of Boyce Ditto Library, Weaver Collection.)

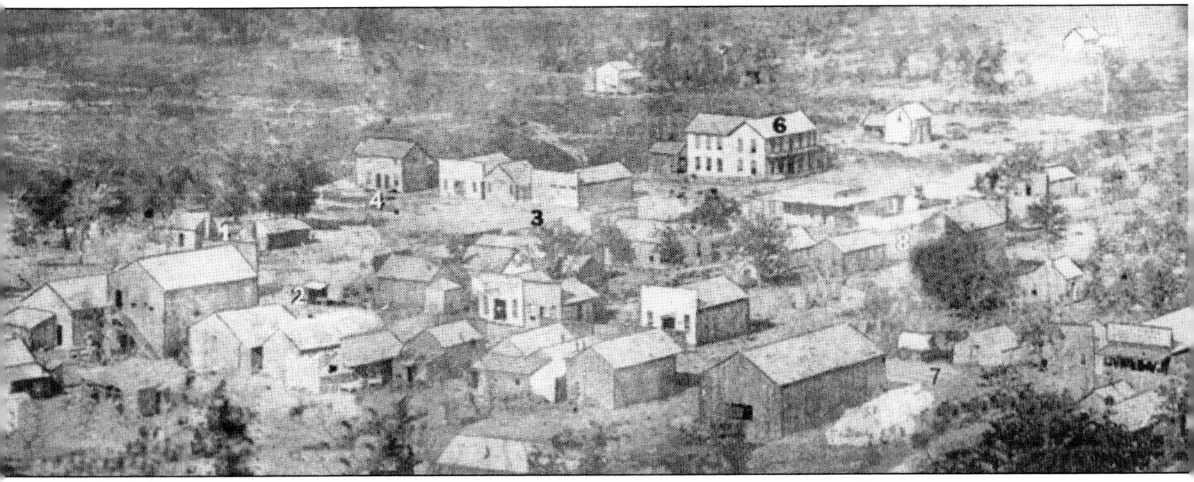

This photograph is an early panoramic view of Mineral Wells, taken in 1882 from East Mountain, looking to the southwest. Numbers on the photograph represent specific locations: 1.) Judge James A. Lynch's cabins at the location of the first mineral water well; 2.) Northeast First Avenue, where a second well was dug though it was dry; 3.) Oak and Hubbard Streets; 4.) the present location of the fire and police stations; 5.) South Oak Avenue; 6.) the Commercial Hotel, later the location of the gas company; 7.) the Northeast First Avenue business district; and 8.) North Oak Street. (Courtesy of Boyce Ditto Library, Weaver Collection.)

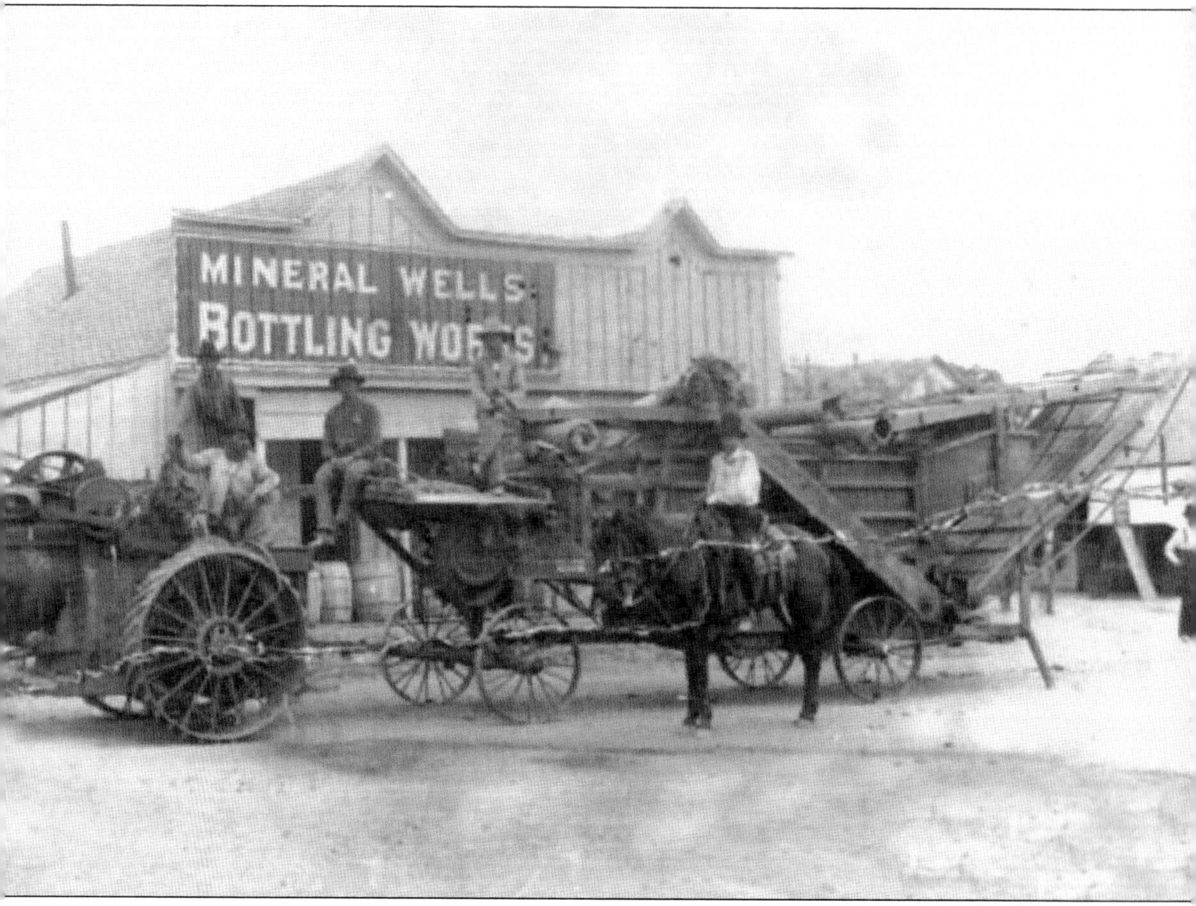

A number of the early mineral water wells bottled their product and sold it nationwide for its reputed health benefits. Since the name of the particular well associated with the 1900 endeavor in this picture is not identified, it may well have been the innovator of the bottled water industry. This photograph shows new equipment being delivered. What appears to be a scar on the tractor wheel indicates the original picture was probably damaged and was repaired. Later development of the crystallizing process eliminated the substantial shipping cost of water and adversely affected the bottled water industry. The concentrated crystals greatly expanded the distribution of the beneficial minerals inherent in the water and created its own industry. (Courtesy of Boyce Ditto Library, Weaver Collection.)

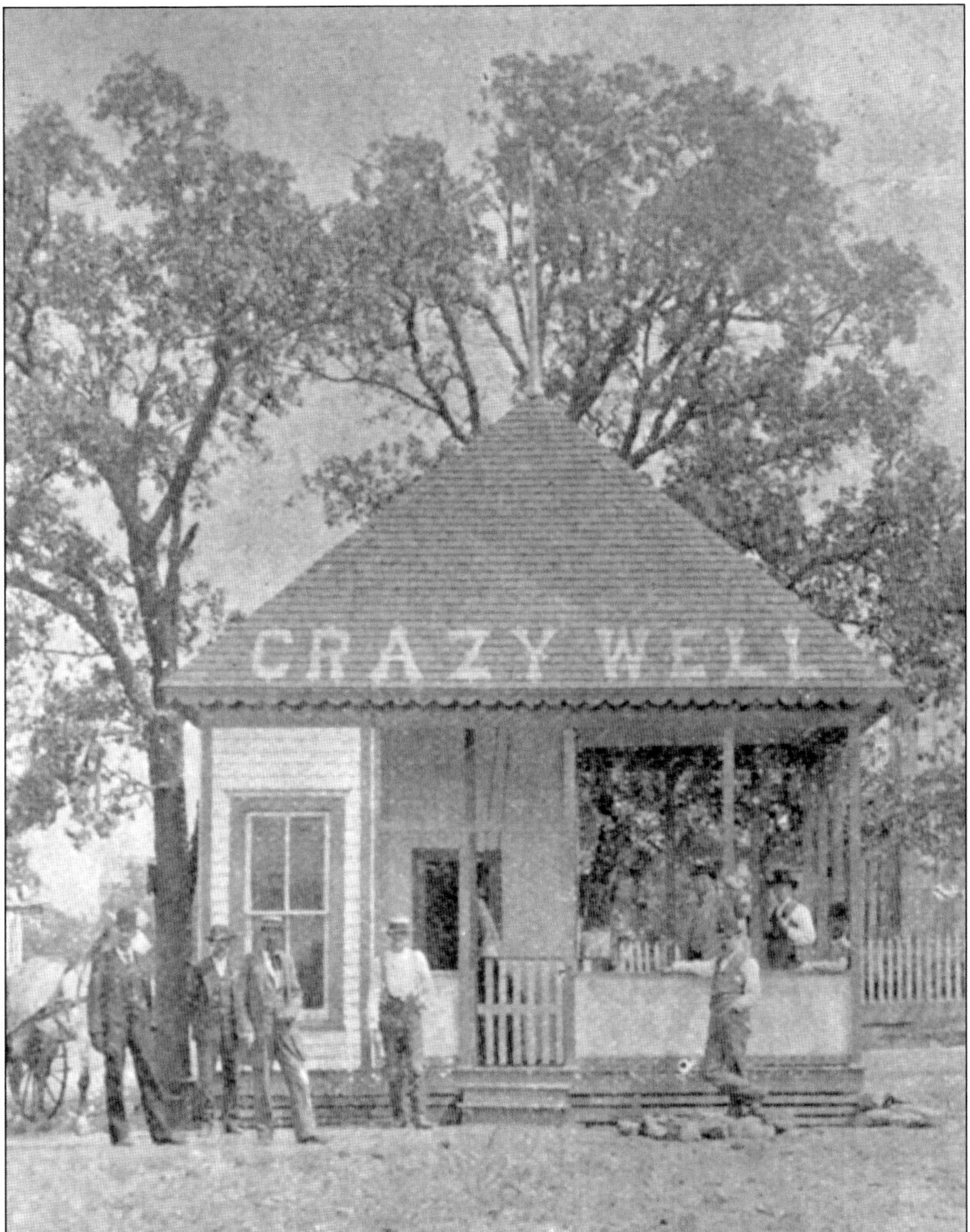

This is the Crazy Well drinking pavilion, the first such service facility in Mineral Wells. When "Uncle" Billy Wiggins dug the third well in town, it was frequented by a "crazy lady" who was eventually cured of her dementia by drinking of the water, as the well water contained lithium. Because of the word-of-mouth publicity, people came from miles around to drink the water. A house was built around the well for the convenience of customers. The highly successful business attracted competition, and one of the most popular health spas in the nation grew from these beginnings. (Courtesy of Boyce Ditto, Weaver Collection.)

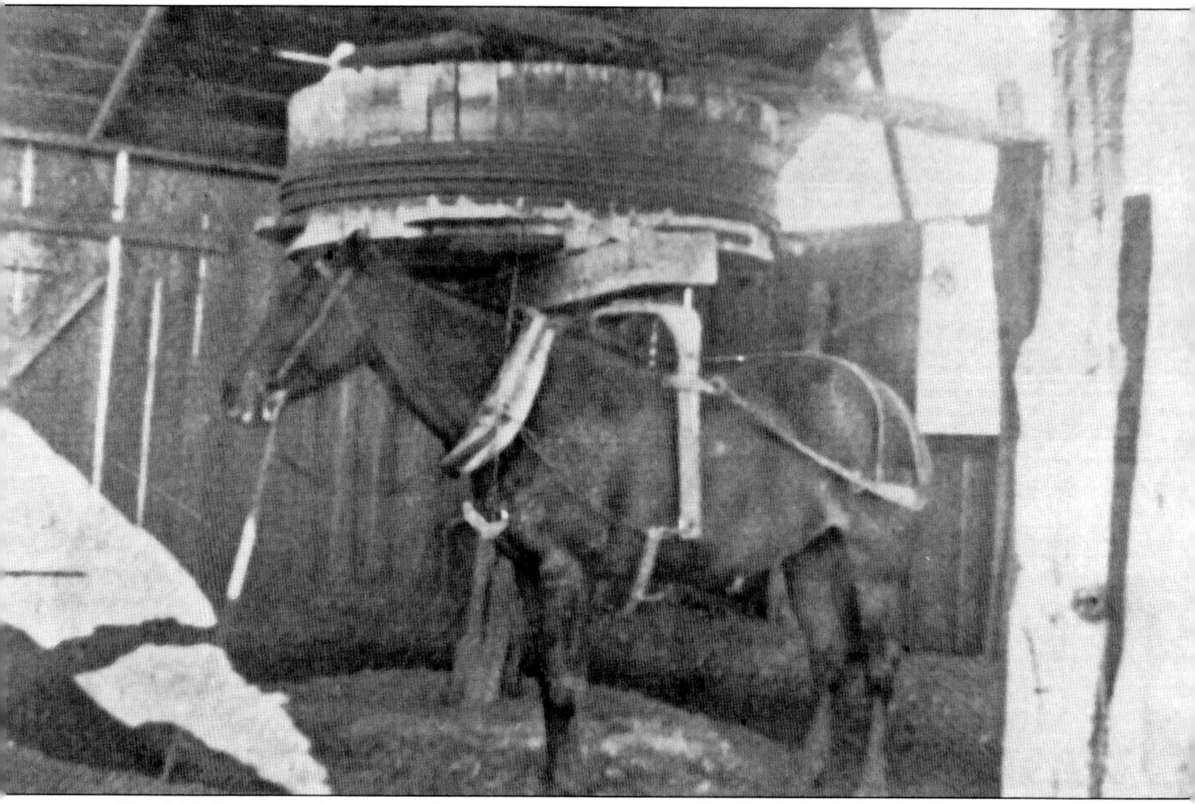

Blind Nellie was a fixture at the Austin Well for years. Col. W. R. Austin came from Kentucky to Palo Pinto County about 1880 and settled on Staggs Prairie. When an infection in his eye responded to mineral water treatment, he established the Austin Well, which was later operated by his son-in-law, Tom Sims. A unique method of bringing water to the surface was an added attraction at the well. Instead of drawing it up by hand or using a power pump, Austin used a mare named "Blind Nellie," who was trained to walk around in circles to pull the water up from below. She would pause long enough for the water to empty and, as if on a hidden cue, would go around again as the receptacle lowered back into the well, repeating her performance accurately each time. A cowboy had ridden Blind Nellie into Mineral Wells one day and auctioned her off to the highest bidder, J. H. Coleman, who bid $1.50. In later years, when she became confused in her ritual and was retired, Blind Nellie selected a place in her pasture, and during the working hours of the day, she walked her circle in a size corresponding to the one she had walked for so many years at the Austin Well. She died in 1912. (Courtesy of Boyce Ditto, Weaver Collection.)

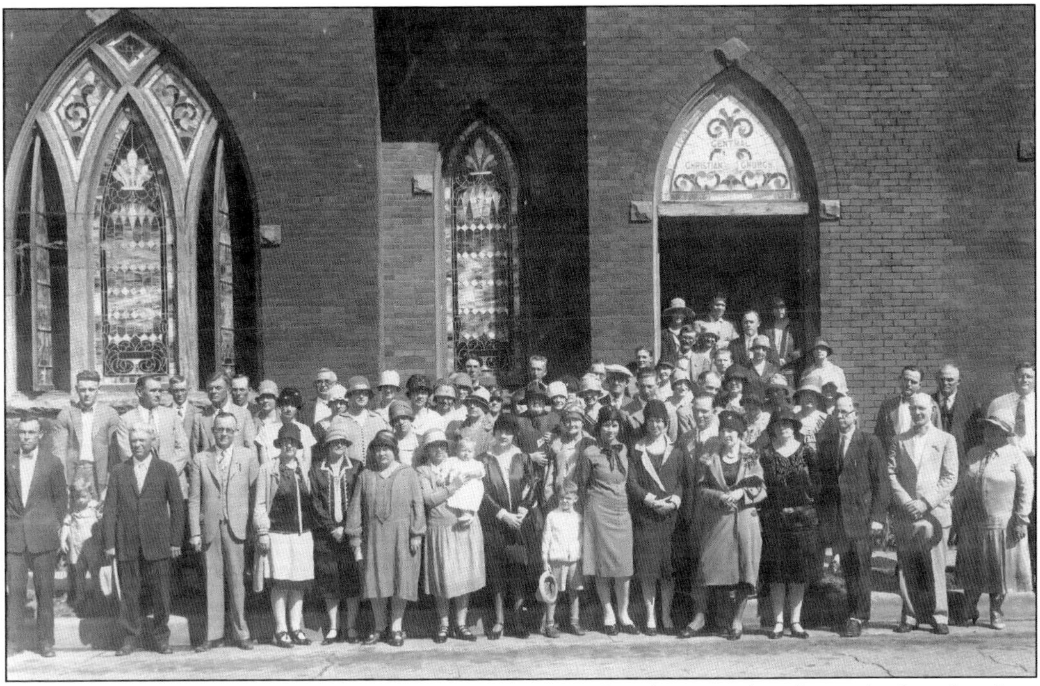

Although this photograph was taken in the 20th century, the Christian church was the first church in Mineral Wells, and James and Armanda Lynch were members. Central Christian Church (now First Christian) was located on Northeast First Street and Northeast First Avenue. This structure was the second Christian church in Mineral Wells. The first one was wooden and burned. The third church, First Christian, was built on the site of the old Gibson Well. (Courtesy of Lou Hayes Warren.)

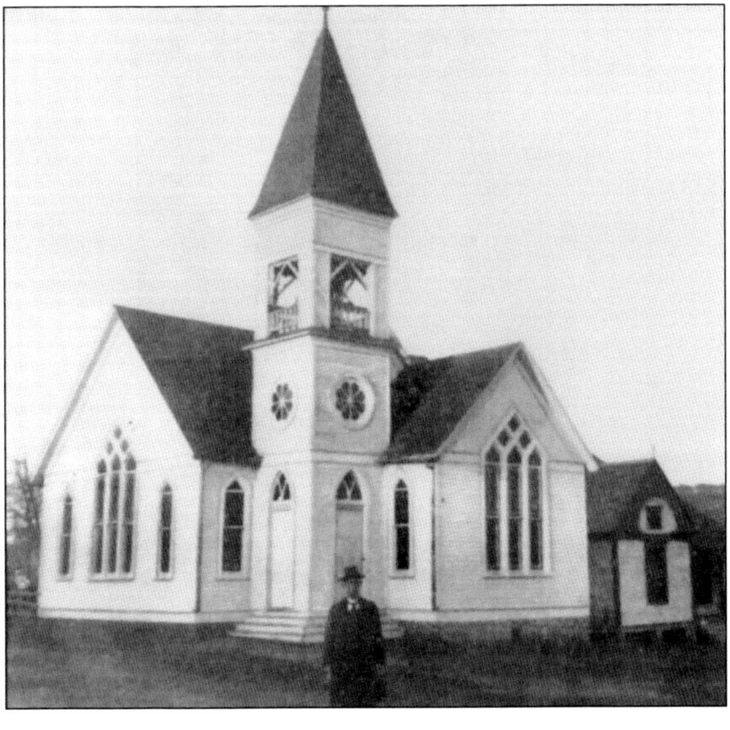

On the back of this photograph is written, "Presbyterian Church & Manse N.W. 4th Ave. & 2nd St. Built 1896, Burned 1908." This was the first Presbyterian church of Mineral Wells. After it burned in 1908, it was replaced in the same location the following year with a unique domed church that endured for some 70 years. Deterioration of the second foundation necessitated a third replacement at this same location in the early 1980s. It still stands on Northwest Fourth Avenue. (Courtesy of Boyce Ditto Library, Weaver Collection.)

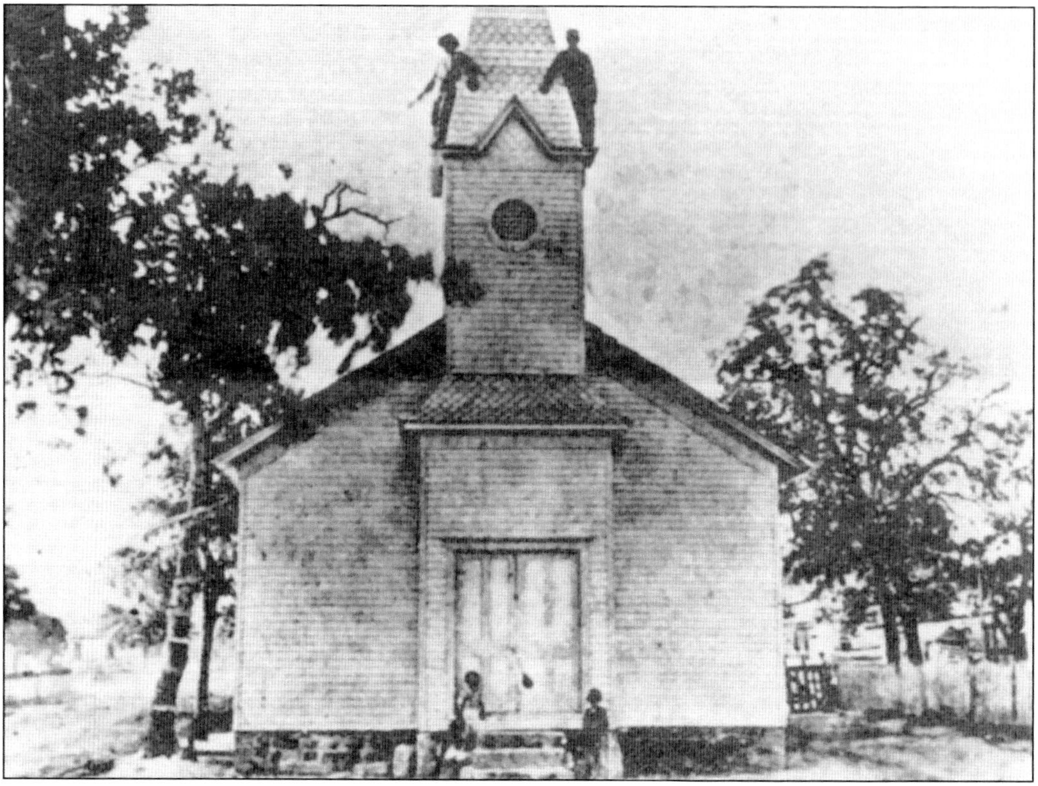

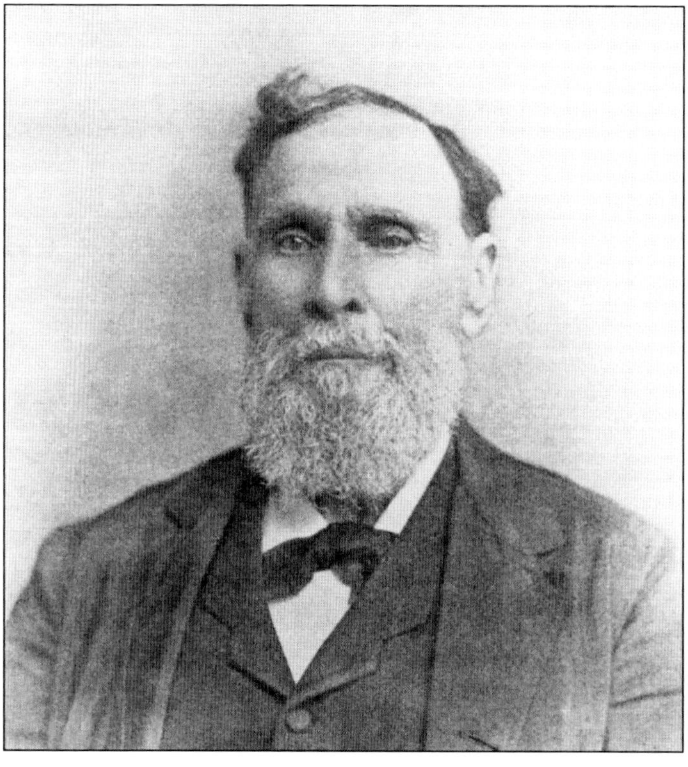

The first Baptist church was built in Mineral Wells in 1883. It was located in the Crazy Water Hotel block in a building that was initially built for the Presbyterian congregation who had outgrown the facility. (Courtesy of Louise Dillard.)

The Reverend George Webb Slaughter (1811–1895) was a Palo Pinto County pioneer, Republic of Texas soldier, Native American fighter, and self-educated doctor. He was a cattleman who provided beef for the Confederacy during the Civil War, and he was the founder of the First Baptist Church of Mineral Wells. (Courtesy of Louise Dillard.)

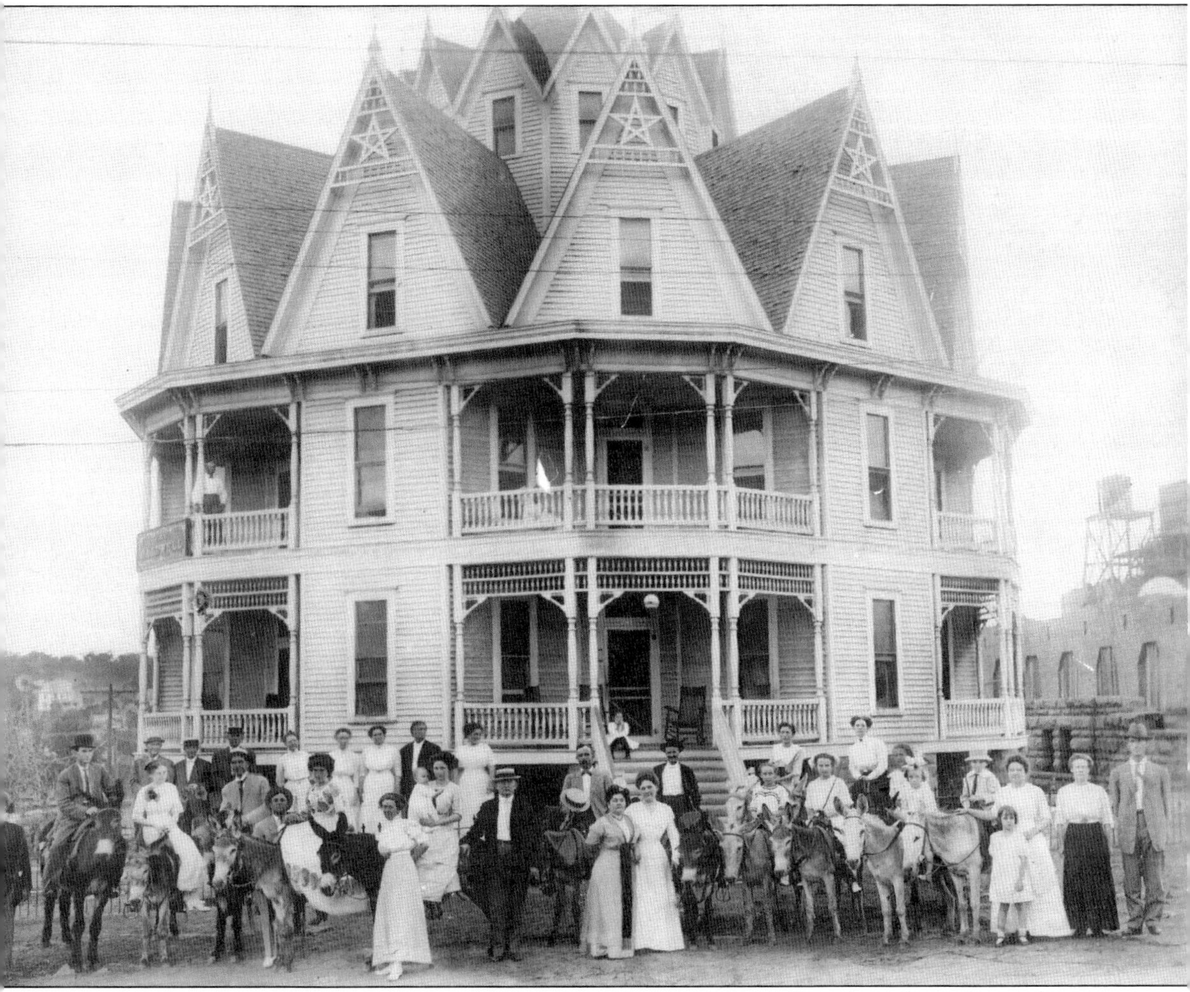

The Hexagon House Hotel was designed and built by David G. Galbraith and was located in Mineral Wells in the 700 block of North Oak Street. Construction started in 1895 and completed in 1897. The hotel was the first electrically lighted hotel in the city, and the hexagon shape was designed to achieve maximum air circulation 61 years before air-conditioning became available. Galbraith was the inventor of the paper clip and, along with five other men, inventor of synthetic fiber acetate. A large group of people is shown here in front of the hotel, most sitting on the donkeys that were used to transport visitors to the top of East Mountain for a view of the city of Mineral Wells. The building behind the Hexagon House Hotel is the electricity generating plant. This hotel was used by patrons of the wells. It was torn down in September 1959. (Courtesy of Boyce Ditto Library, Weaver Collection.)

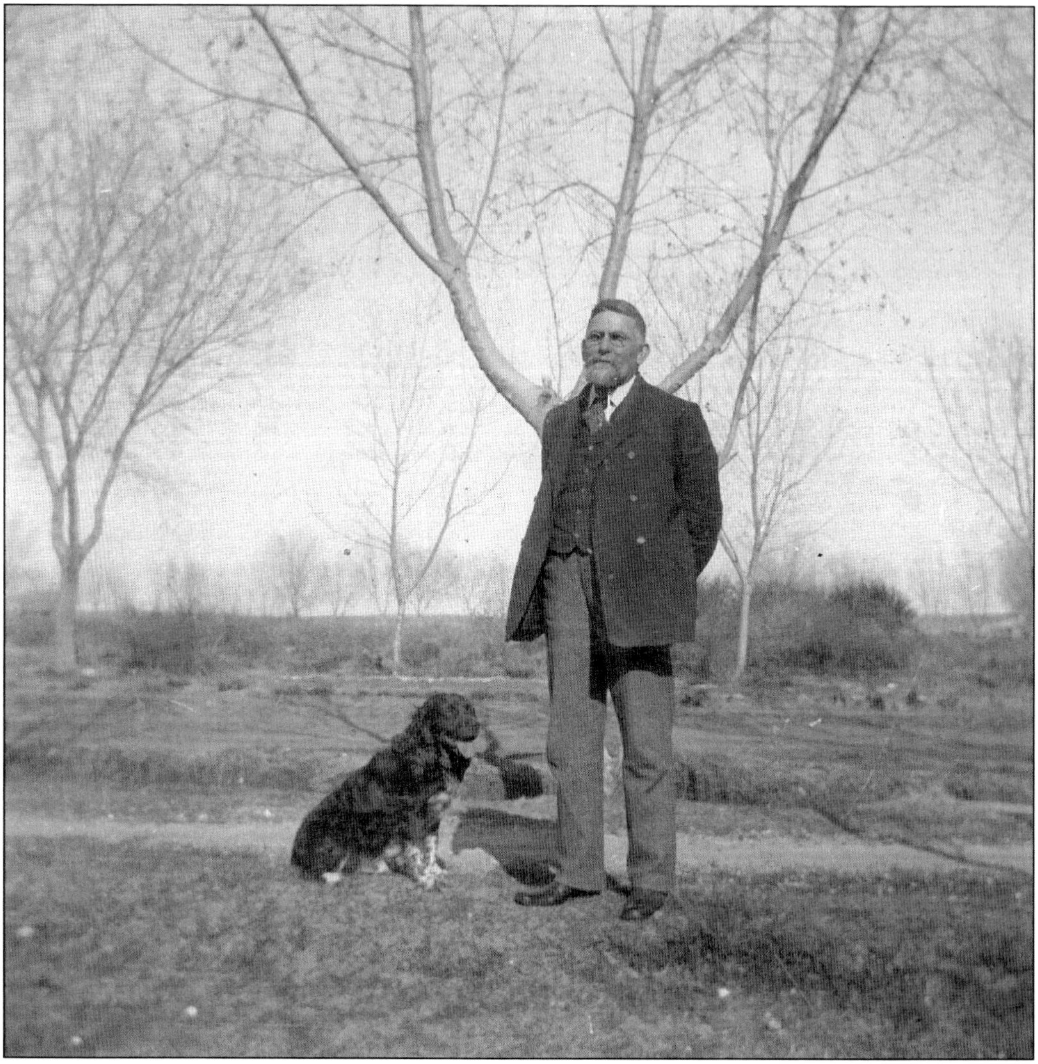

Judge James A. Lynch bought 80 acres, laid out the city of Mineral Wells, and was the first self-appointed mayor. The city incorporated in 1882, and Jim Laverty became the first mayor of the newly incorporated Mineral Wells. In 1894, the city adopted a change of charter, and a new corporation was formed, which elected G. C. Green as the first mayor of this new corporation. This photograph shows Jim Laverty and his dog in 1882. (Courtesy of Boyce Ditto Library, Weaver Collection.)

George Thomas Hayes, teamster, and Marguerite Louiza Smith Hayes were settlers and businesspeople in the early days of Mineral Wells. Hayes owned a hauling business. Among other jobs, he hauled bricks to build the highway from Mineral Wells to Millsap and dug out dirt to build the Baker Hotel. (Courtesy of Lou Hayes Warren.)

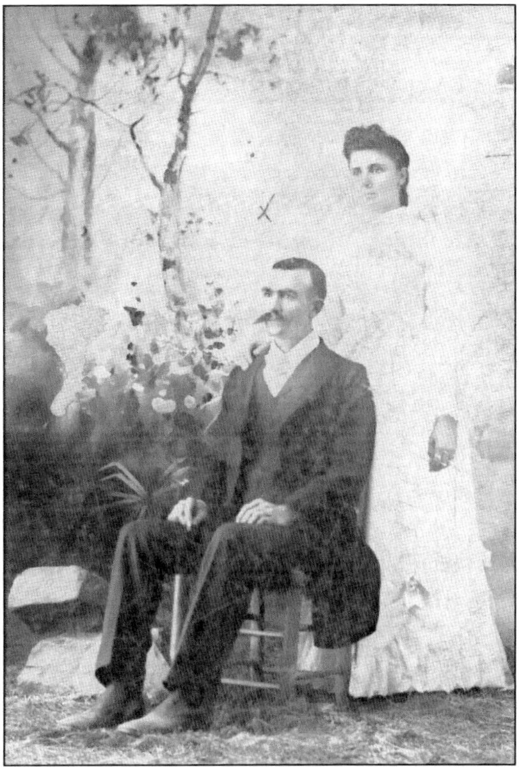

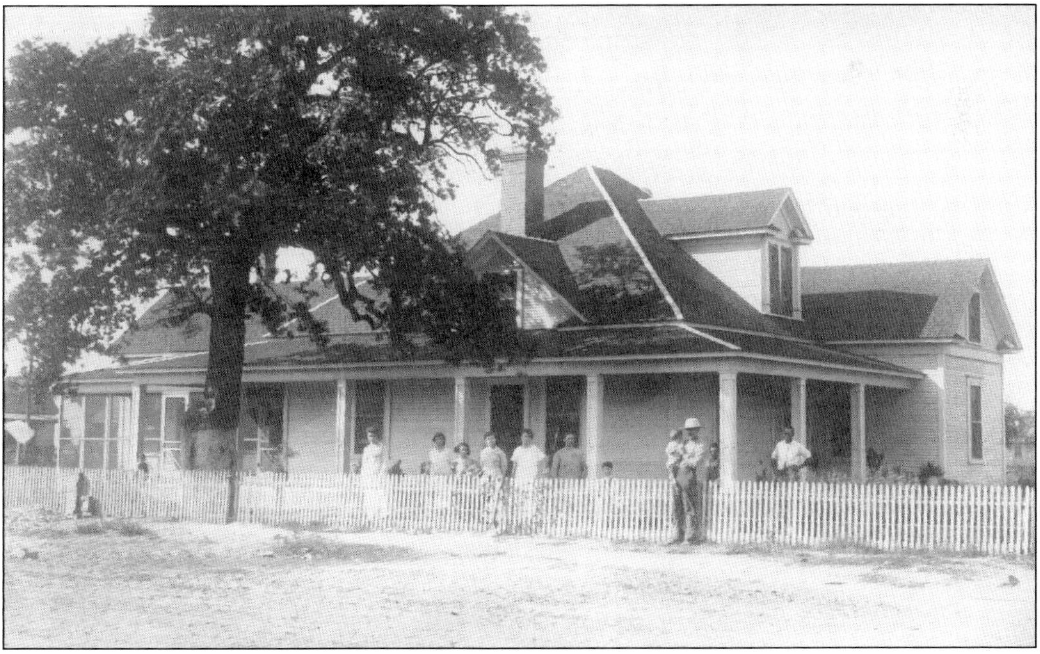

The George Thomas Hayes home sat on the lot across from present-day Sim's Lumber Company. Hayes is in front of the fence holding one of his children, while his son John stands to the left behind him on the porch holding the rail. The family moved from this home to the country in 1919. (Courtesy of Lou Hayes Warren.)

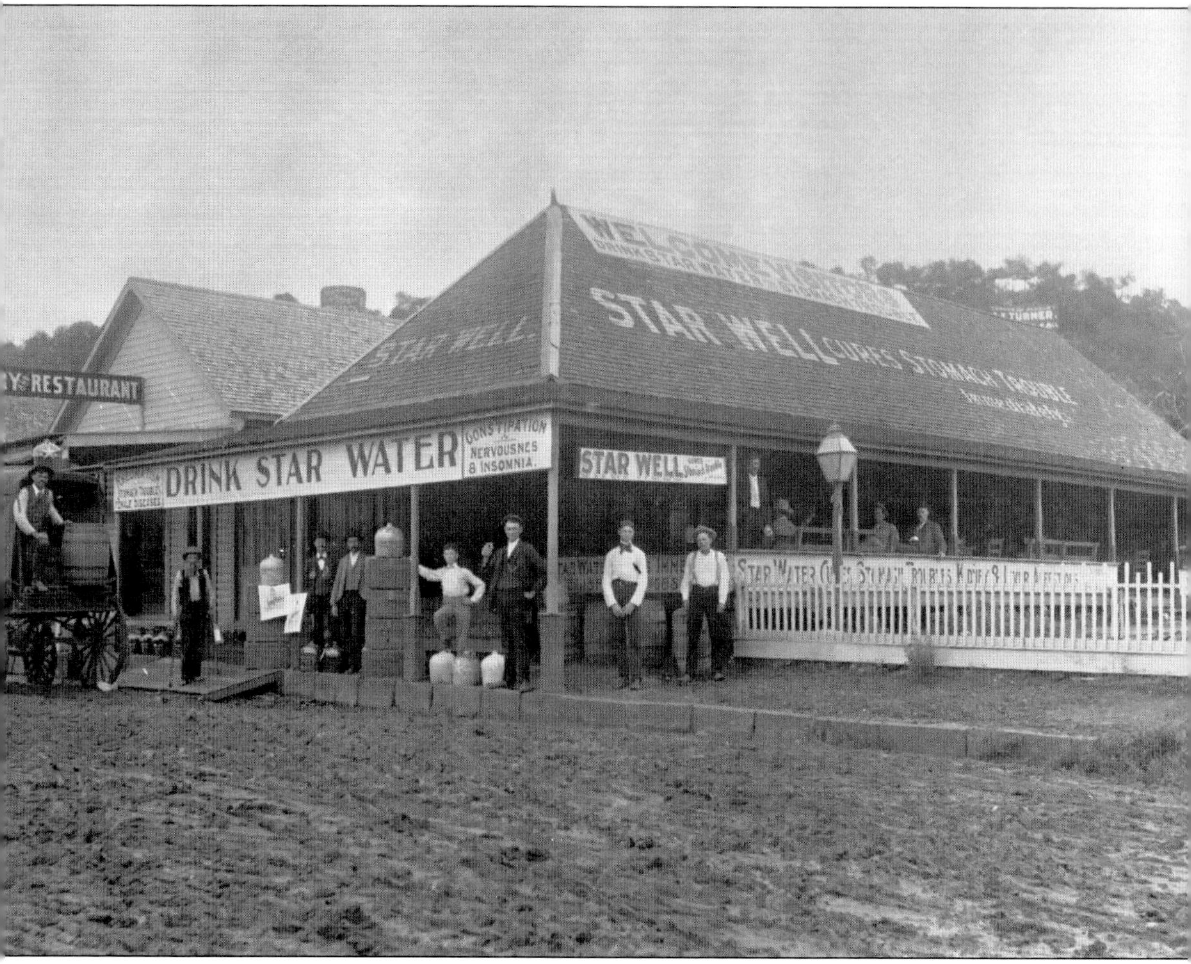

A legend on the photograph reads, "Winter Scene, shipping Star Well water, From Min. Wells, Texas." The Star Well was located in the 200 block of Northeast First Avenue, across the street and north of where the Baker Hotel now stands. It was managed by Frank Richards, who purchased a block of land in the northern part of Millsap Valley on which two wells were dug that proved to have an abundant supply of the very strongest mineral water. Mineral water was expensive to ship, so furnaces were built at the new location, pumps were installed, and a modern evaporating plant was built to produce hundreds of pounds of crystals annually. Richards's new land and wells became known as the Pike Well. Signs on the building claim that the water "cures stomach trouble" as well as constipation, nervousness, insomnia, rheumatism, and female diseases. (Courtesy of Boyce Ditto Library, Weaver Collection.)

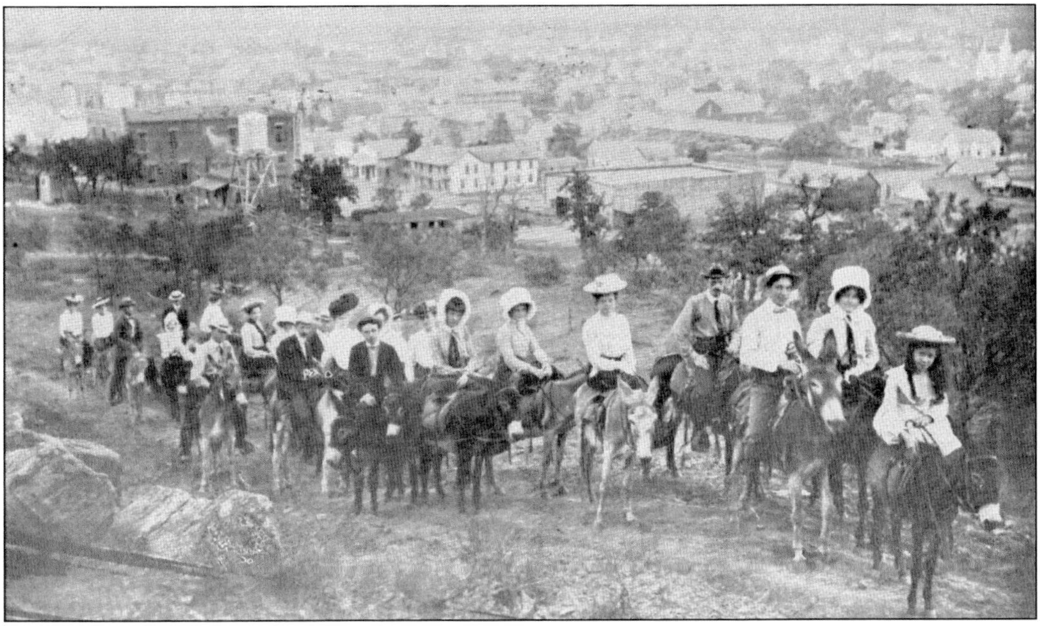

A group takes a trail ride with donkeys up East Mountain. Tourists who visited Mineral Wells to take the water cures also enjoyed the spectacular scenery of the area. The land in and around Mineral Wells and all through the Pinto Hills is now known as North Texas Hill Country. Donkeys were used a lot in the hills because they were more sure-footed than horses as they climbed up and down the hills. (Both, courtesy of Lou Hayes Warren.)

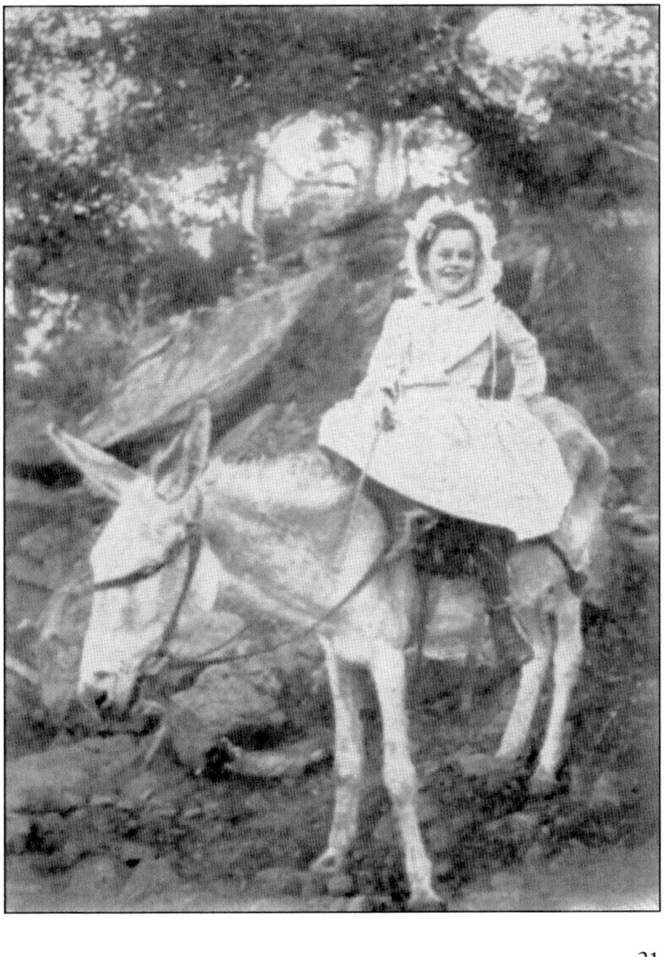

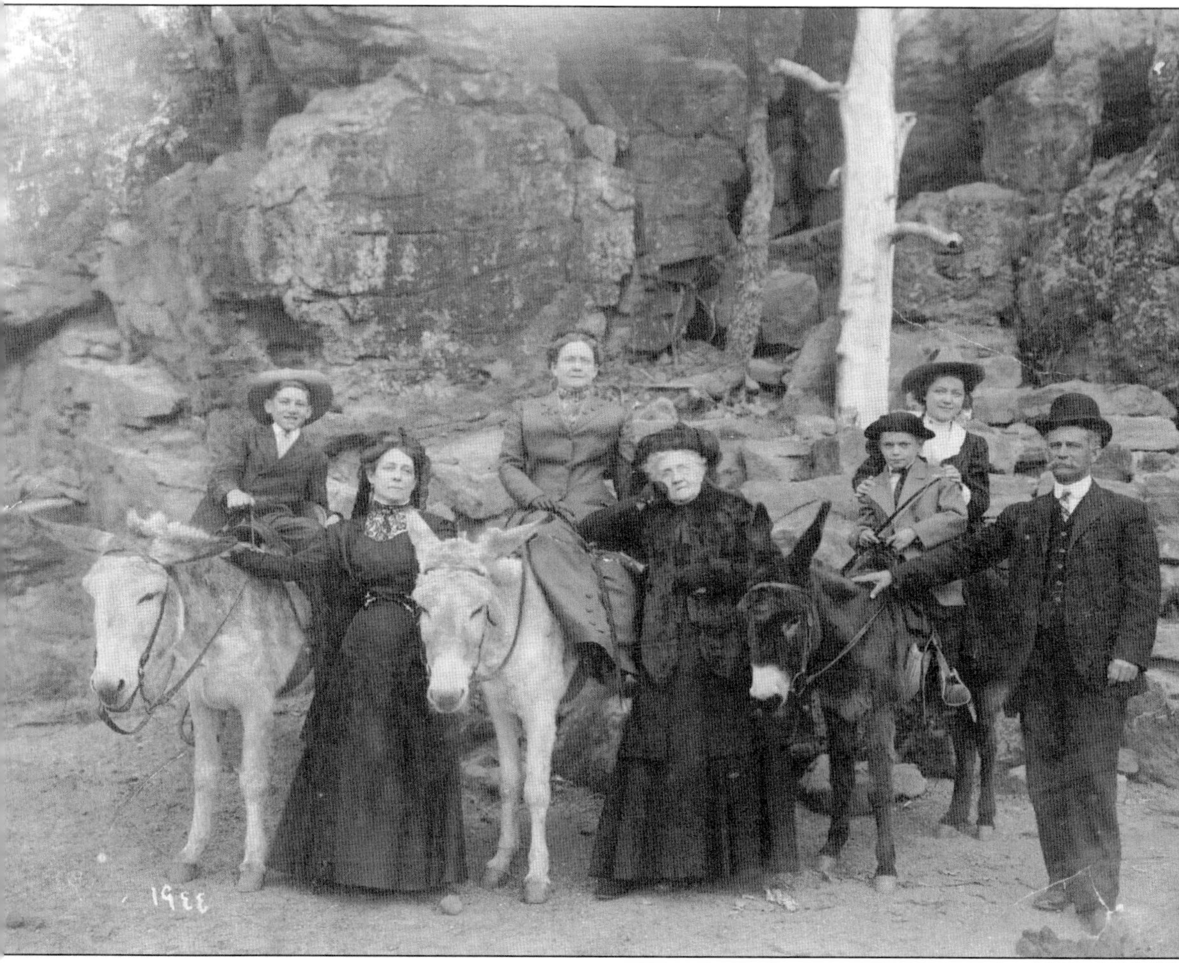

At the beginning of the 20th century, entertainment for the many visitors to Mineral Wells was provided, in part, by riding donkeys up a trail to the top of East Mountain. The donkey trail crossed the 1,000-step staircase about halfway up. The stairs went to the top of the mountain and were built in 1905. Photographers, first J. C. McClure and then J. L. Young, took souvenir photographs of the visitors at this crossing. This photograph of the Belcher family was taken by J. D. McClure. John M. Belcher stands on the right, and his son John E. Belcher sits on a donkey at the left of the picture, with his mother standing beside him. (Courtesy of Boyce Ditto Library, Weaver Collection.)

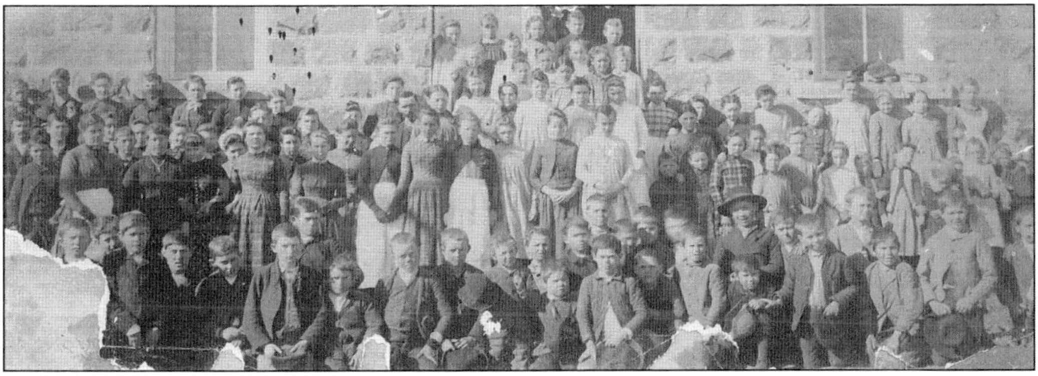

Built in 1884, the Little Rock Schoolhouse, Mineral Wells' first public school, is now a Mineral Wells museum. The back of this photograph, which appears to be of the students and teachers, has three notes: "Taken in front of school house about 1885," "Donated by James H. Perry," and "Some are dead. Some are married, and we are all scattered, never to meet on earth again." (Courtesy of Boyce Ditto Library, Weaver Collection.)

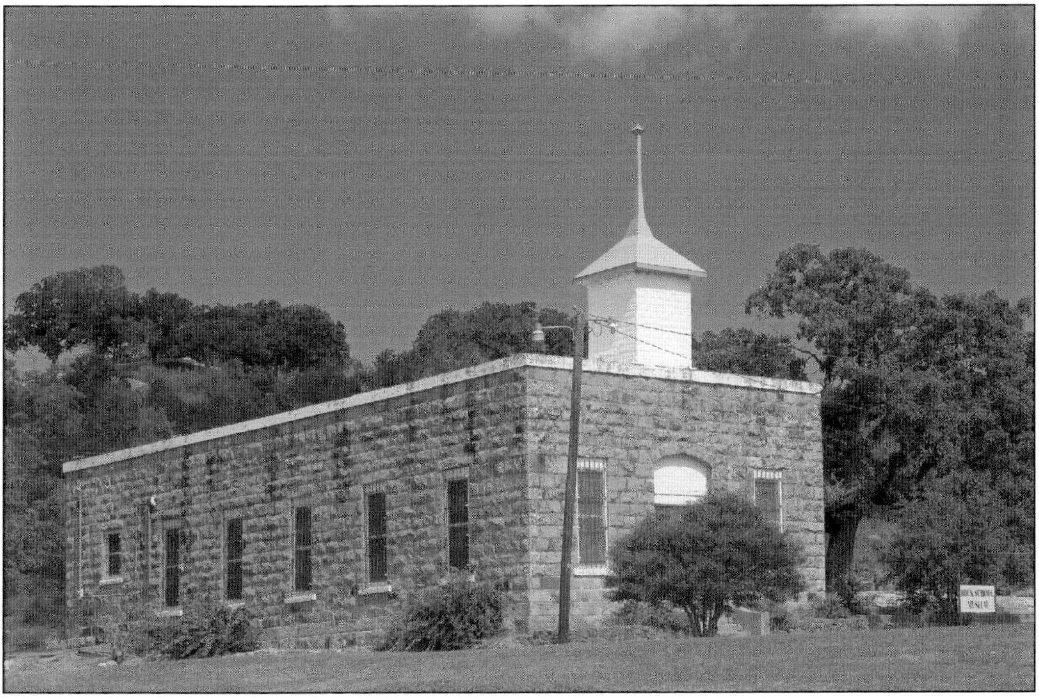

The Little Rock Schoolhouse, shown here as it appears today, was the first school in Mineral Wells. It was built in 1884, only seven years after James and Armanda Lynch settled in Millsap Valley. This building, now a museum, houses much information about the town and its history. A scale replica of the Hexagon House Hotel is on display there as well as much memorabilia about Crazy Water and the industry that it started. (Photograph by Raf Seibert.)

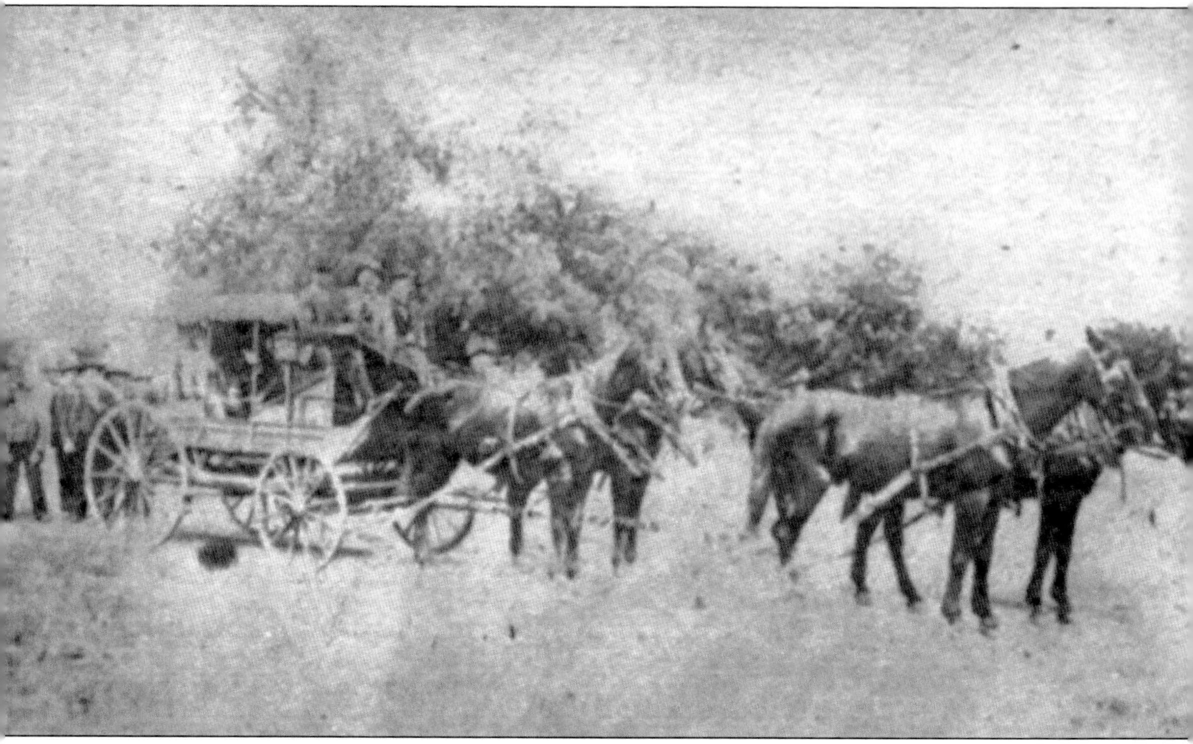

This big yellow stagecoach was a welcome sight to settlers before the start of the 20th century because it brought news from back East. For Mineral Wells, it also brought tourists who were flocking here to drink the waters and be cured. The first stagecoach arrived in Mineral Wells in 1882. (Courtesy of Lou Hayes Warren.)

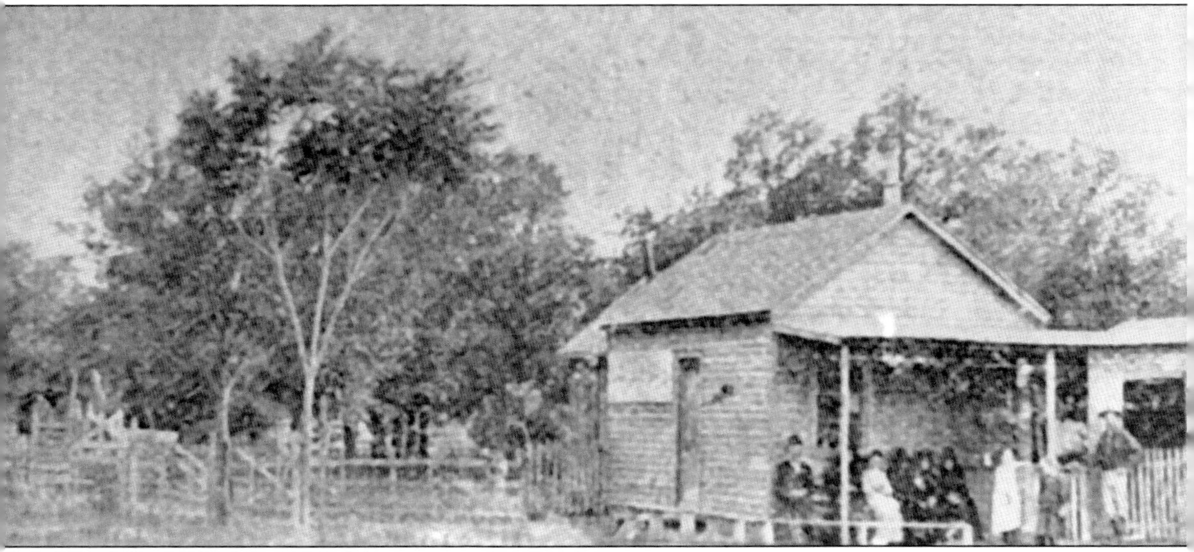

The Gibson Well, located in the 700 block of Northwest Second Avenue, was one of the first wells in Mineral Wells to establish a drinking pavilion for the convenience of its customers. In time it became one of the largest pavilions and parks in the city. An expanded pavilion replaced the one pictured here and became one of the more popular social gathering places in town. The First Christian Church now occupies the entire city block on which the Gibson Well was located. (Courtesy of Boyce Ditto Library, Weaver Collection.)

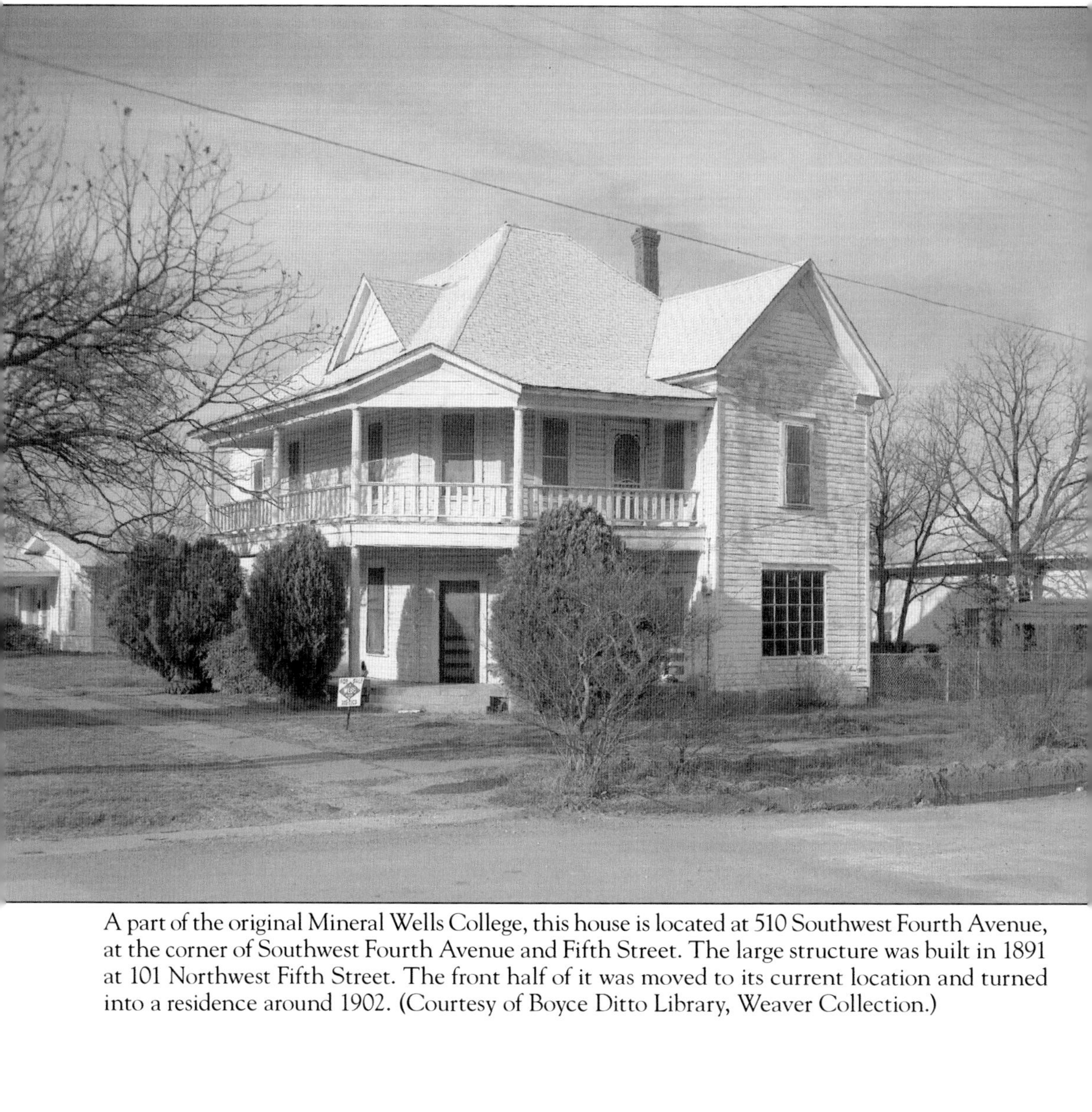

A part of the original Mineral Wells College, this house is located at 510 Southwest Fourth Avenue, at the corner of Southwest Fourth Avenue and Fifth Street. The large structure was built in 1891 at 101 Northwest Fifth Street. The front half of it was moved to its current location and turned into a residence around 1902. (Courtesy of Boyce Ditto Library, Weaver Collection.)

Pat Gallagher was born in Tennessee in 1839. He married Hannah Brooks, and together they moved to Palo Pinto County. They had five sons—Emerson, George, Spence, Bell, and Bill—and one daughter, Maude. Pat and Hannah settled in what is now the Union Hill area northwest of Mineral Wells, and he worked as a stonemason around the county building many beautiful stone structures from rock quarried on what is now the BARK Ranch. An example of his work is shown in his own home pictured below. Pat stands third from left in the image with the white beard and vest. (Both, courtesy of Bob and Ruth Kimbrough, BARK Ranch.)

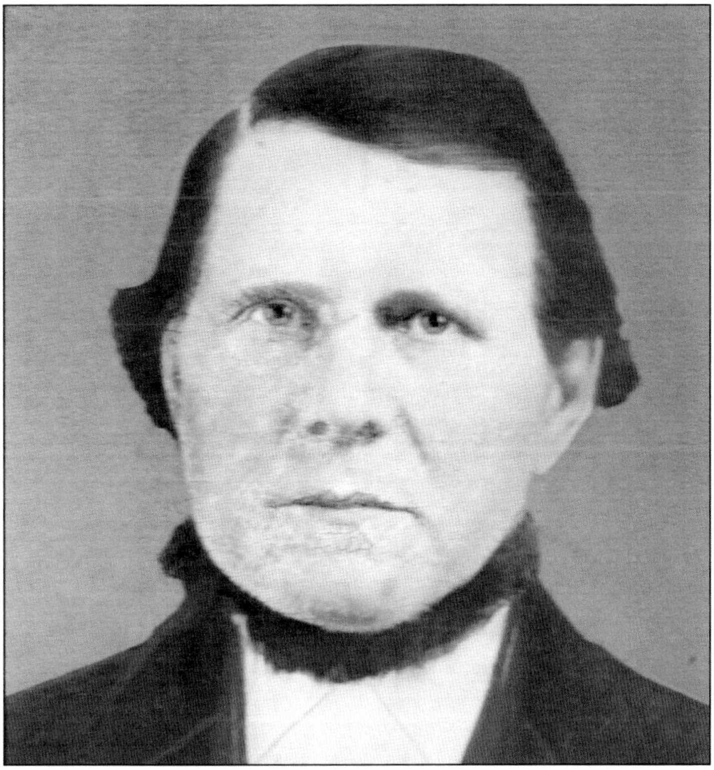

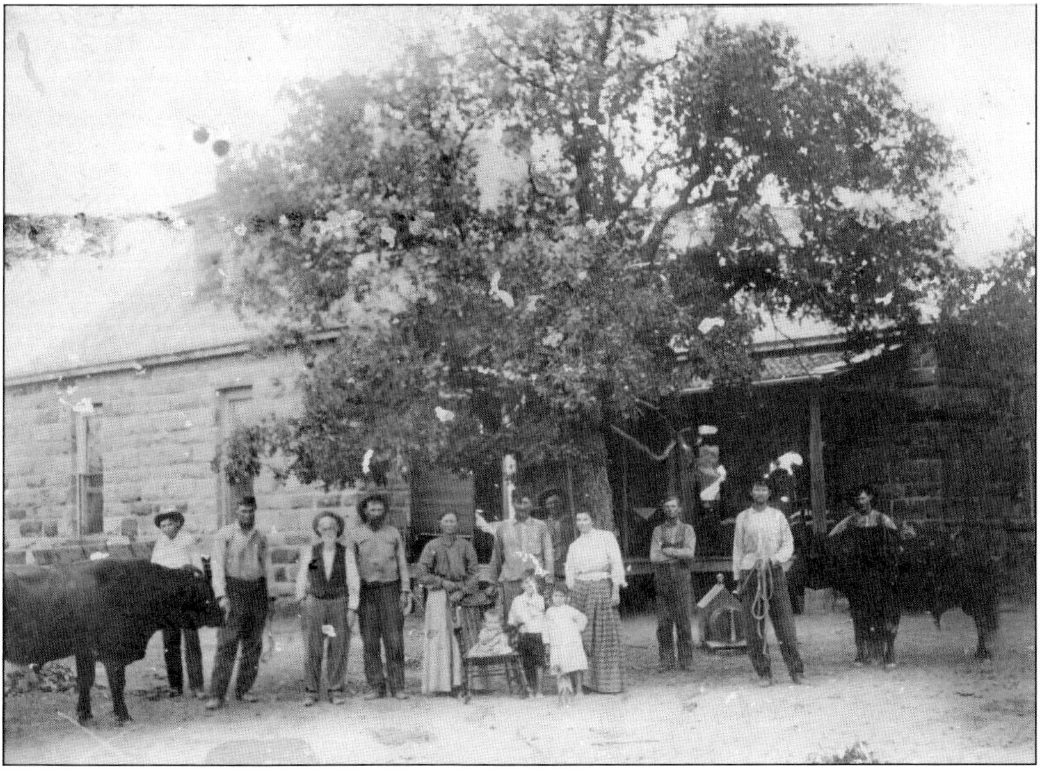

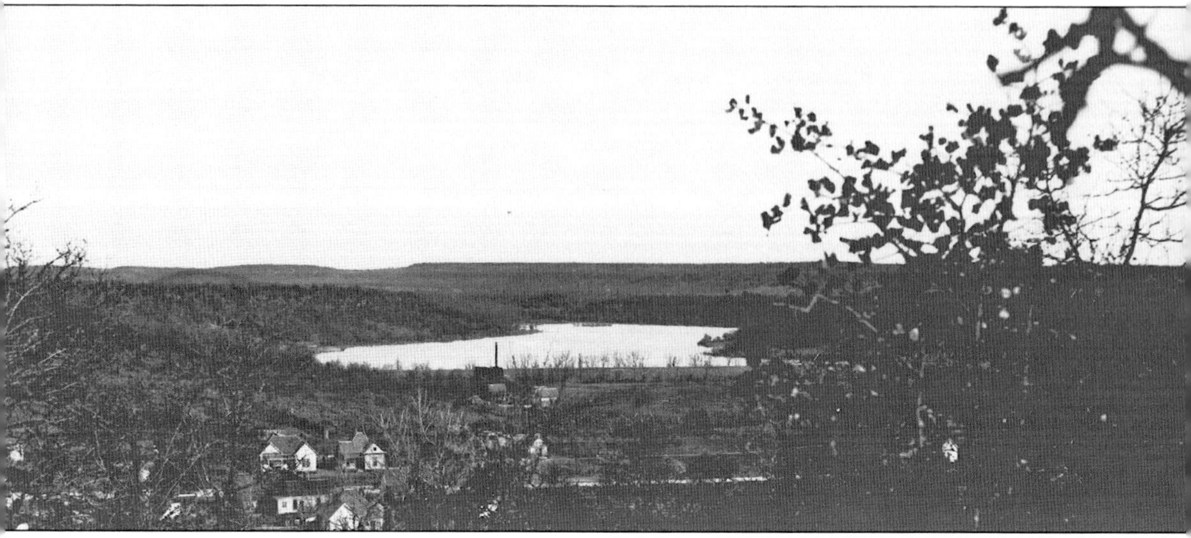

By 1889, many property owners in early Mineral Wells had their own water wells, but the city pumped water to a small standpipe on East Mountain for distribution to Mineral Wells. When the wells became insufficient to supply the city's needs, Barber Lake was built in the northeast part of town as Mineral Wells' first city water supply lake. Then around 1905, Cicero Smith and Ed Dismuke built a dam across Pollard Creek, west of the city, to form Lake Pinto, the city's next water supply. Barber Lake can still be found southeast of Cullen Grimes School, which is a block east of North Oak Street at about Thirteenth Street. It was built near Dr. G. P. Barber's log cabin. (Courtesy of Boyce Ditto Library, Weaver Collection.)

Three

A Spa Town Is Born 1900–1960s

At the start of the 20th century—only 23 years after Judge James A. Lynch founded the town of Mineral Wells—there were 2,048 citizens in the community and many guests taking the cure and living in a tent city set in the eastern lee of West Mountain.

The "town built on water" was surely running on it. Mineral Wells' Lake Pinto was dammed by Cicero Smith and Ed Dismuke in 1905, and tourists flooded the area to view the beauty of the land. Lake Pinto, located between West Mountain and West City Park, was a trendy recreation spot for tourists but is now part of the Upham Ranch.

Other businesspeople took advantage of the tourist trade: Donkey rides up East and West Mountains, dinky car rides to the lake, restaurants, and tourist shops were established. The train brought people in every day to take the cure or to play.

The Famous Water Company, located at 209 Northwest Sixth Street, still stands at the location established by Ed Dismuke and continues to sell mineral water in four grades, as it did when it opened in 1914. Dismuke also developed Pronto-Lax, Residuum, Dismuke's Famous Crystals, and Dismuke's Eyebath from the mineral water, which were sold around the world.

Celebrities came to Mineral Wells as a destination vacation and resort. People like Judy Garland and Will Rogers visited and proclaimed the area as a haven for those seeking good health.

The town's population continued to grow: 7,890 in 1920; 6,303 in 1940; 11,053 in 1960; 18,411 in 1970. By 1966, Mineral Wells had 365 businesses, including 35 manufacturers, 37 churches, two newspapers, a hospital, a radio station, and a business college.

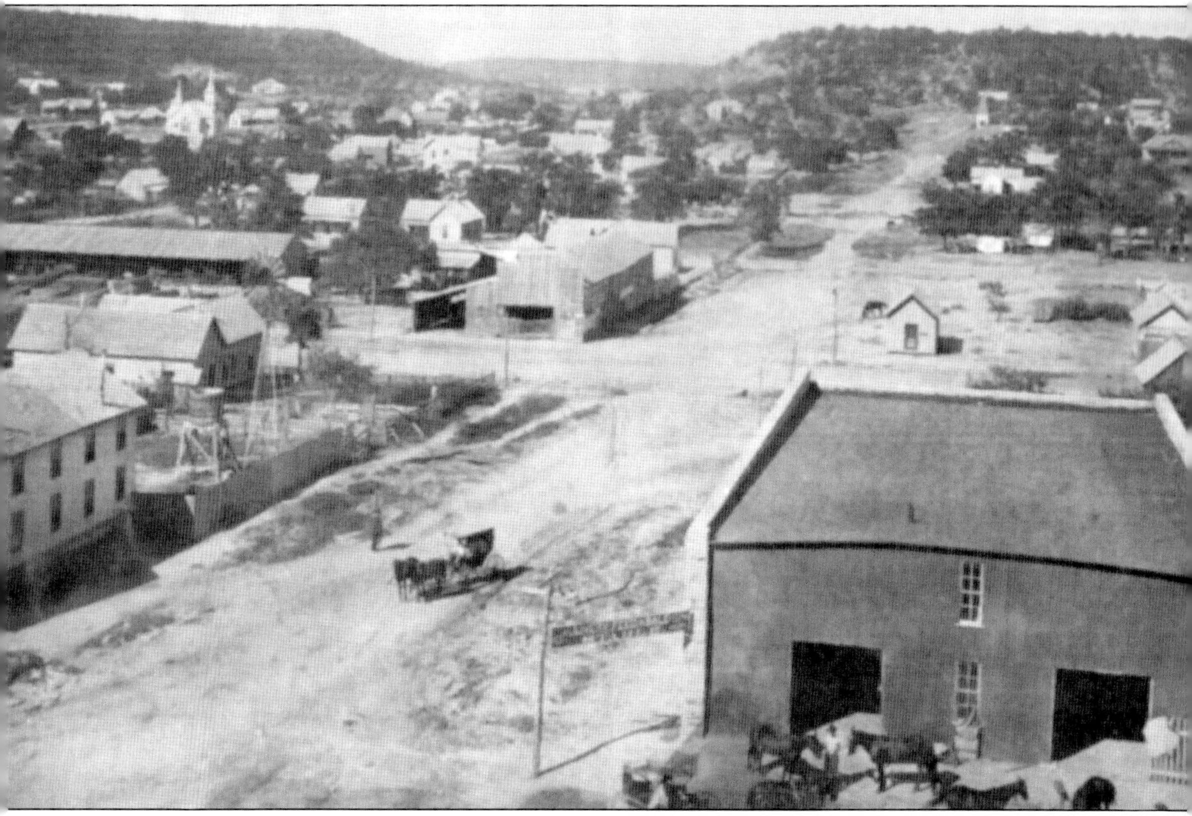

This is Mineral Wells in 1900. The Scott Livery Stable in the foreground is where Whatley Motor Company is located today. Across the street at left was the two-story Holmes Hotel. The barn at the corner, in the center of the photograph, was the T. J. Green Transfer Company. Mat Birdwell, who purchased horses for the government, had his headquarters in the Green barn. Other spots include the Frost Lumber Yard, next to the Green barn; the Old Baptist Church steeples, top left, at the location of the present First Baptist Church; and the Presbyterian church, top right, that later burned. (Courtesy of Boyce Ditto Library, Weaver Collection.)

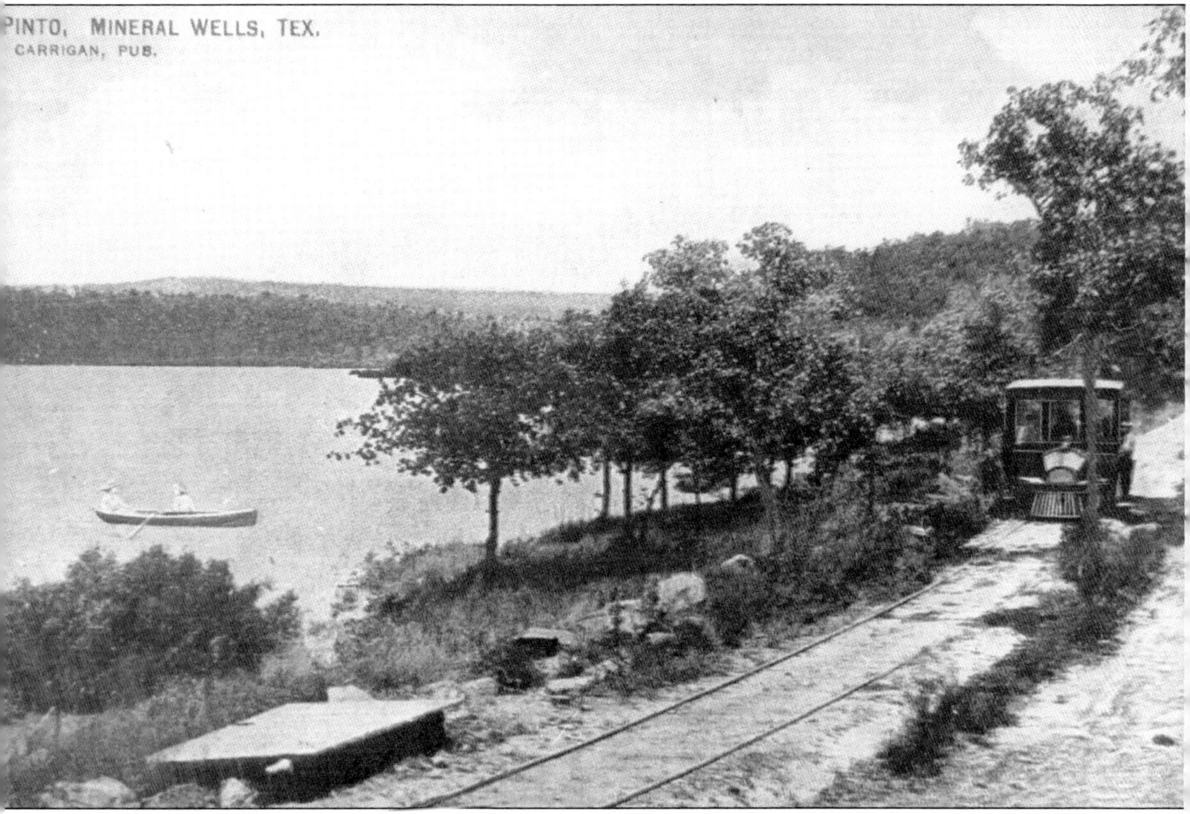

Lake Pinto, the second water supply for the town of Mineral Wells, was built around 1902 by Cicero Smith and Ed Dismuke because Barber Lake was too small for the population. The dam was built across Pollard Creek, west of West Mountain. This photograph shows a dinky car on its tracks by the side of the lake. The original earthen dam burst, draining Lake Pinto and flooding the area to the south of it. The C. R. Upham family now owns this area. The dam has since been replaced by a concrete structure, and the new lake covers much of the original area of the old one. (Courtesy of Boyce Ditto Library, Weaver Collection.)

Lake Pinto supplied water to the city of Mineral Wells from the time of its creation in 1902 until Rock Creek in Parker County was dammed in 1919 to form Lake Mineral Wells, the third lake built as a water supply for the popular resort town. The lake has been a popular recreation area from its beginning. This view shows the public swimming hole, part of what is now Lake Mineral Wells State Park. In the background, the dam is shown, and in the foreground, a second dam is shown that successfully held water for the pool. Lake Mineral Wells was the water source for Mineral Wells until 1964, when Lake Palo Pinto, in south central Palo Pinto County, was impounded from Pinto Creek. (Courtesy of Lou Hayes Warren.)

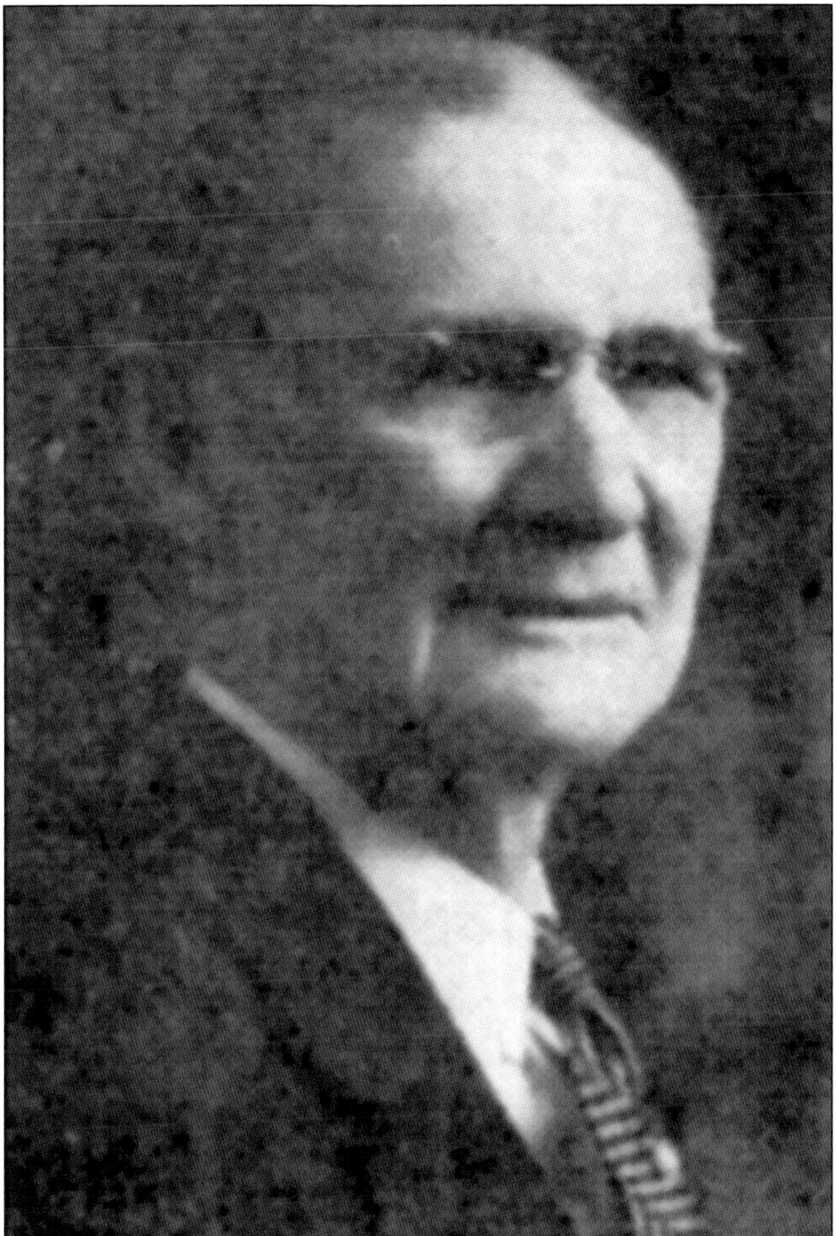

The history of the Famous Water Company began in the early 1900s when Ed Dismuke, a druggist from Waco, Texas, was given a death sentence from his doctors at the age of 40. He headed northwest about 100 miles to an acclaimed health resort town tucked away in the beautiful Palo Pinto Hills. In the town of Mineral Wells, the pharmacist went on a drinking binge of mineral water, and his ailments soon disappeared. As a believer and beneficiary of the mineral water's curative powers, Dismuke quickly sold his 25-year-old pharmacy in Waco and moved to Mineral Wells. It was in 1904 that he founded the Famous Mineral Water Company. The current Famous Pavilion was built in 1914, complete with a game parlor and a fortune-telling booth. Drawing on his experience as a pharmacist, Dismuke developed products from the curative waters. (Courtesy of Lou Hayes Warren.)

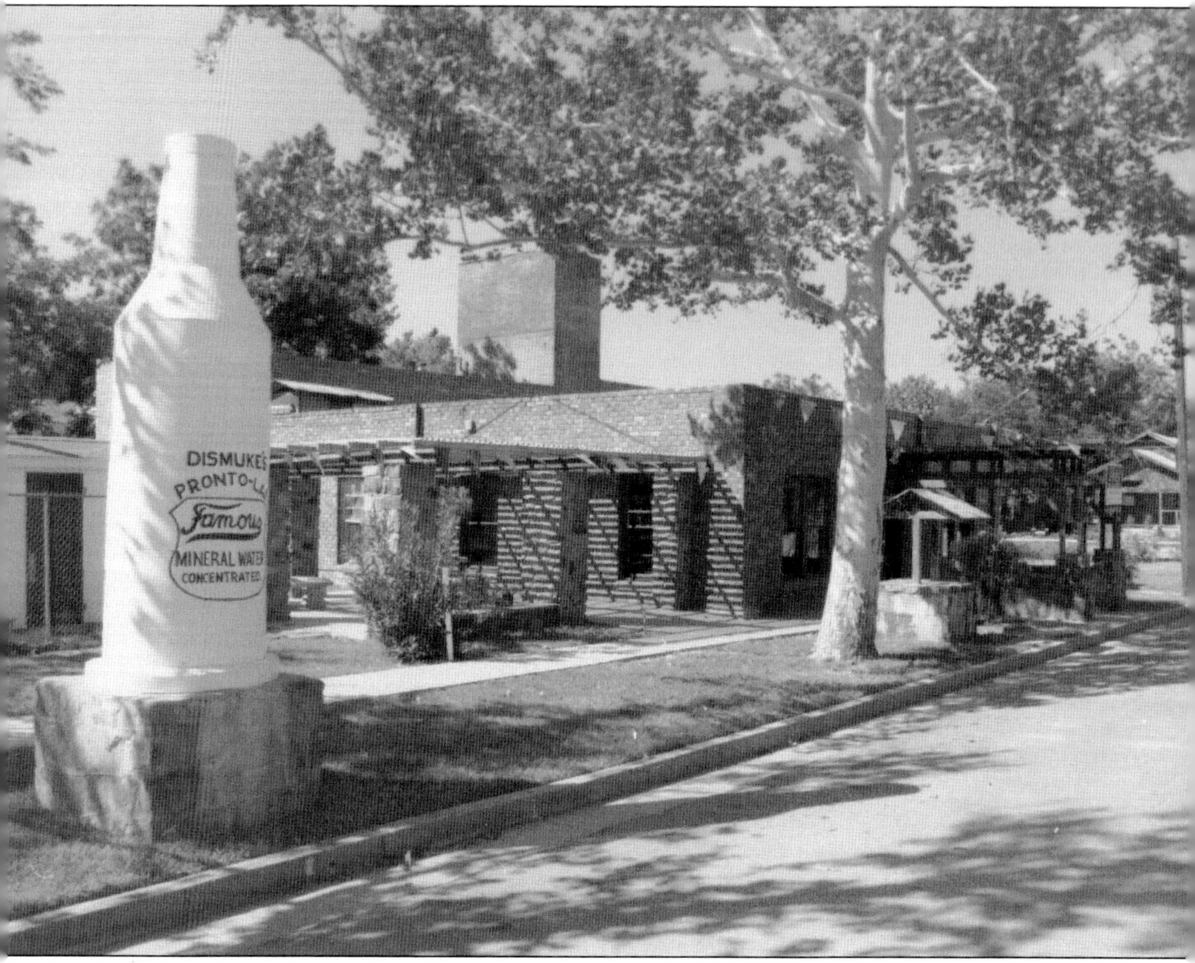

The Famous Water Company, founded by Ed Dismuke, is still located at 215 Northwest Sixth Street. It has been restored and still sells mineral water. The large concrete bottle depicts the original shape of the product. The Famous Water Company currently sells four grades of water: regular full-strength mineral water, deep-well (400 feet) water, deep-well water that has been ionized and filtered by reverse osmosis, and a blend of the ionized and reverse osmosis water. On April 15, 1994, the Famous Mineral Water Company was leased from the Palo Pinto Historical Foundation by Zephyr Water Company and was operated by Sherry Holland. The foundation sold the property to its present owners—Bill and Helen Arneson and Carol and Scott Elder—on October 1, 1999. Now celebrating more than 100 years of service to the area, loyal patrons continue to purchase bottles of the waters. Some customers bring their own containers and have them filled inside the original Famous Pavilion. (Courtesy of Boyce Ditto Library, Weaver Collection.)

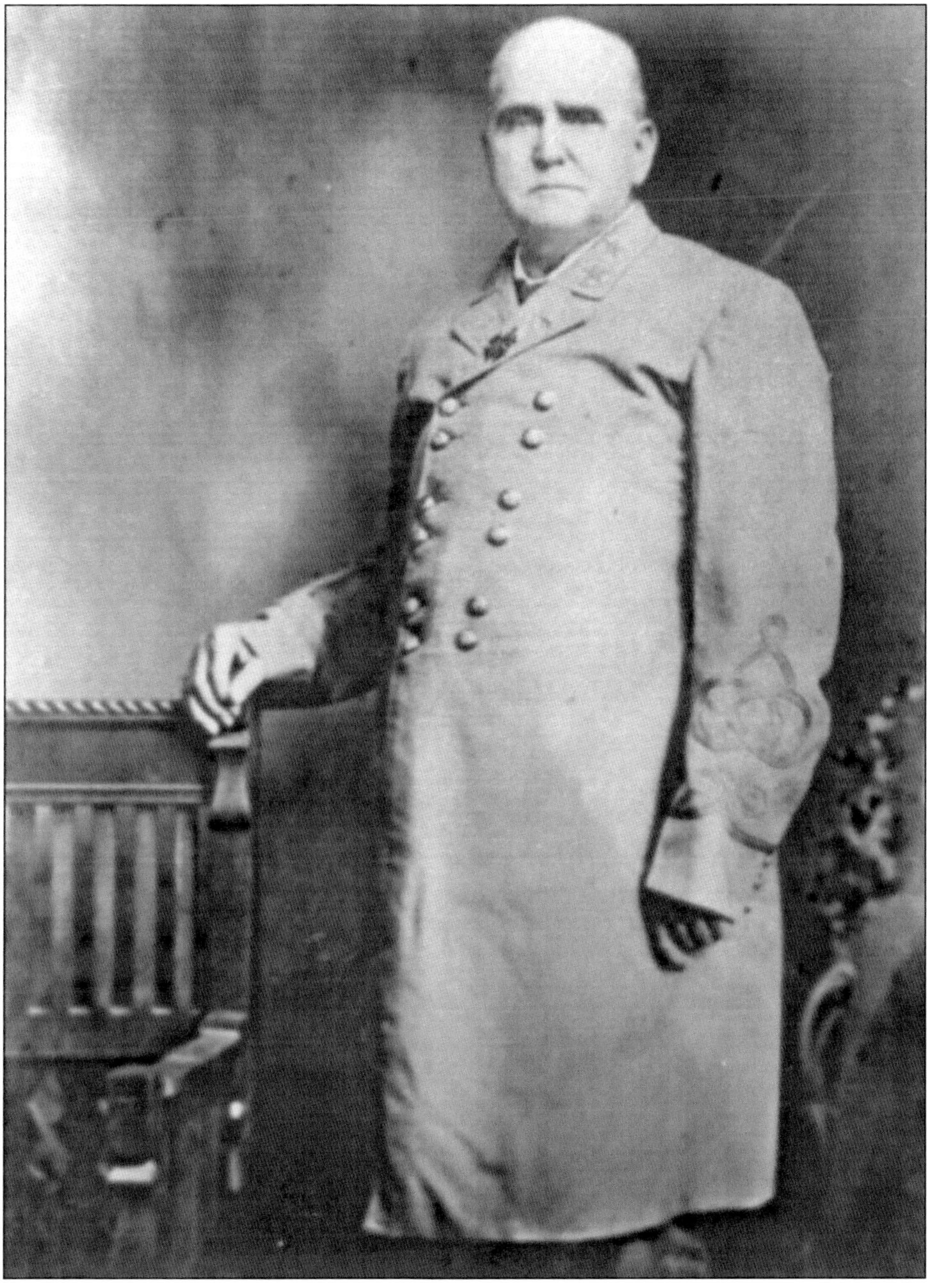

Cicero Smith—entrepreneur, bank president, and business owner—posed here in his United Confederate Veterans uniform. Smith was instrumental in the growth and expansion of Mineral Wells as a tourist and recreational destination. He was born on April 25, 1845, in LaFayette, Georgia, and died February 2, 1914, in Mineral Wells. He was the son of Jesse Smith and Nancy Kite. Cicero saw what was going on in Mineral Wells and developed the tourist industry. He built Mineral Wells Lakewood Motor Car Scenic Railway, which ran from Northwest Sixth Street, where the Famous Water Company was located, to Pinto Lake every 15 minutes and cost 15¢ per ride. The scenic railway trains were actually dinky cars, which are small gasoline-powered vehicles that ran on railroad tracks. (Courtesy of Doris Perry McConnell.)

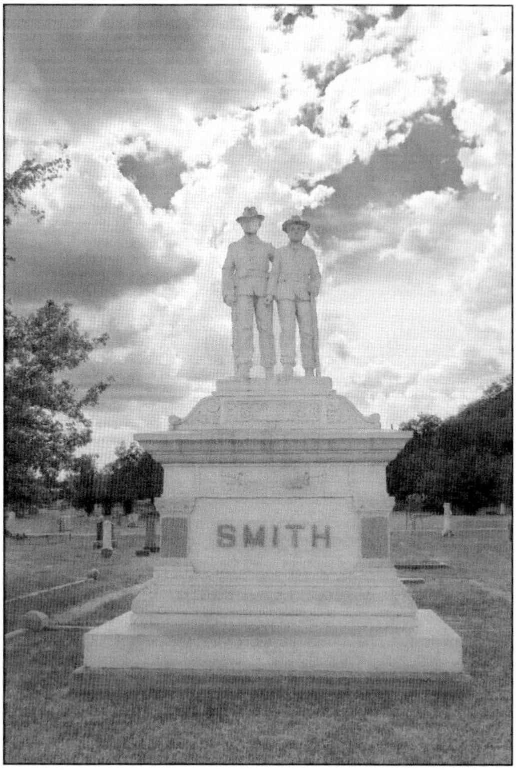

Cicero Smith and his brother John Henry Smith are buried in the Elmwood Cemetery on Highway 180 in Mineral Wells. Their statues show them in their Confederate uniforms of which they were so proud. (Photograph by Raf Seibert.)

The Ben Hur motorcar, owned and operated by Cicero Smith, was a new large gasoline-powered car that operated on Mesquite Street in the 200 block of Northeast First Avenue. It joined two dinky cars named "Esther" and "Susie" on the Mineral Wells Lakewood Park and Scenic Railway in 1908. The railway ceased operation in 1909. Mineral Wells was probably one of the few cities in the United States that had gasoline-powered streetcars. (Courtesy of Boyce Ditto Library, Weaver Collection.)

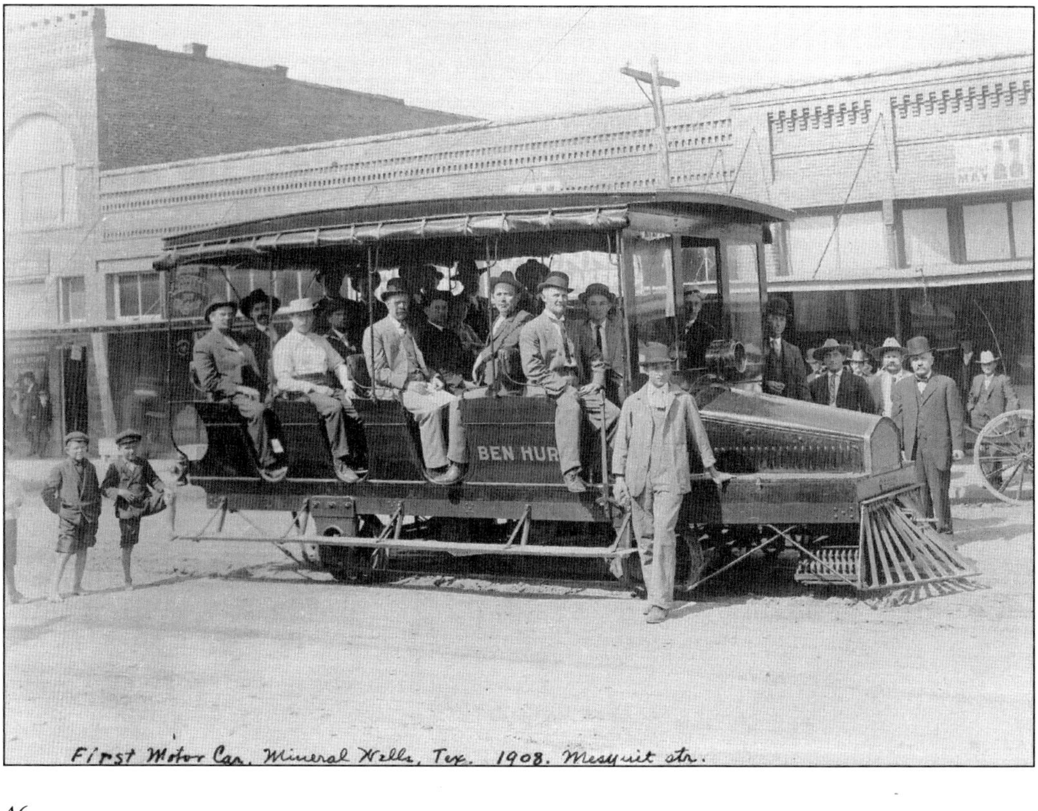

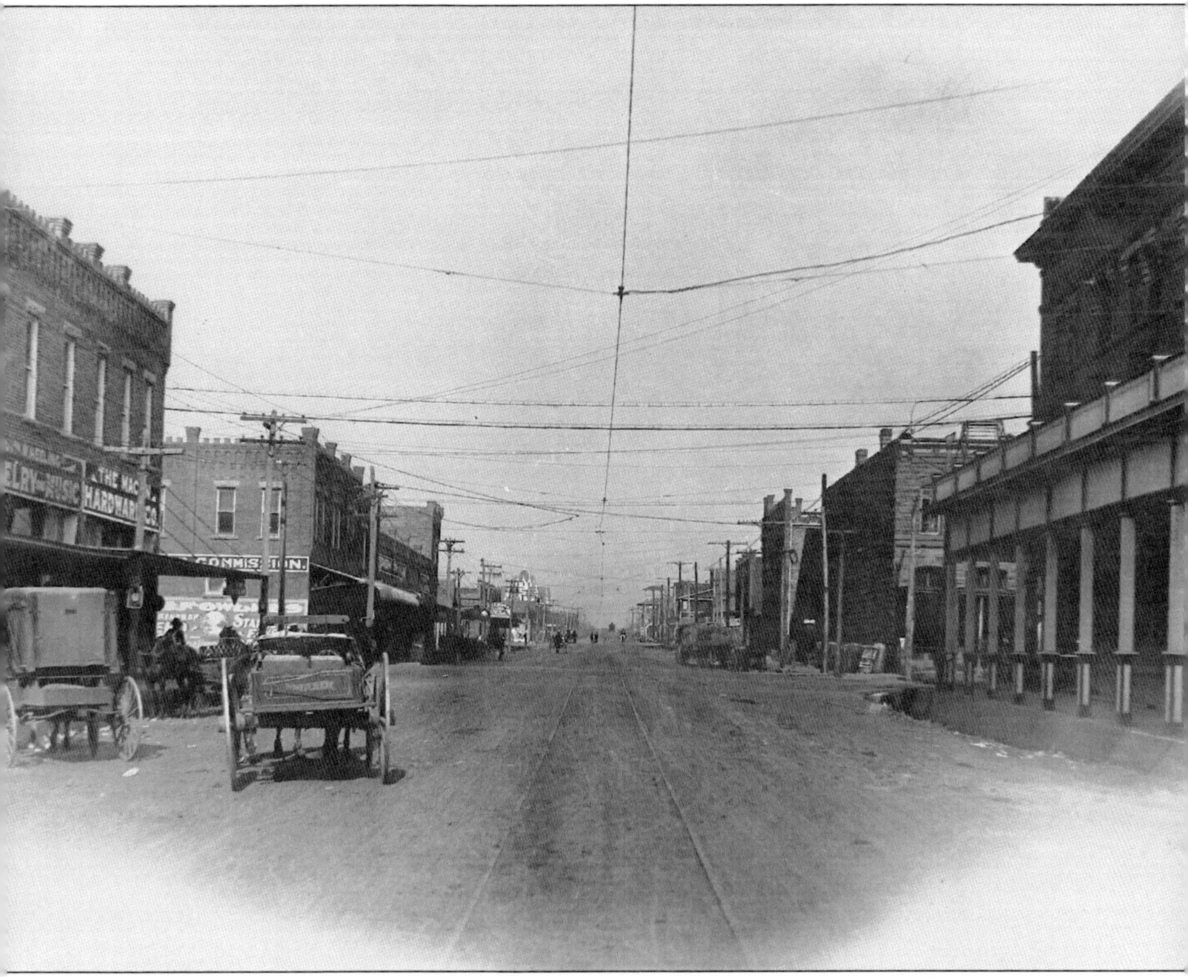

This street scene in Mineral Wells was taken around 1900. Looking north on North Oak Street, near the intersection of West Hubbard Street, streetcar tracks line the middle of the road, and the Hexagon House Hotel, opened in 1897, is visible toward the north end of town. Streetcar service ran from 1907 to 1913. The streets in Mineral Wells were not paved until 1914. (Courtesy of Boyce Ditto Library, Weaver Collection.)

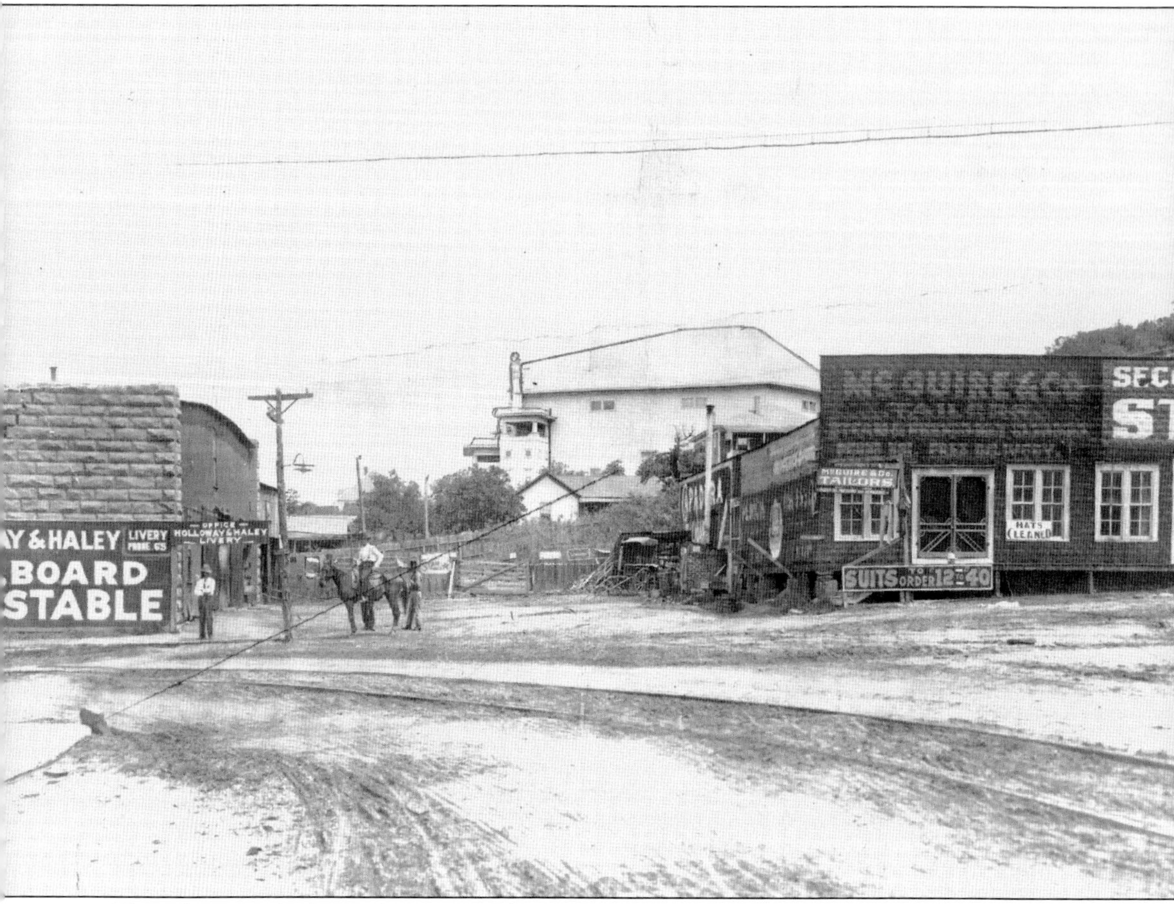

This photograph shows the corner of Mesquite and Coke Streets (now Northeast First Avenue and Northeast Second Street). The picture was taken in 1905 after the Ben Hur motorcar stopped running, but the tracks can still be seen. The Whatley Motor Company is now located where the livery stable, seen at left, was located at the time. The old post office, now the Woman's Club, replaced the buildings on the right, and the Chautauqua, an adult educational facility for lectures, plays, and musical performances, was the large white building a block farther up the street at the center. (Courtesy of Boyce Ditto Library, Weaver Collection.)

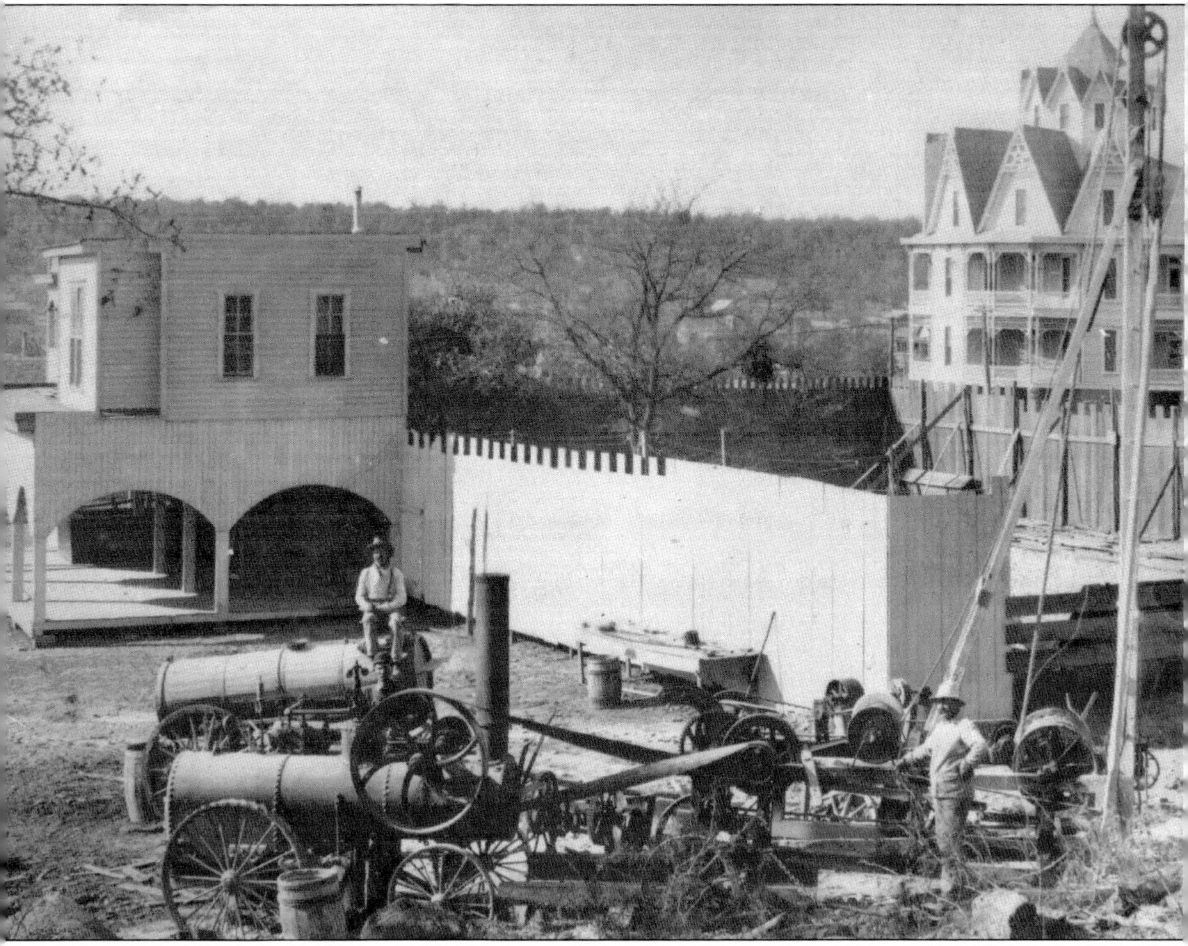

Drilling of the Vichy Well was done by J. W. "Doon" Deberry in the 600 block of North Oak Street. The Vichy Well Natatorium, later "the Beach" and then the Standard Well, was located across North Oak Street from the Hexagon House Hotel, which can be seen at the right edge of the photograph. The Standard Pavilion boasted a variety of attractions, including a swimming pool, movie theater, bowling alley, and dance floor. It was torn down during World War II and replaced by a United Service Organization (USO) canteen to serve the soldiers training at local Camp Wolters. At the end of the war, the USO was given to the city and utilized as a community center and later as a senior center. (Courtesy of Boyce Ditto Library, Weaver Collection.)

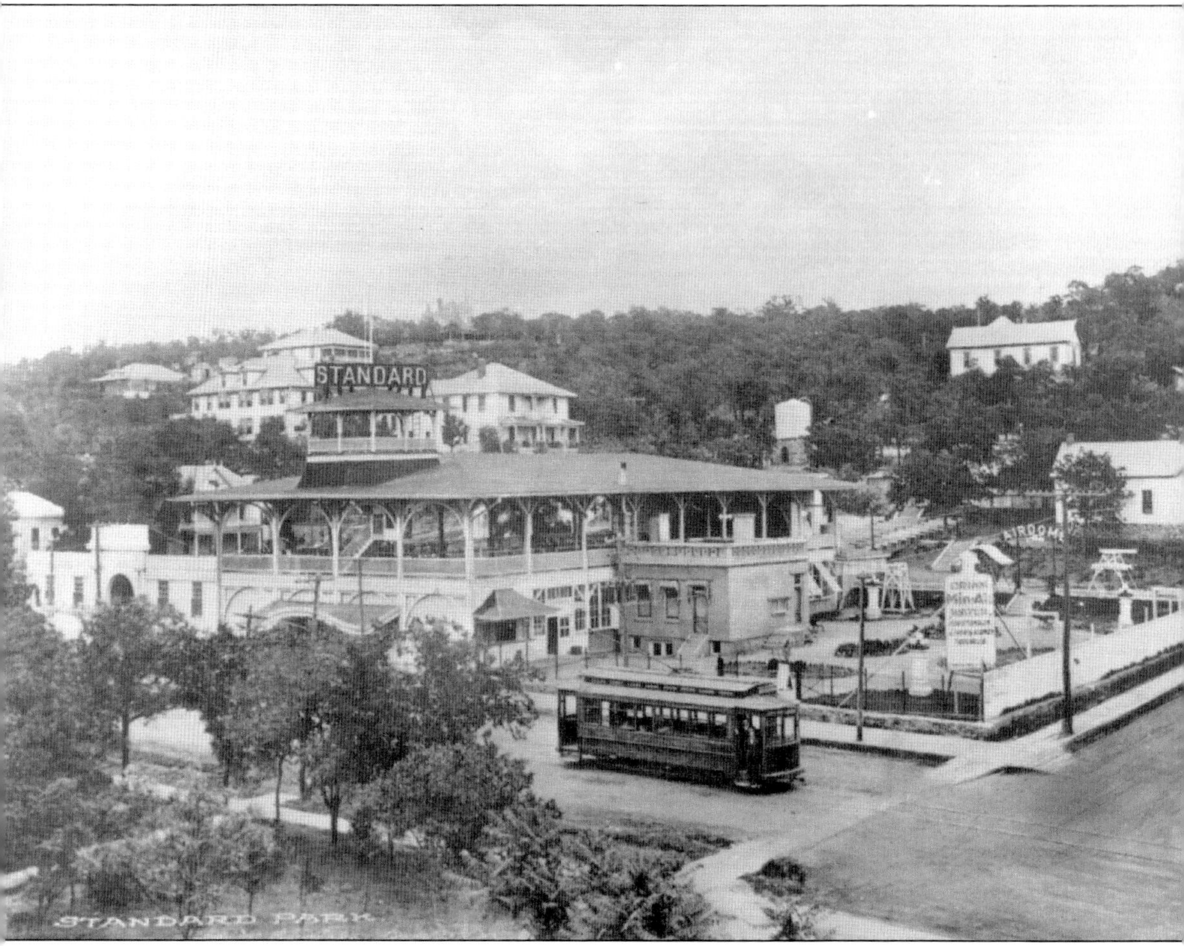

The Standard Pavilion contained many entertainment venues for health-seekers. A trolley to it operated on North Oak Street from 1907 to 1913. The Standard was torn down in World War II, and the USO club was built there. The USO building was given to the city after the war and renamed the North Oak Community Center. The Kingsley Hotel, above left of the Standard, was built into the side of East Mountain and was later destroyed by fire. (Courtesy of Boyce Ditto Library, Weaver Collection.)

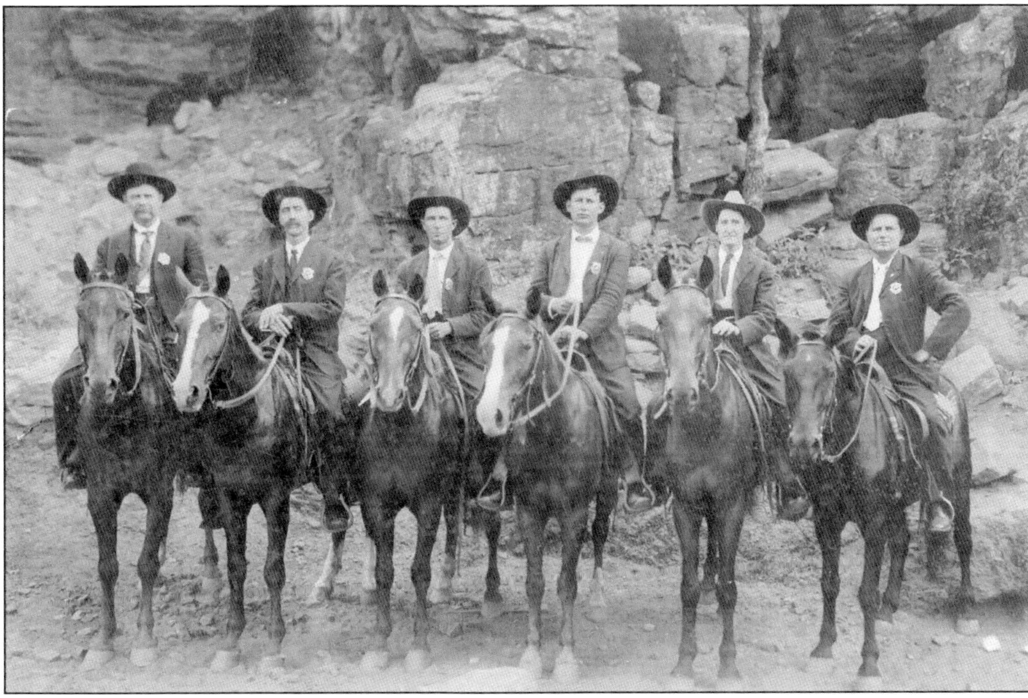

By the start of the 20th century, the mounted police of Mineral Wells were using horses as well as donkeys. Here they are posing on the way up East Mountain. (Courtesy Lou Hayes Warren.)

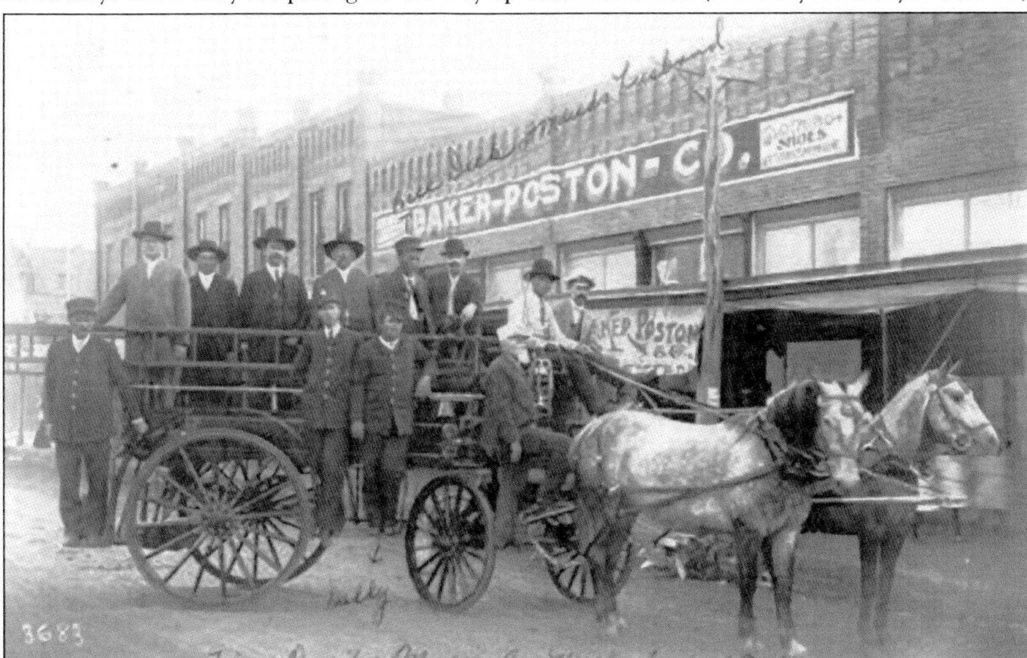

By 1900, Mineral Wells had a fire department, pictured here in front of the Baker-Poston Company on North Oak Street. This building later became Poston Dry Goods and is now the Palo Pinto County Courthouse Annex in Mineral Wells. (Courtesy of the I. B. Chapman family of Chapman Family Ranches.)

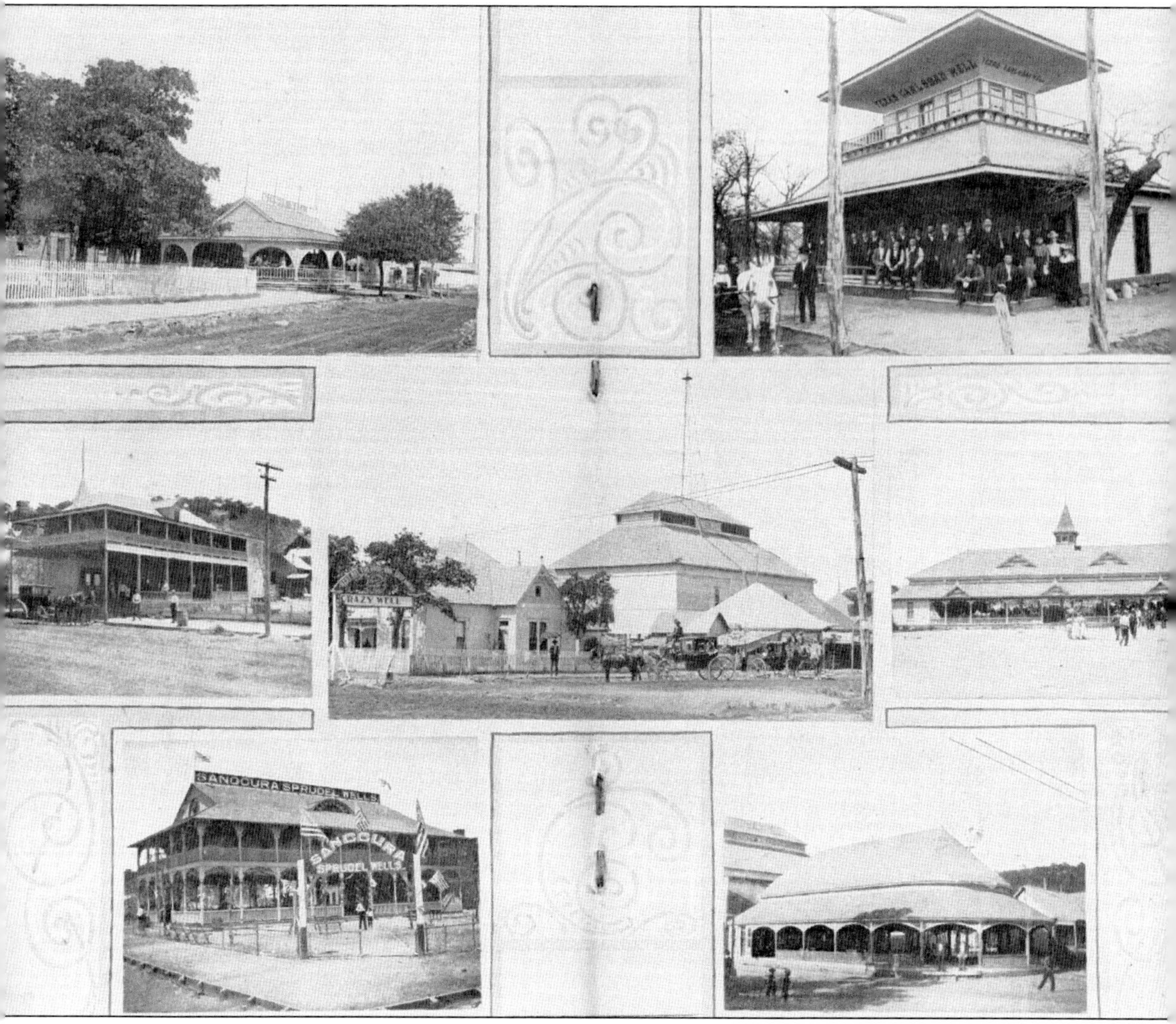

Many wells were dug in the beginning of the 20th century, each one trying to outdo those before it by being more ornate and providing many tourist attractions, with drinking pavilions for people seeking healthful cures. (Courtesy of Lou Hayes Warren.)

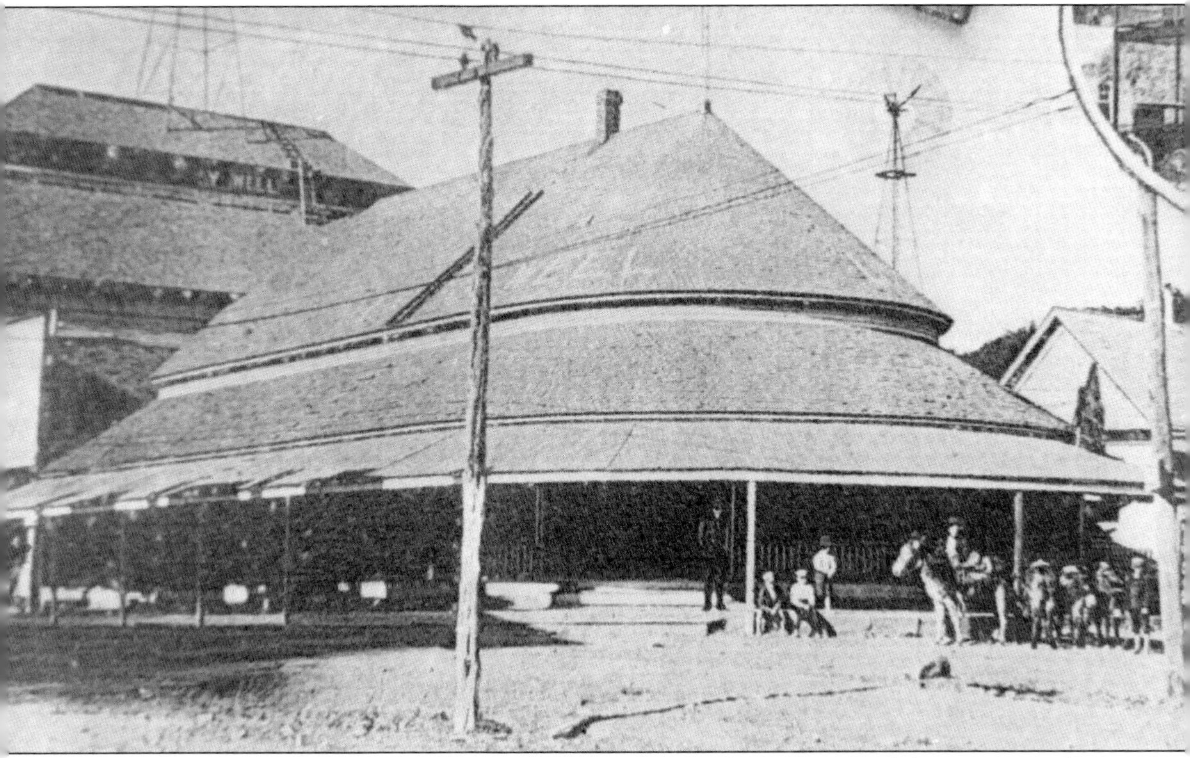

The Lithia Well and Drinking Pavilion was located on the southwest corner of the Crazy Hotel Block at what is now 400 Northwest First Avenue, the location of the Crazy Retirement Home. The second Crazy Well Pavilion is the large building at the upper left of the photograph. Note the three burros next to the horse. Riding burros up a trail on East Mountain was a popular tourist pastime in addition to drinking and bathing in the mineral waters. (Courtesy of Boyce Ditto Library, Weaver Collection.)

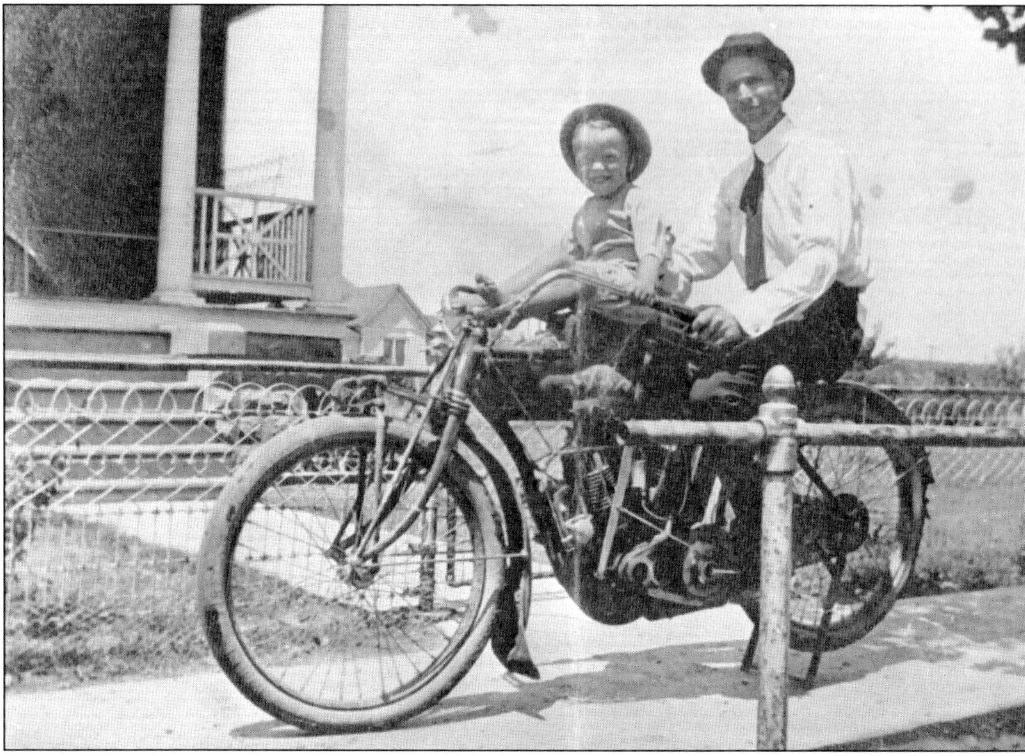

Pictured in 1908 is Frank Richards, owner of the first motorcycle bought in Mineral Wells. Frank Richards was the owner of the Star Well during Mineral Wells' heyday as a popular health spa resort, and the boy on the bike with him was his son Robert Frank Richards, father of Bobby Richards, a local businessman. (Courtesy of Boyce Ditto Library, Weaver Collection.)

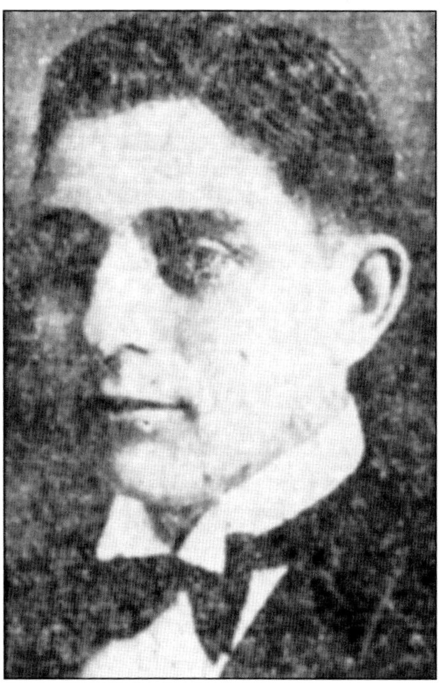

D. C. Harris owned the second motorcycle in Mineral Wells. Harris was the postmaster and served as mayor of the city at one time. His mother was the first white child born in Palo Pinto County. (Courtesy of Lou Hayes Warren.)

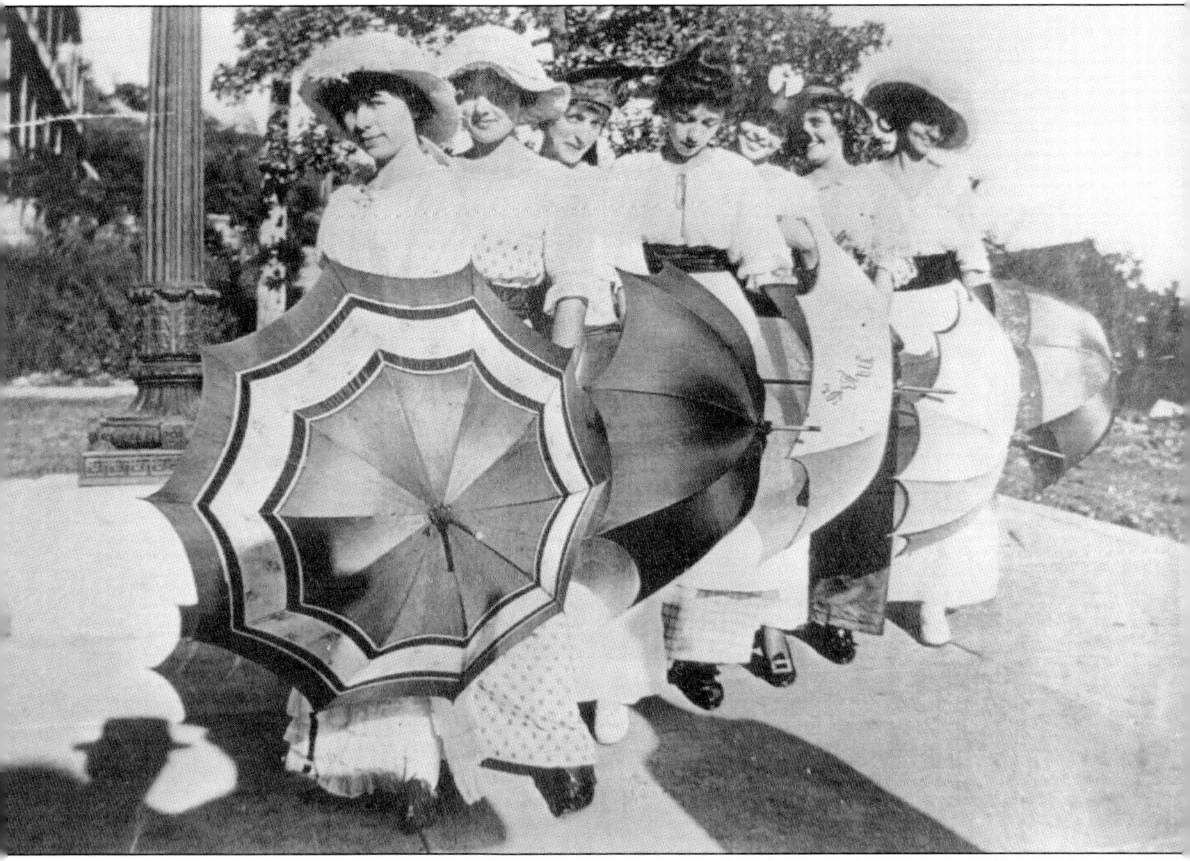

The Sllew La Renim Club was Mineral Wells spelled backward. The members pose in front of the old post office in 1913. Pictured from left to right are Anna Mae Guinn, Ernestine Pollard, May Belle Smith, Ann Locke Galbraith, Ruby Andrews, and Mattie Withers. The ladies of the time used parasols to shade themselves from the sun. There are seven ladies in the picture, but only six are identified. As deduced from the notes on the back of the picture, Mary Lee Hayes is believed to be the third lady in line in the picture. The Mineral Wells Sanitarium, originally known as the Exchange Hotel, is shown in the upper left of the picture. (Courtesy of Boyce Ditto Library, Weaver Collection.)

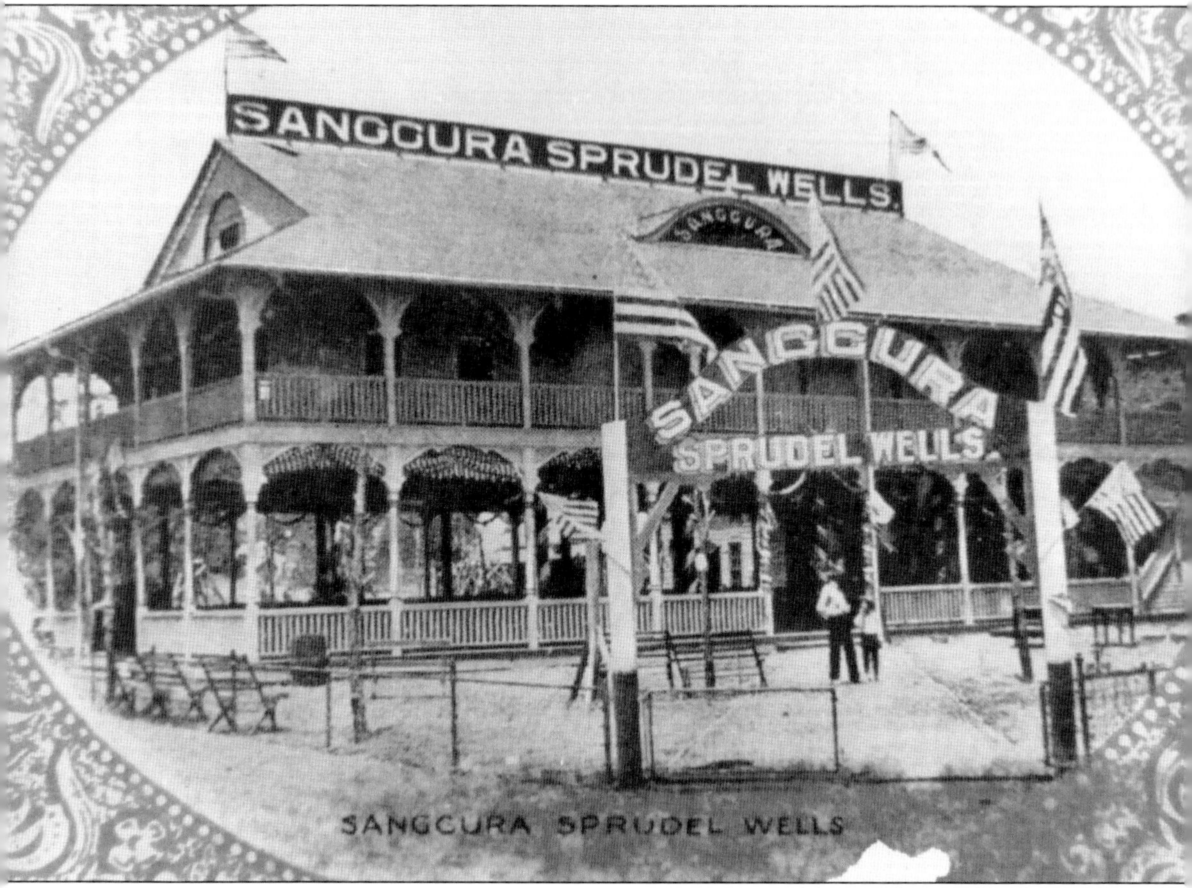

Sangcura Sprudel Wells was a water drinking pavilion located at 800 Northwest Second Avenue. The building was later moved to 314 Northwest Fifth Street. The porches were enclosed, and it was turned into a rooming house, but it later burned down. (Courtesy of Boyce Ditto Library, Weaver Collection.)

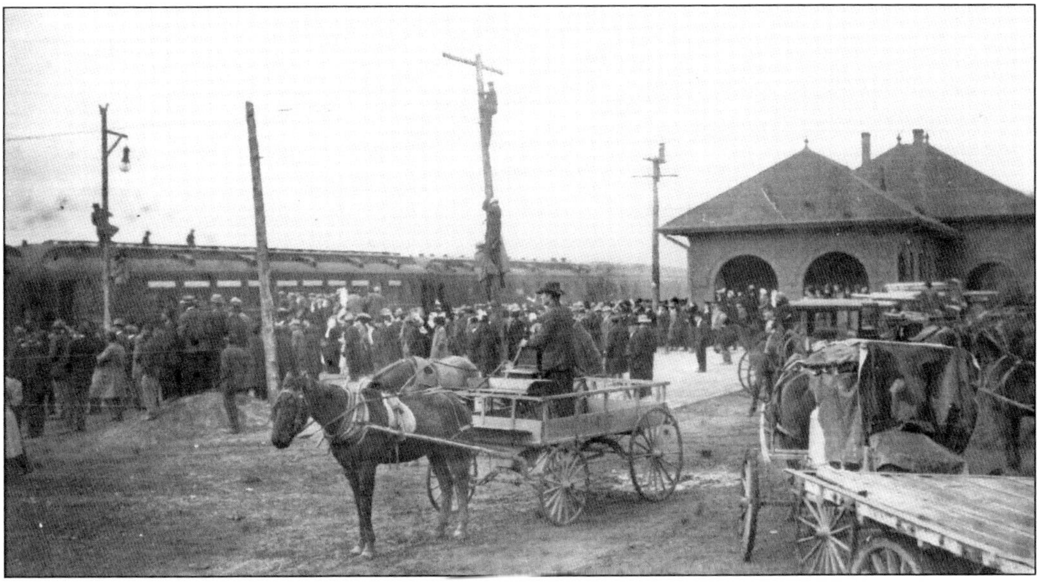

Before the advent of automobiles, hacks met tourists and health-seekers at the depot to take them to their favorite hotel or rooming house in Mineral Wells. These pictures are typical of weekend visitors from the Fort Worth/Dallas Metroplex who came to Mineral Wells to drink the healing mineral water and take the relaxing baths and massages. The men on the telephone poles were spotters who sought to deliver clients to local hotels and rooming houses. (Both, courtesy of Boyce Ditto Library, Weaver Collection.)

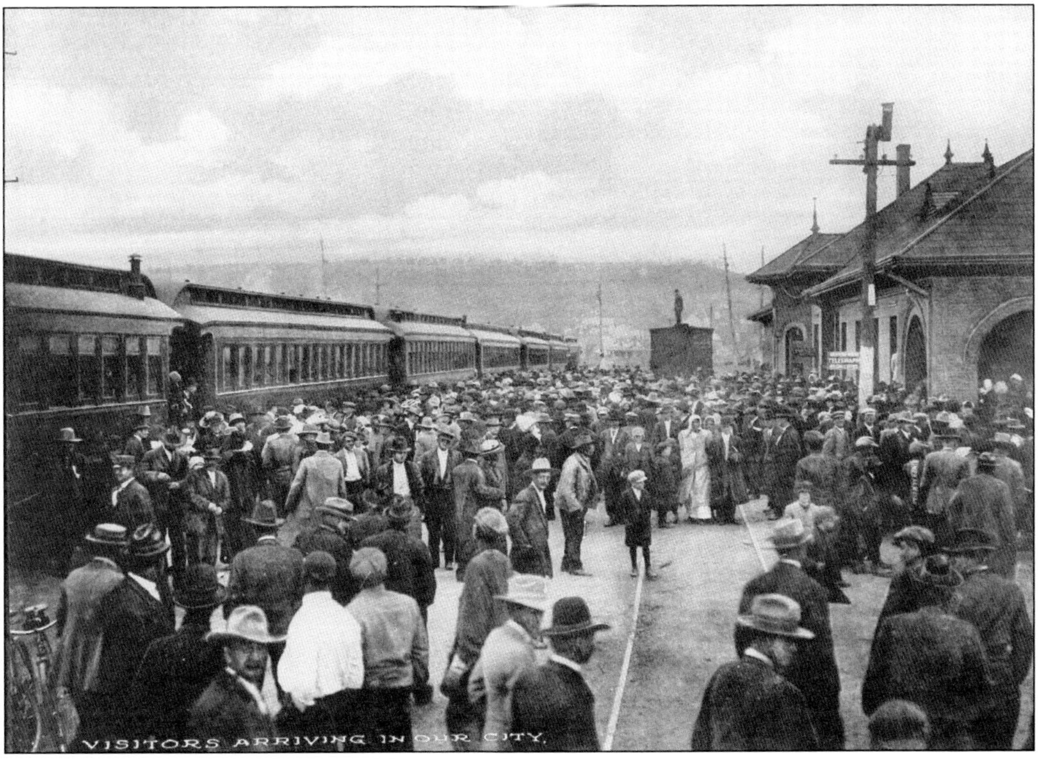

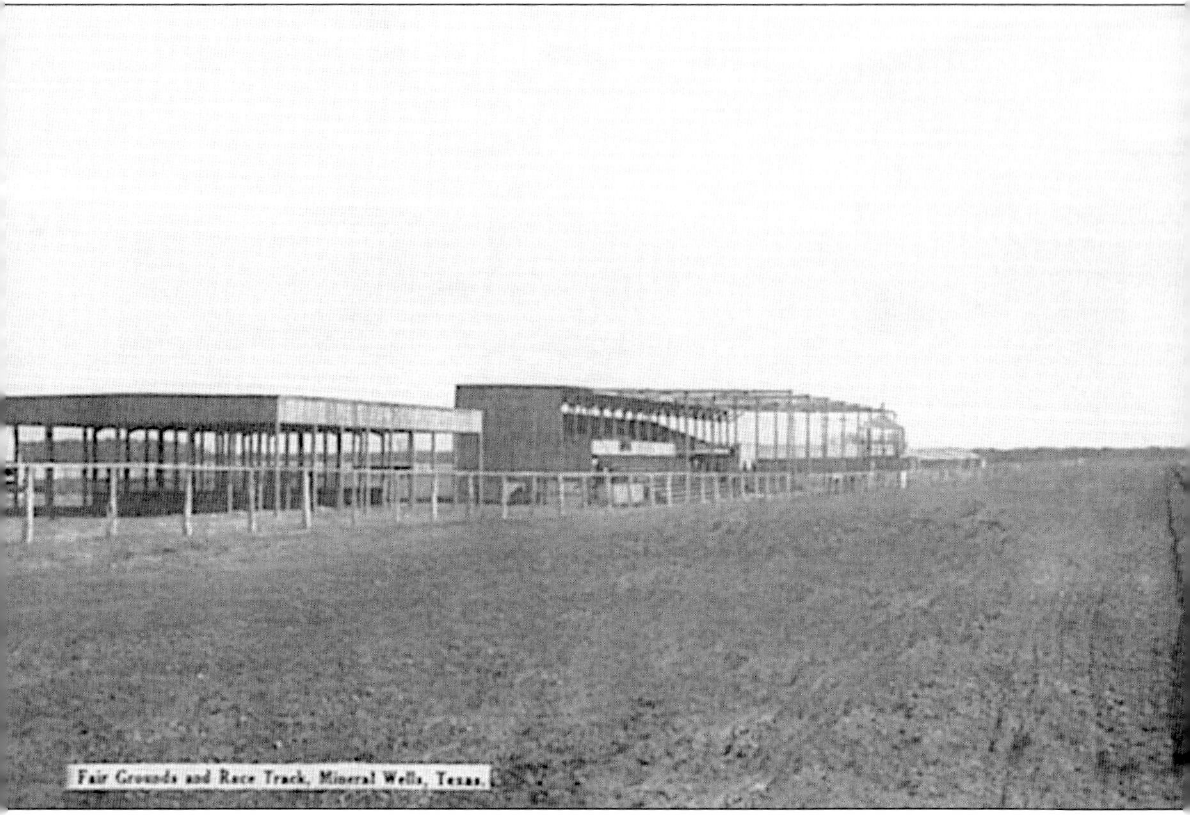

At the turn of the 20th century, a horse racetrack and fairgrounds was located southeast of town. It is not certain if thoroughbred horses raced here, but sulkies are known to have raced here. This course was the first of its kind in Mineral Wells. After it was torn down, another track was constructed in the southwest part of town at Elmhurst Park. (Courtesy of Boyce Ditto Library, Weaver Collection.)

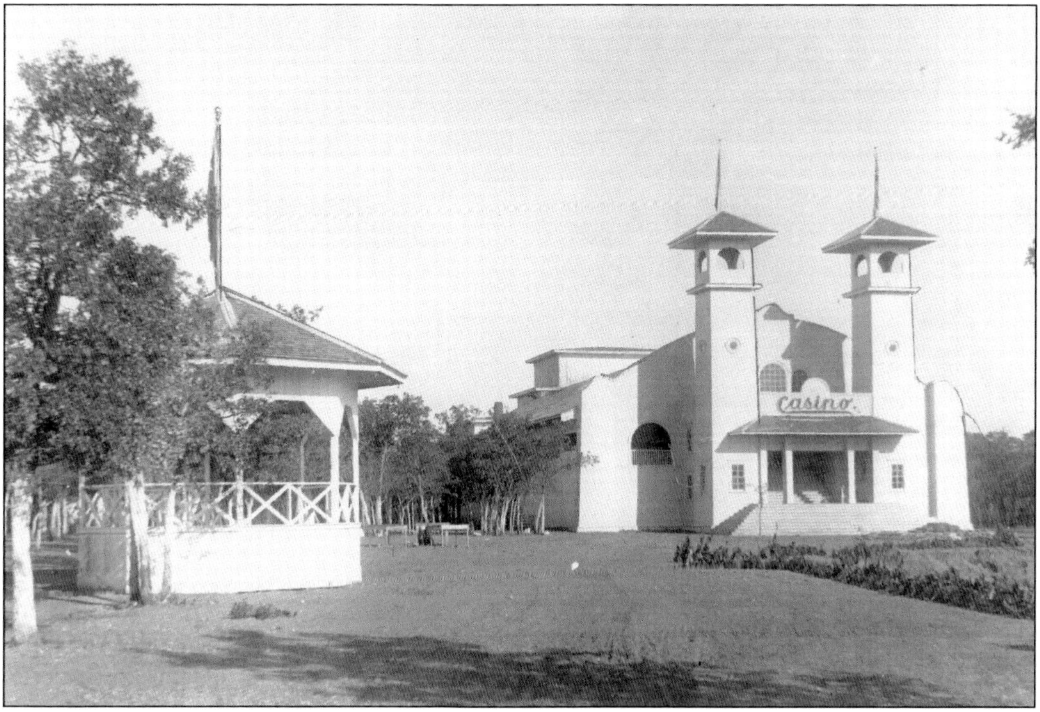

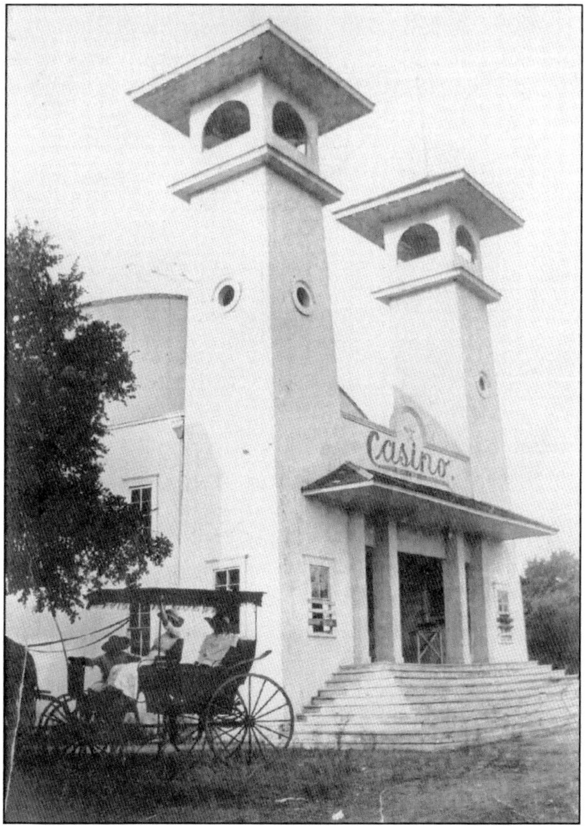

The Casino at Elmhurst Park was in the southwest part of Mineral Wells. The park was a 1920s and 1930s recreational spot for the resort city. It no longer exists, as it was a casualty of state gambling reform laws. The casino is now the site of the city sewage disposal facility. (Both, courtesy of Boyce Ditto Library, Weaver Collection.)

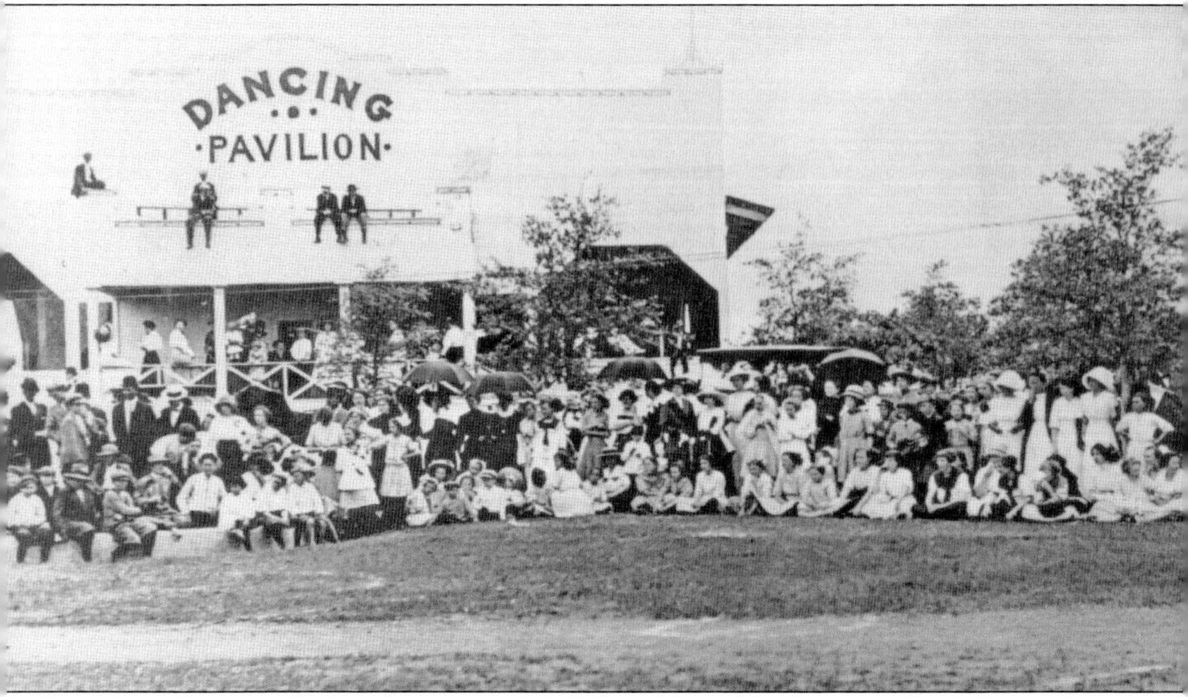

This photograph shows a spring play day at Elmhurst Park in 1910. The popular park once boasted a casino, a dancing pavilion, exhibit halls, and outdoor sports fields. It hosted the county fair and sports events until 1913, when the popularity of automobiles disrupted the once-thriving streetcar business and made that mode of transportation unprofitable. Upon the closure of Elmhurst Park, the City of Mineral Wells became owner of the property. It was used for a housing development during World War II to accommodate families of soldiers and civilian workers at Camp Wolters. The City of Mineral Wells built water treatment facilities there after the war. (Courtesy of Boyce Ditto Library, Weaver Collection.)

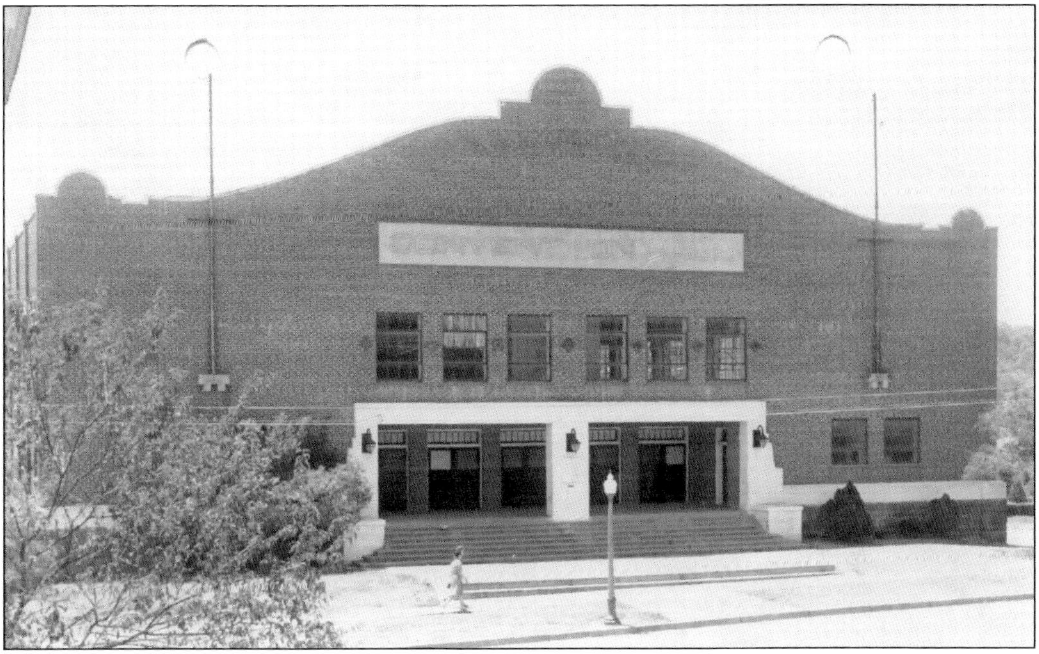

The Mineral Wells Convention Center was constructed north of the Hexagon House Hotel on North Oak Street. It was a popular place for groups such as the Woodmen of the World and the Texas Republican Convention. The photograph below shows part of the group attending a convention of the Woodmen of the World in Mineral Wells in 1905. The picture was taken at the Texas Carlsbad Well, located at 415 Northwest First Avenue. (Above, courtesy of Lou Hayes Warren; below, courtesy of Boyce Ditto Library, Weaver Collection.)

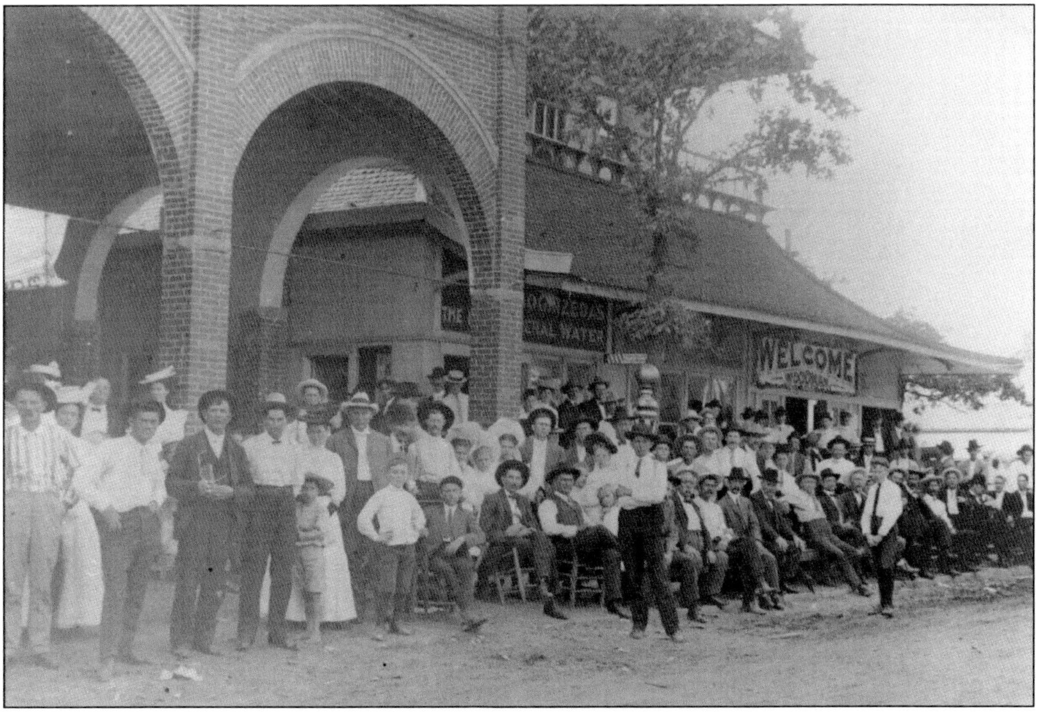

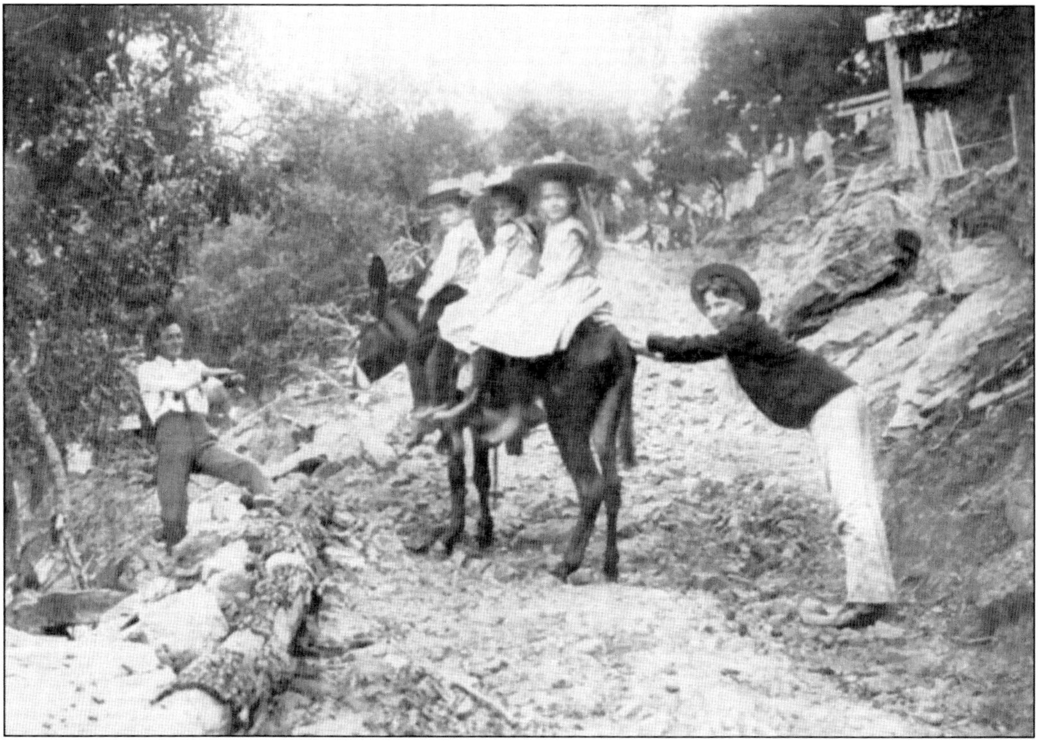

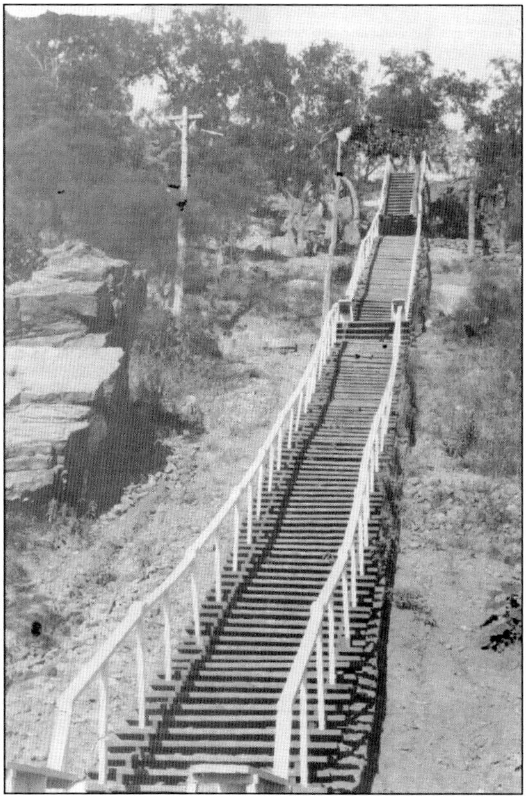

While many people preferred to ride donkeys up East Mountain in Mineral Wells, there were times when the donkey was not happy about the trip and had to be encouraged. (Courtesy of Lou Hayes Warren.)

There were other times when folks chose to use the "Fat Man's Misery Steps" that led up the side of East Mountain. It was quite a climb, but it was very good for the health. (Courtesy of Lou Hayes Warren.)

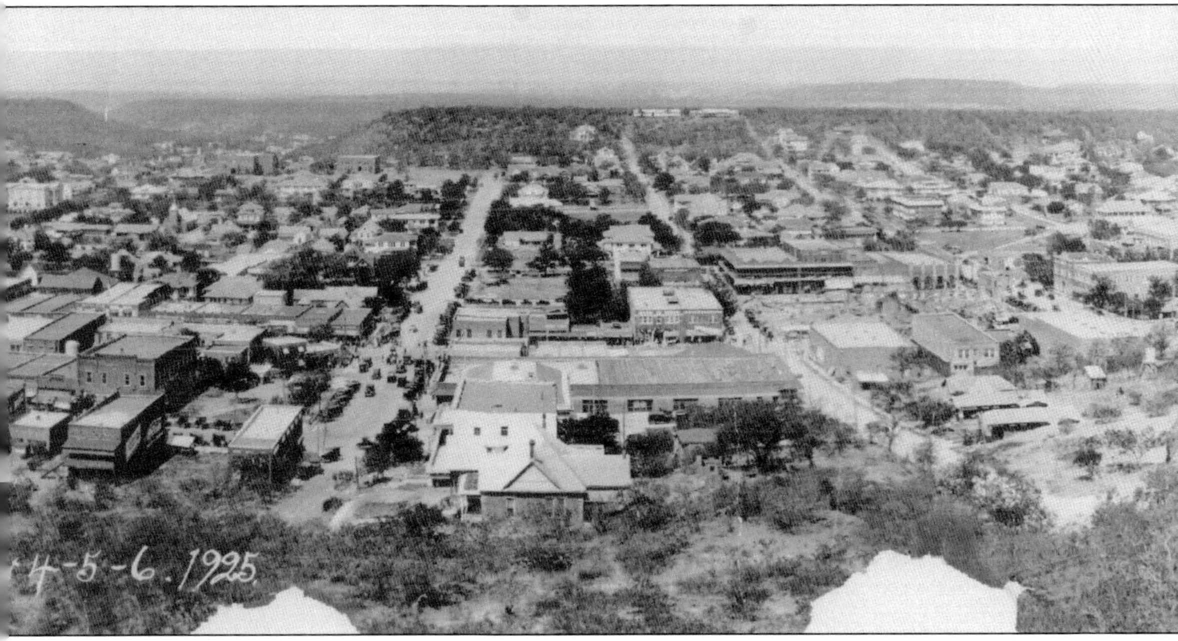

This photograph was taken two months after the Crazy Water Hotel burned in 1925. Although there is no Crazy Hotel in this picture, the Crazy Well building behind the hotel did not burn and is shown here in the vacant lot on the wide street at right. Looking west toward West Mountain, the two buildings on top were owned by the Troop F cavalry. That is where their horses were kept. The old high school, the Little Rock School, and the West Ward School can be seen in the upper left of the picture at the south end of West Mountain. (Courtesy of Boyce Ditto Library, Weaver Collection.)

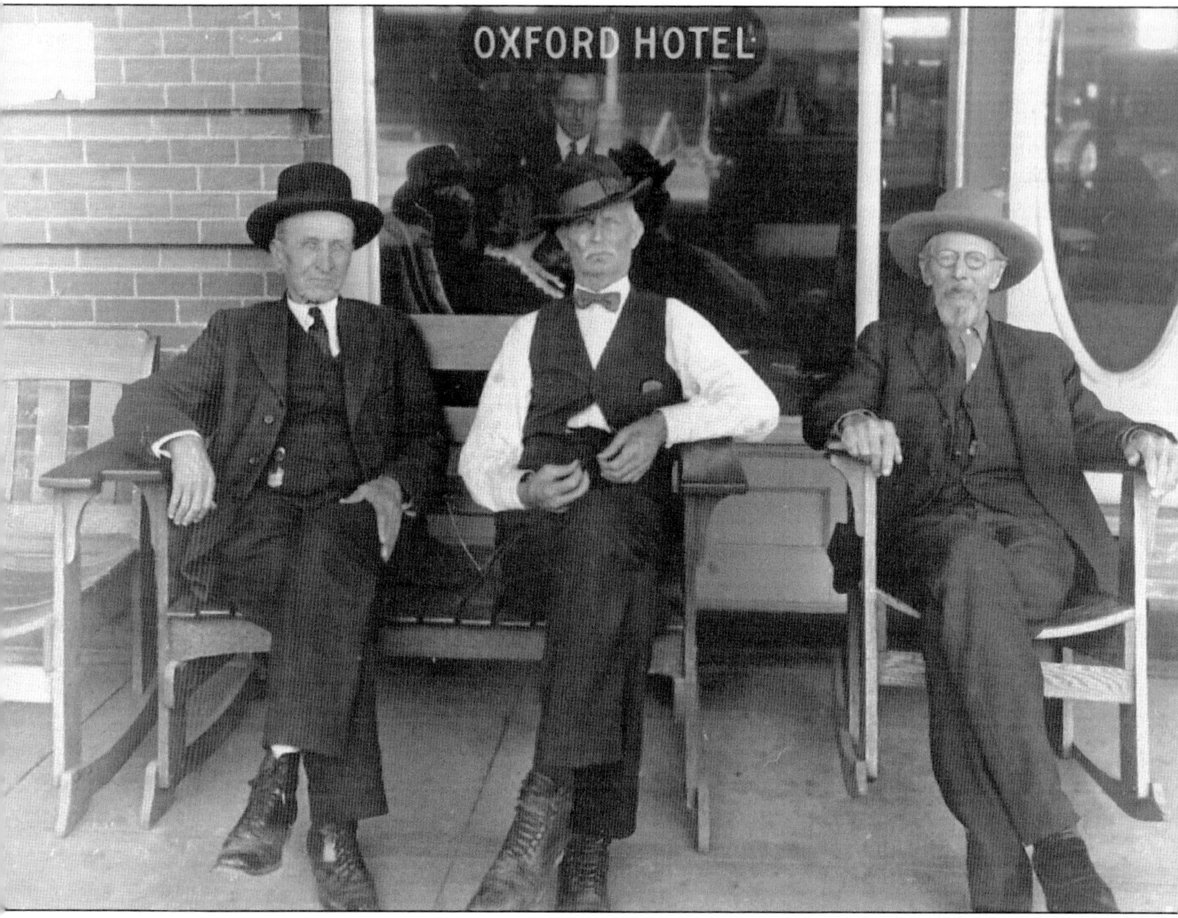

In front of the Oxford Hotel are, from left to right, R. B. Preston, Mr. Dick from Millsap, and Stith Edmondson, who was an early sheriff of Palo Pinto County. Dr. J. H. McCracken can be seen in the window. The First State Bank and Trust Company was located in the corner of this building, later called the Firstron Building. A sign on the left corner of the building promotes public decorum: "$15.00 Fine for Spitting on Sidewalk." (Courtesy of Boyce Ditto Library, Weaver Collection.)

Col. Willis Riess Austin and his wife, Maggie, came from Kentucky to Palo Pinto County around 1880 and established the Austin Well. Austin settled on Staggs Prairie, where he farmed and ranched. He became interested in mineral waters when he had an eye infection. Austin moved into Mineral Wells, and continuous use of the waters restored his sight. At first he engaged in the dairy business but later entered the field of mineral water production, establishing the Austin Well, which was later operated by his son-in-law, Tom Sims. (Courtesy of Boyce Ditto Library, Weaver Collection.)

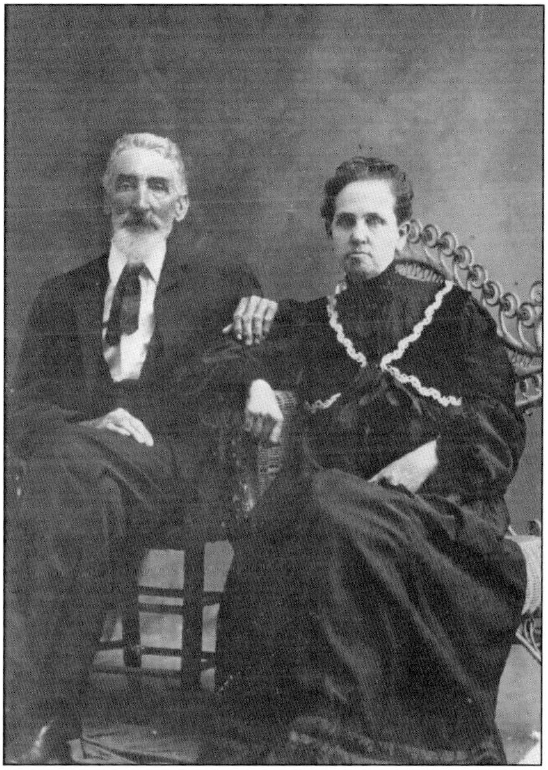

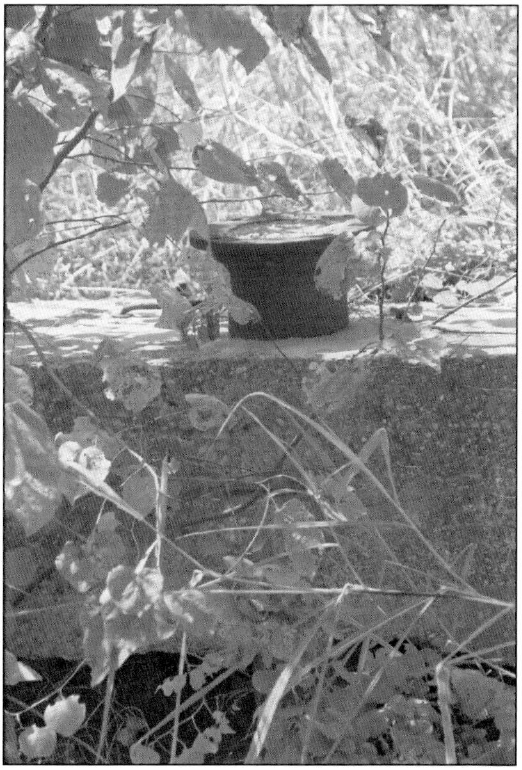

This is the Austin Well today. Wells like this are still a common sight when driving through Mineral Wells, especially in the northwest part of town. (Photograph by Raf Seibert.)

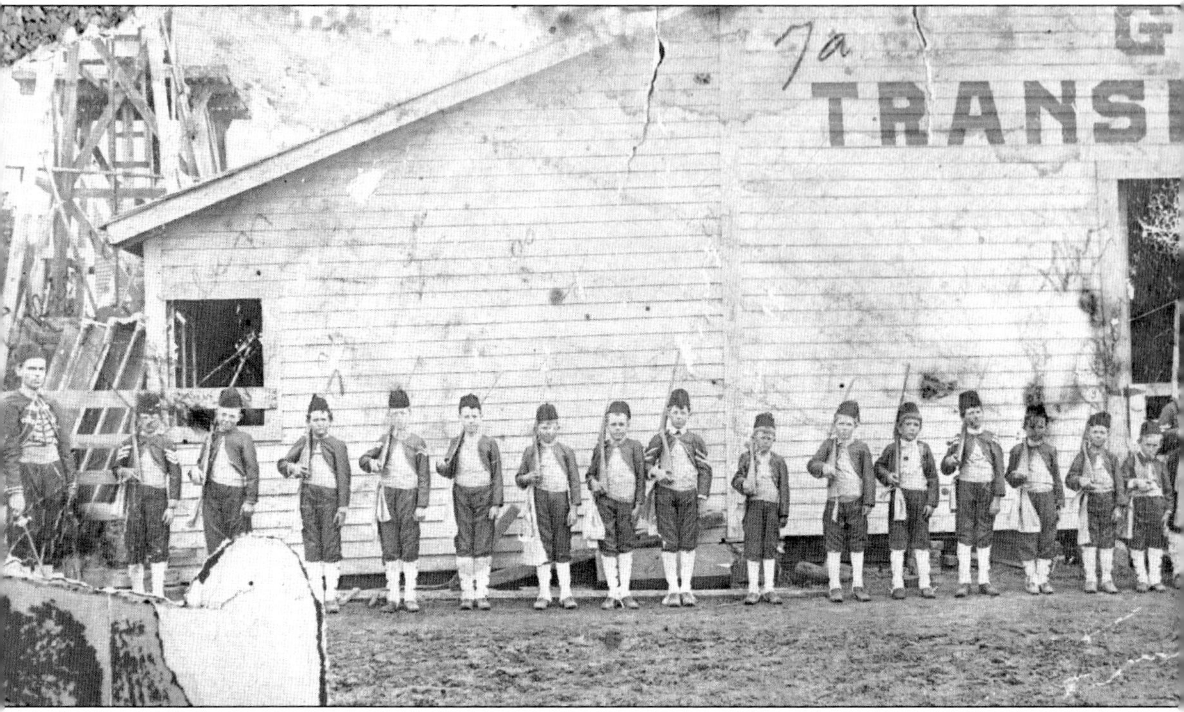

This photograph of the first organized boys' club in Mineral Wells, perhaps a youth division of the Shriners, was taken in front of the Greens Transfer Building around 1902. It was a precursor to the Boy Scouts movement that started six years later in England and spread to America in 1910. This group was organized by Frank Creighton (far left) and met in the Sangcura Sprudel Well Pavilion. (Courtesy of Boyce Ditto Library, Weaver Collection.)

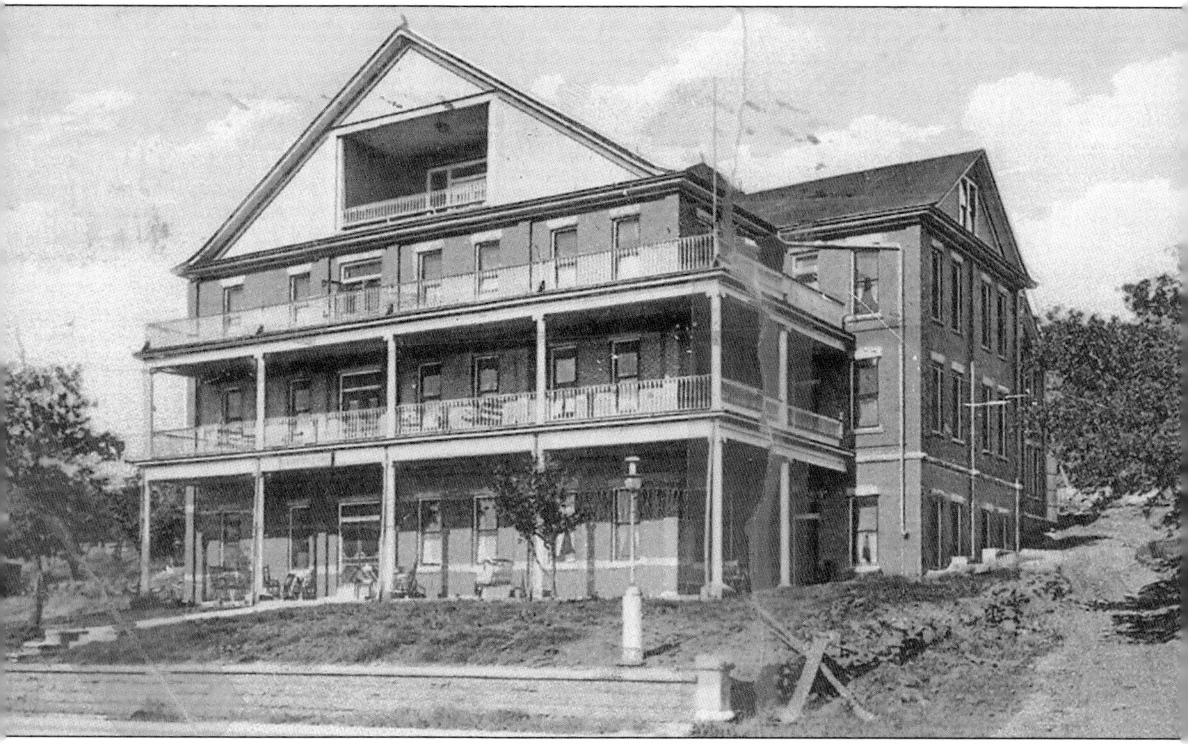

The Fairfield Inn, built by Col. Walter H. Boykin around the start of the 20th century, was a very popular boardinghouse in the early days of Mineral Wells. It was located at 814 North Oak Street, across Oak Street and one block north of its contemporary, the Hexagon House Hotel. Part of the retaining wall still exists. Boykin built his home at 1501 Southeast Fourth Avenue. The home was later sold to William Whipple Johnson, who operated the Rock Creek coal mines in eastern Parker County around 1910. Johnson, with his brother Harvey, had previously opened the coal mines at Thurber on the Palo Pinto–Erath county line in 1908. (Courtesy of Boyce Ditto Library, Weaver Collection.)

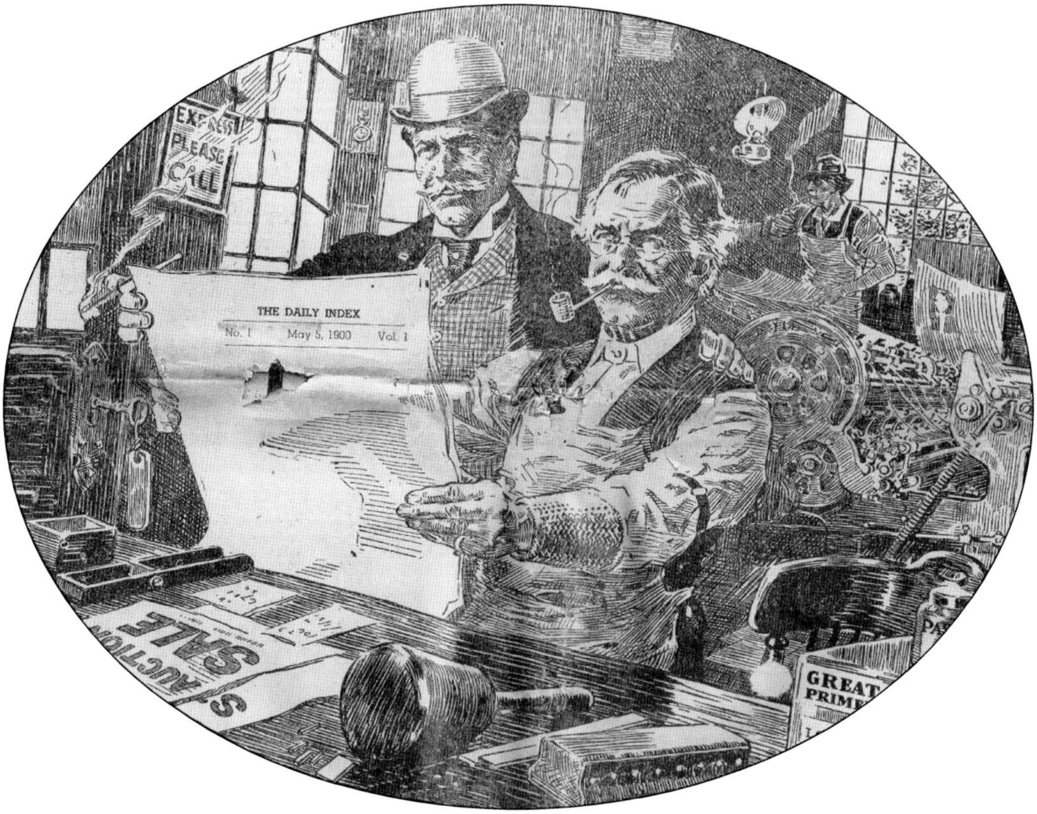

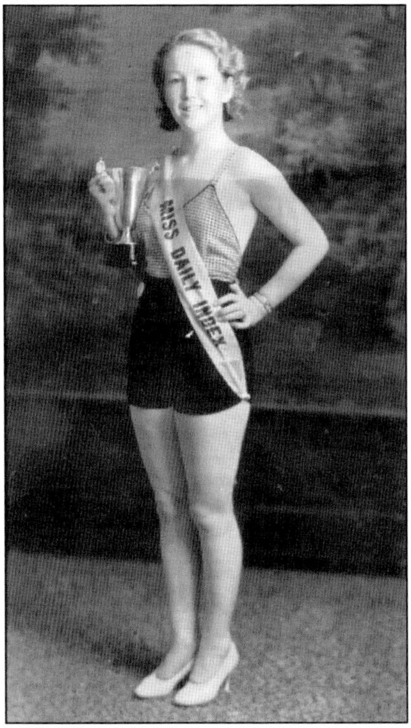

The *Mineral Wells Index* began its life as the *Daily Index* on May 5, 1900. At the time, it published six days a week and was locally owned and operated. Now, 110 years later, it is owned by Community Newspaper Holdings, Inc., of Birmingham, Alabama. The *Index* has gone through many changes. As well as publishing a newspaper, it also publishes two magazines—the *North Texas Star* and *Serendipity*. In the early days, the paper sponsored a Miss Daily Index contest. This unidentified young lady was a winner. (Both, courtesy of Lou Hayes Warren.)

Around 1905, Fr. Edwin Wickens obtained permission to hold the first Episcopal Mass in Mineral Wells. After that, services were held irregularly in hotels, a schoolhouse, or a room above the jail until W. S. and Frances W. McCutcheon moved to Mineral Wells from El Paso. Services were held in the McCutcheon basement, called the Catacombs Chapel, and later the McCutcheons donated land east of their house on Northwest Sixth Street to the church. St. Luke's Episcopal Church still stands where its final structure was built in 1930. Frances is shown in the photograph at right, and below is an early Christmas service held in the Catacombs Chapel. (Both, courtesy of St. Luke's Episcopal Church.)

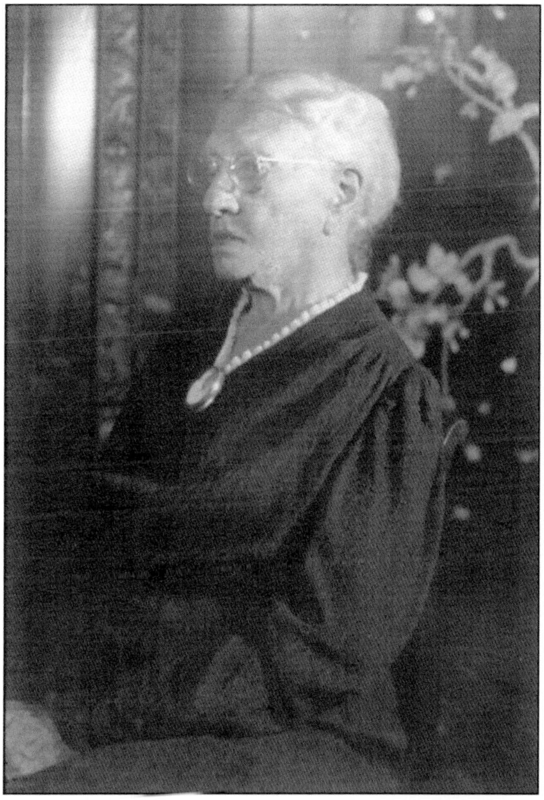

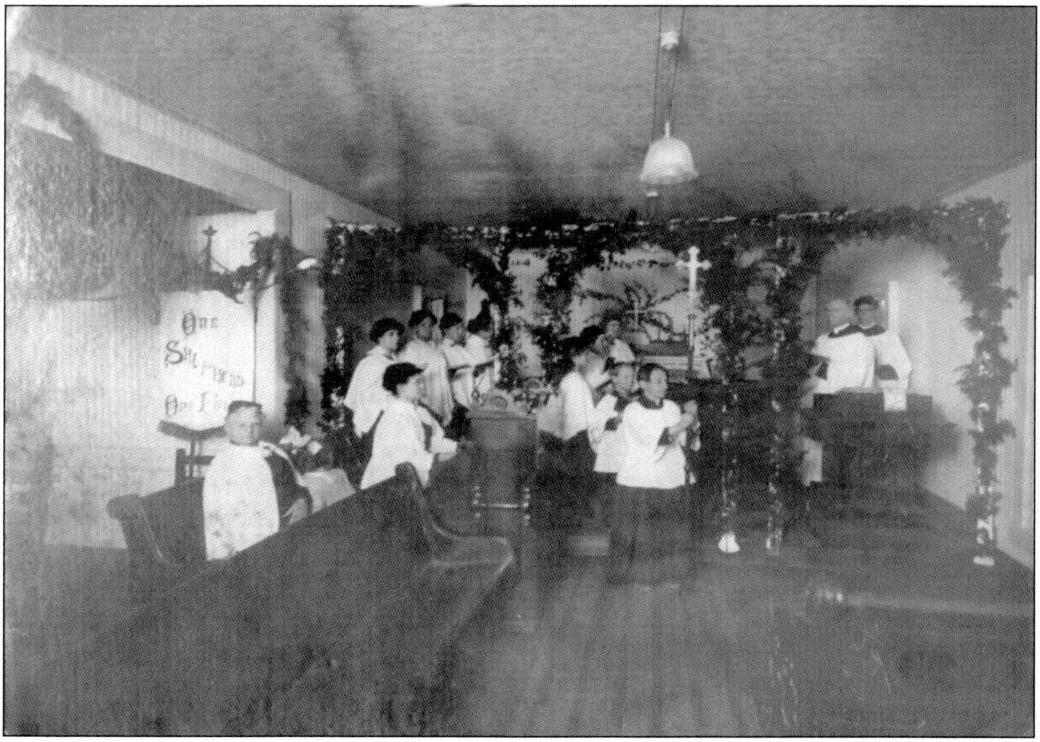

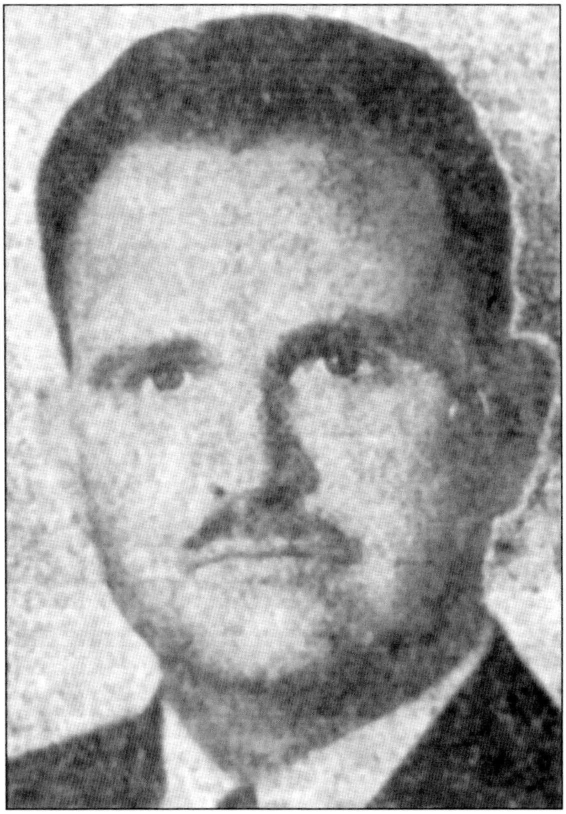

Dr. H. H. Milling, one of Mineral Wells' most progressive business and professional men, was the owner of the Milling Sanitarium, located in the 2500 block of Southeast Sixth Avenue. Today this building is home to the Veterans of Foreign Wars (VFW). Milling was the first of the town's many "rubbing doctors," and he treated patients from almost every state in the union. He served as president of the Mineral Wells School Board for several terms, and he donated land for Milling State Park, north of town. No longer a state park, this park is now called Pollard Creek Park and is the site of Texas Frontier Trails productions. (Both, courtesy of Lou Hayes Warren.)

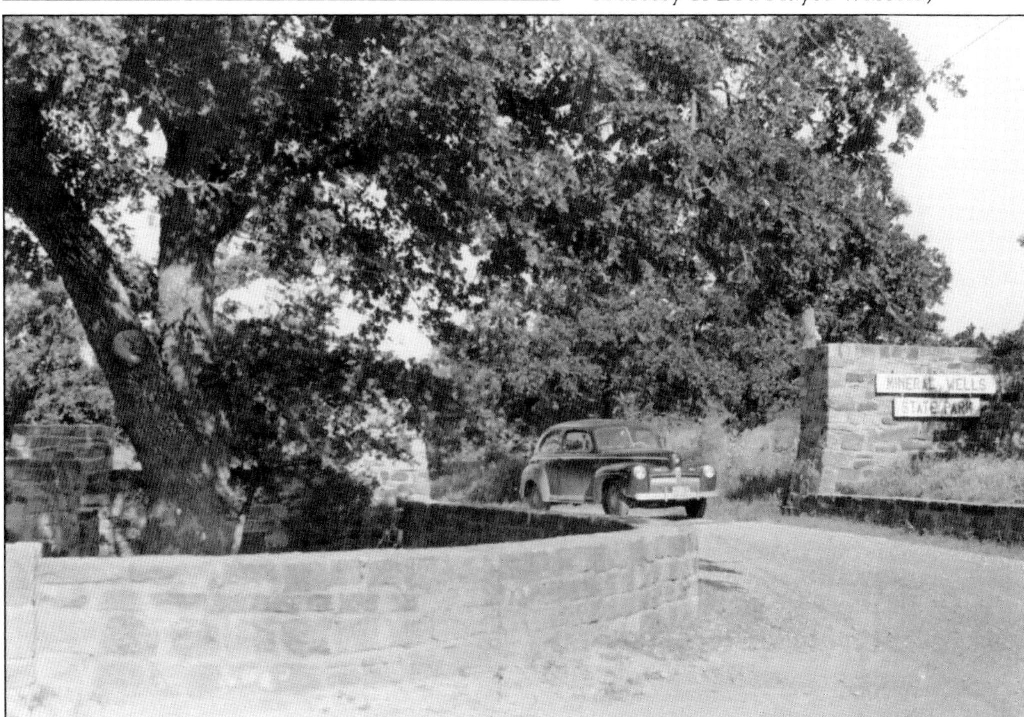

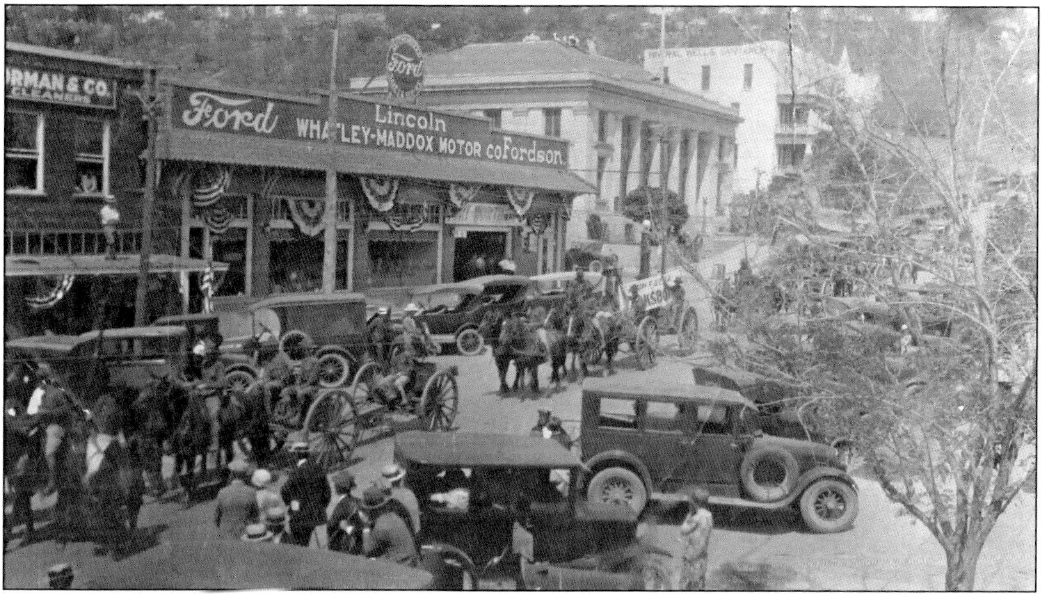

The 1925 West Texas Chamber of Commerce Parade was capped with a military contingent. The parade is proceeding west in the 100 block of Northeast Second Street. The Mineral Wells Sanatorium is in the upper right of the photograph, just east of the old post office, with Whatley Motors in the center. (Courtesy of Boyce Ditto Library, Weaver Collection.)

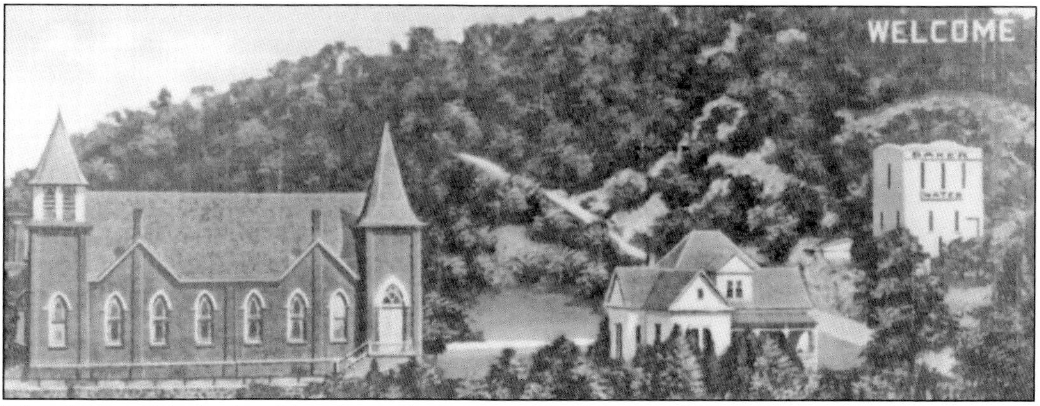

The old First Methodist Church can be seen in this photograph from around 1930. Also shown is the Baker Hotel water storage building and the welcome sign that was on East Mountain. The home in the center, which is also shown on the following page, was that of Dr. C. F. Yeager. The Methodist church has since been rebuilt, the water storage building has been removed, and the welcome sign has been relocated farther east to greet visitors from its new location overlooking Elmwood Cemetery. (Courtesy of Boyce Ditto Library, Weaver Collection.)

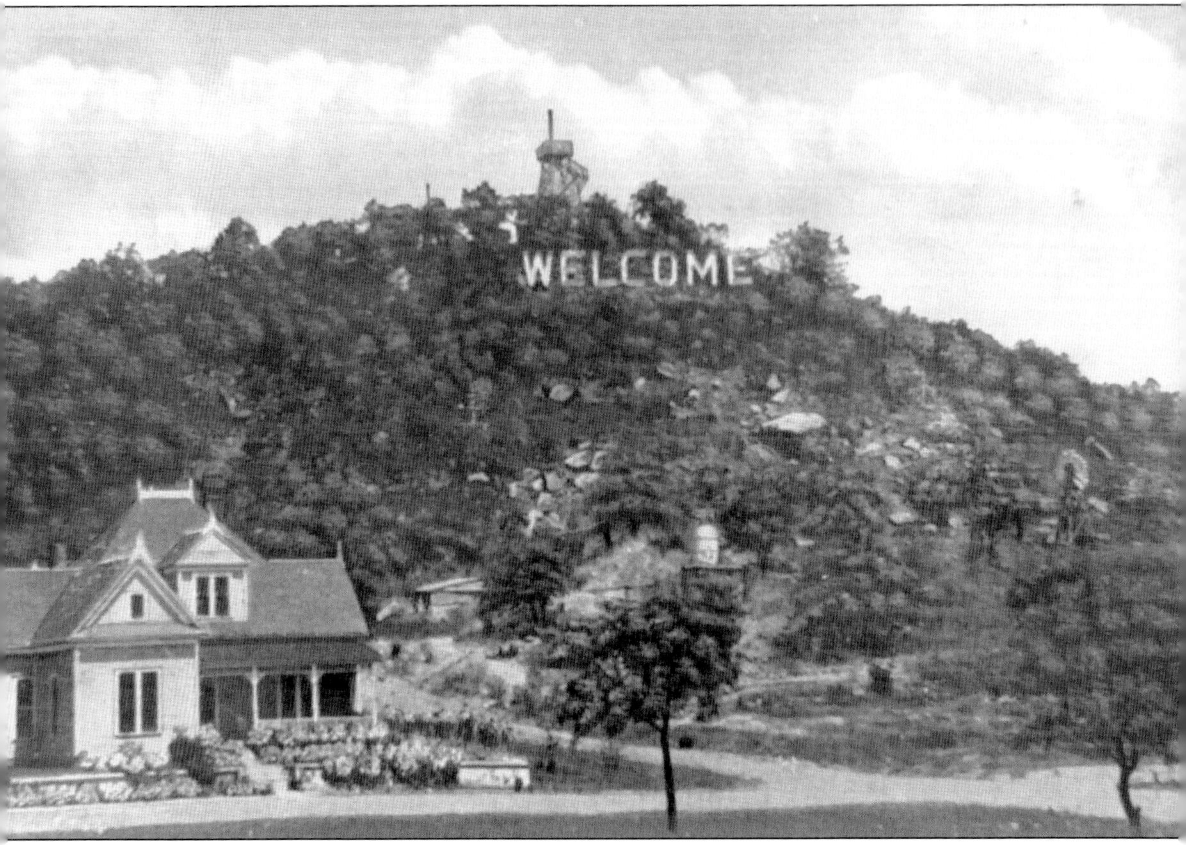

The welcome sign was donated to the City of Mineral Wells in 1922 by George Holmgreen, president of the Texas Rotary Club, following the Rotary Convention in Mineral Wells that year. East Mountain was a popular place for viewing the city, especially for photographers. The lookout tower atop West Mountain was destroyed by a tornado in 1930. This sign inspired D. W. Griffith to promote the Hollywood sign in California after his visit to Mineral Wells in 1928. Griffith, a producer and director of the silent movie classic *Birth of a Nation*, also produced the Keystone Kops comedies. A Warrant Officer Corps (WOC) company from Fort Wolters moved the sign from East Mountain in 1972 to the east side of Bald Mountain, where it remains, lighted, today. (Courtesy Boyce Ditto Library, Weaver Collection.)

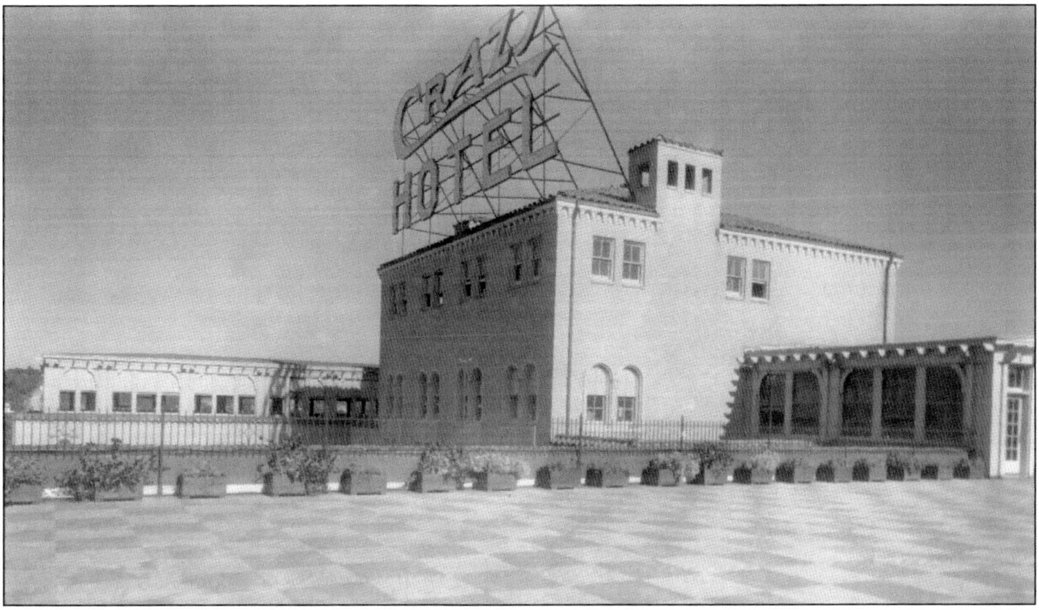

The first Crazy Hotel was built in two sections: The first section was built in 1912, and the second section to the left of it was built in 1914 and joined to the first. A fire started in the hotel drugstore on March 15, 1925, and destroyed the entire city block. The second Crazy Hotel, covering this entire city block, opened in 1927. The original Crazy Well is now in the sidewalk at the northwest corner of the hotel with a cover over it. (Courtesy Lou Hayes Warren.)

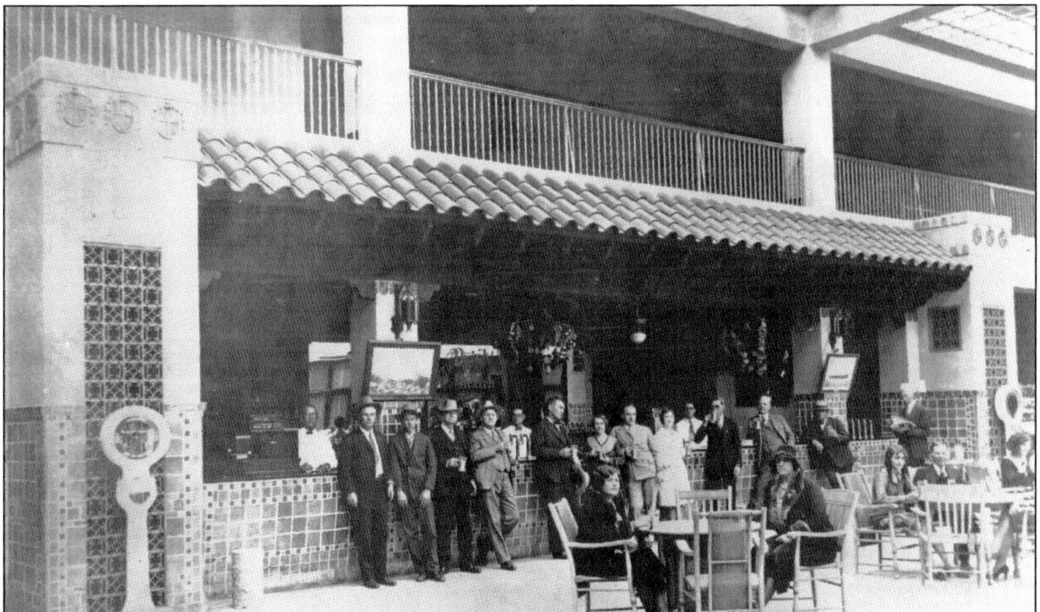

This drinking pavilion at the Crazy Hotel still exists just off the lobby. In this photograph are Boyce Ditto (standing third from right) N. E. Adams (last on the right reading a newspaper), and Mrs. Veale (seated at left), mother of Cecil Young. Ditto left money in his will for Mineral Wells' first public library building. (Courtesy of Boyce Ditto Library, Weaver Collection.)

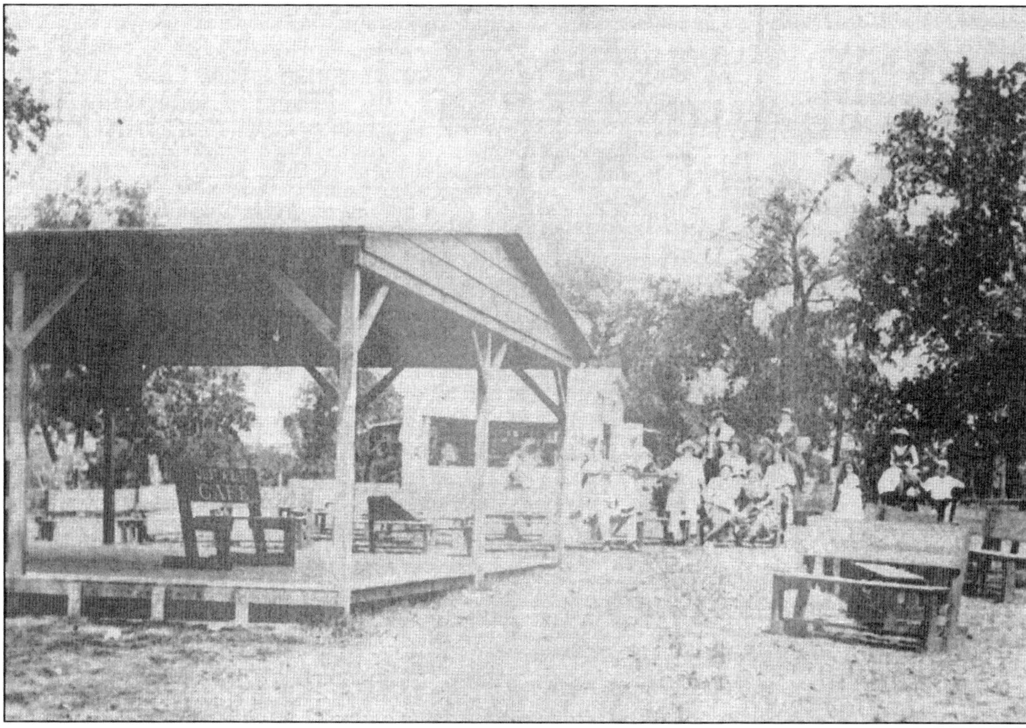

In 1920, Z. Z. Murray had a hamburger stand and open-air dance hall called Just a Bite Café at the top of East Mountain so that tourists could have refreshments and fun after their donkey ride or climb to the top. Town merchants purchased the benches and put advertisements on them. (Courtesy of Joyce Ann Murray Watson.)

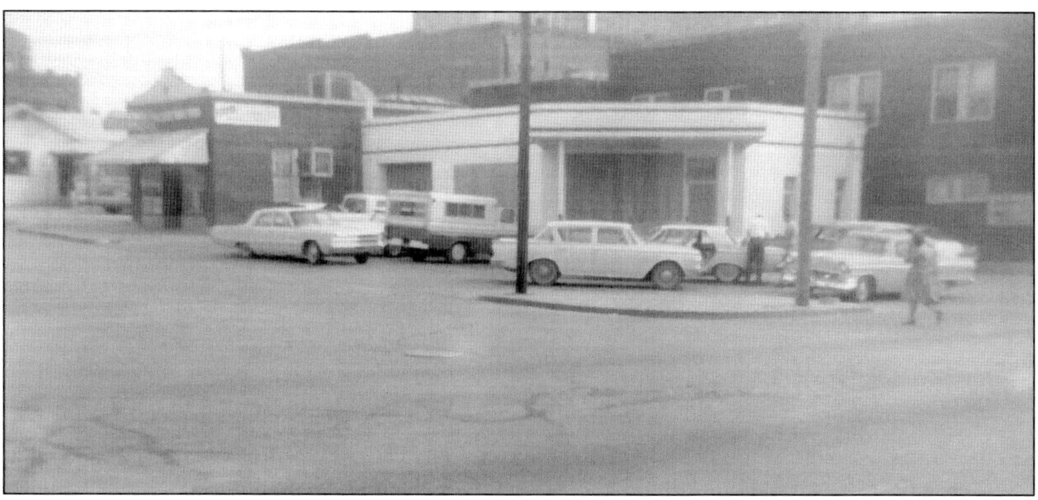

Later, Z. Z. Murray's son Clyde had a grill at the corner of North Oak and Northeast Second Streets. The Murray family had eating establishments in town for many years. (Courtesy of Joyce Ann Murray Watson.)

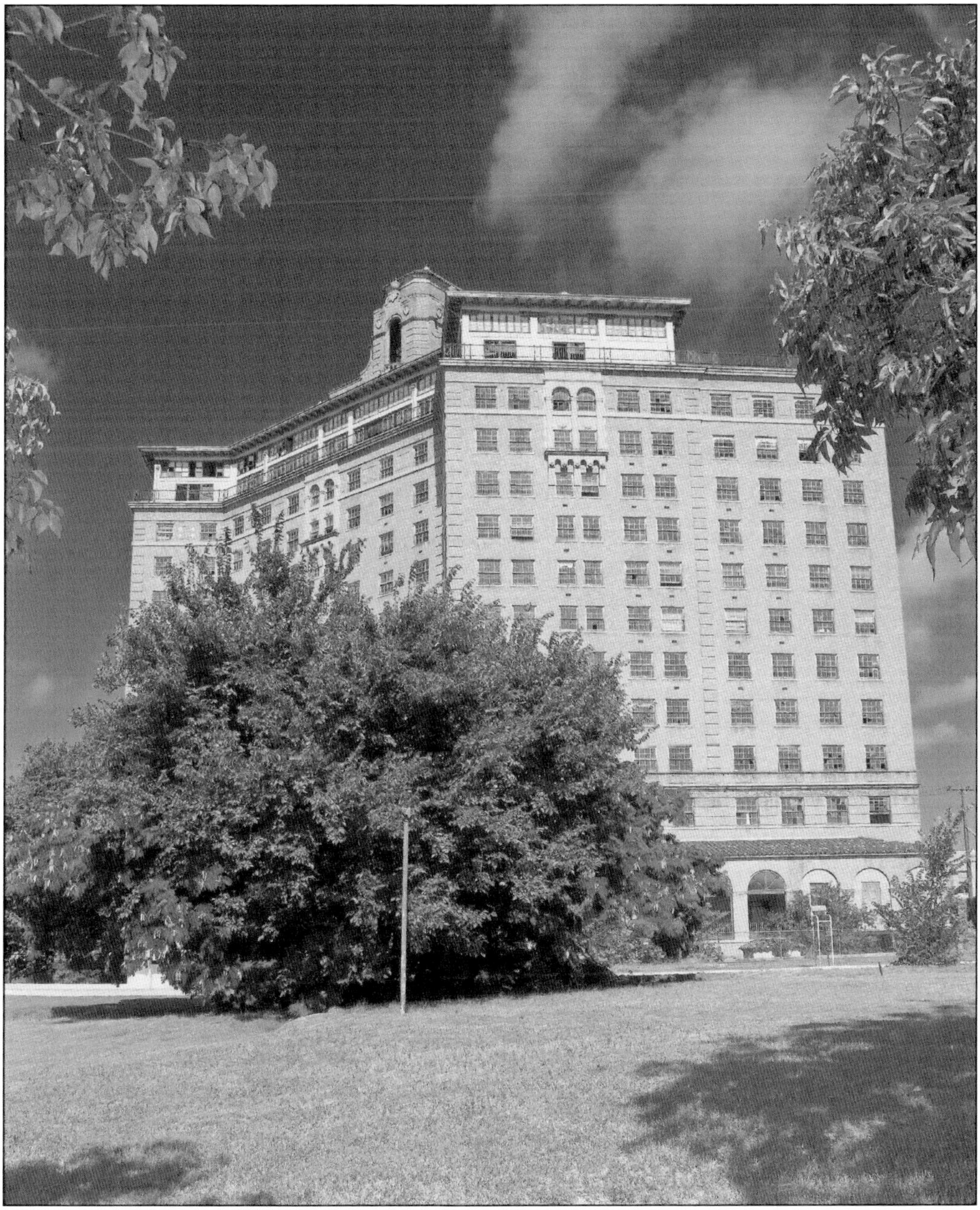

The Baker Hotel was built by hotel magnate T. B. Baker, who already owned the Baker Hotel in Dallas and the St. Anthony Hotel in San Antonio. The Crazy Hotel had proven that there was business for a large hotel, and when it burned in 1925, Baker decided to build a more lavish hotel. The Baker had 11 floors of rooms with space for 50 apartments above the main roofline. These premium rooms had the benefit of the rooftop solarium. The Baker opened its doors just two weeks after the stock market crash of 1929. It filed for bankruptcy in 1932, but new owners kept the building open. It served as military dependent quarters from 1941 to 1944 and remained open until 1963. It reopened briefly from 1965 to 1972, but the doors have been shut since then. (Photograph by Raf Seibert.)

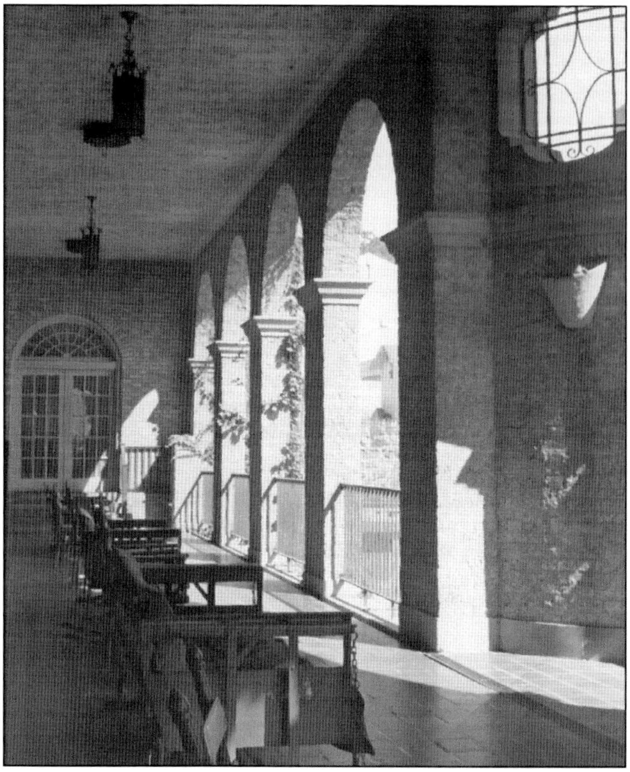

The East Terrace of the Baker Hotel was one of many spaces in the hotel for relaxation and enjoyment. (Courtesy of Lou Hayes Warren.)

The Baker swimming pool was also a place to relax and enjoy the outdoors. It was a place to see and be seen. It was a lively place while it was open, with celebrities like Will Rogers, Tom Mix, Marlene Dietrich, Jean Harlow, Helen Keller, and even the Three Stooges as hotel guests. Entertainers that performed at the Baker include Lawrence Welk, Pat Boone, Mary Martin, Judy Garland, and Paul Whiteman and his orchestra. (Courtesy of Lou Hayes Warren.)

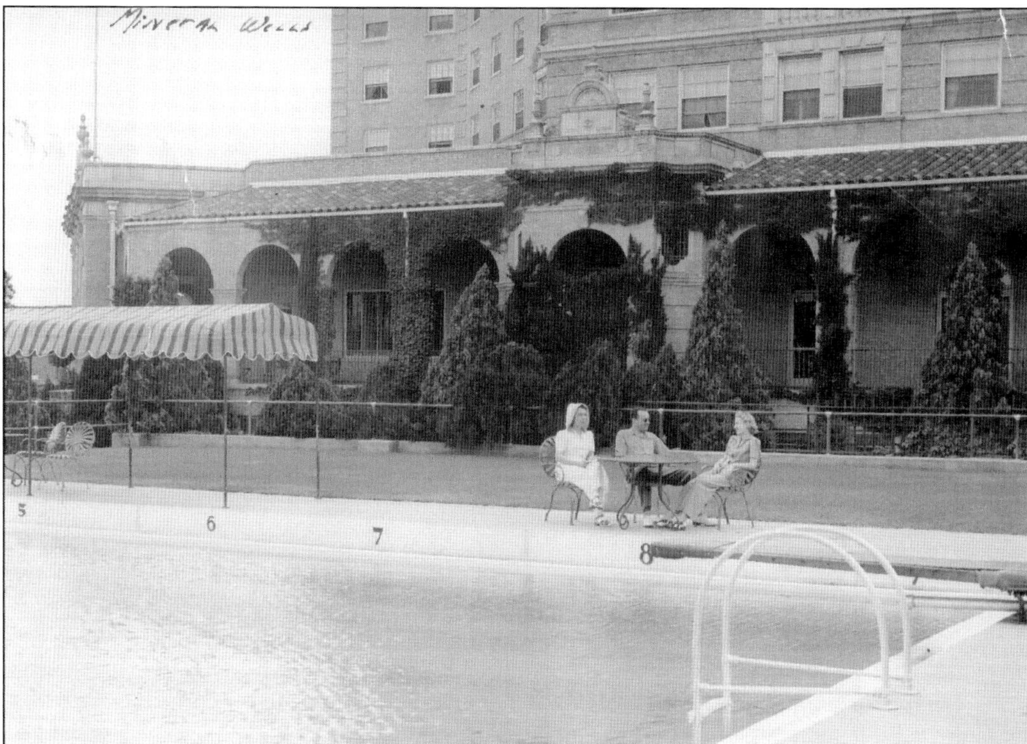

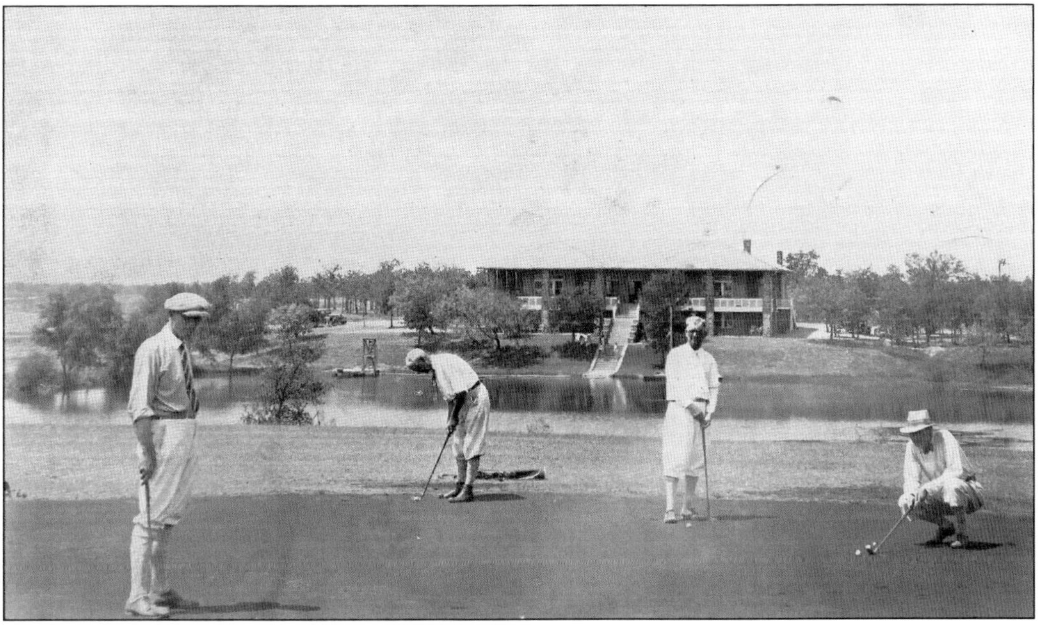

In 1930, four unidentified men in golfing knickers stand on what is now the No. 12 green across the lake from the original Holiday Hills Country Club house. (Courtesy of Boyce Ditto Library, Weaver Collection.)

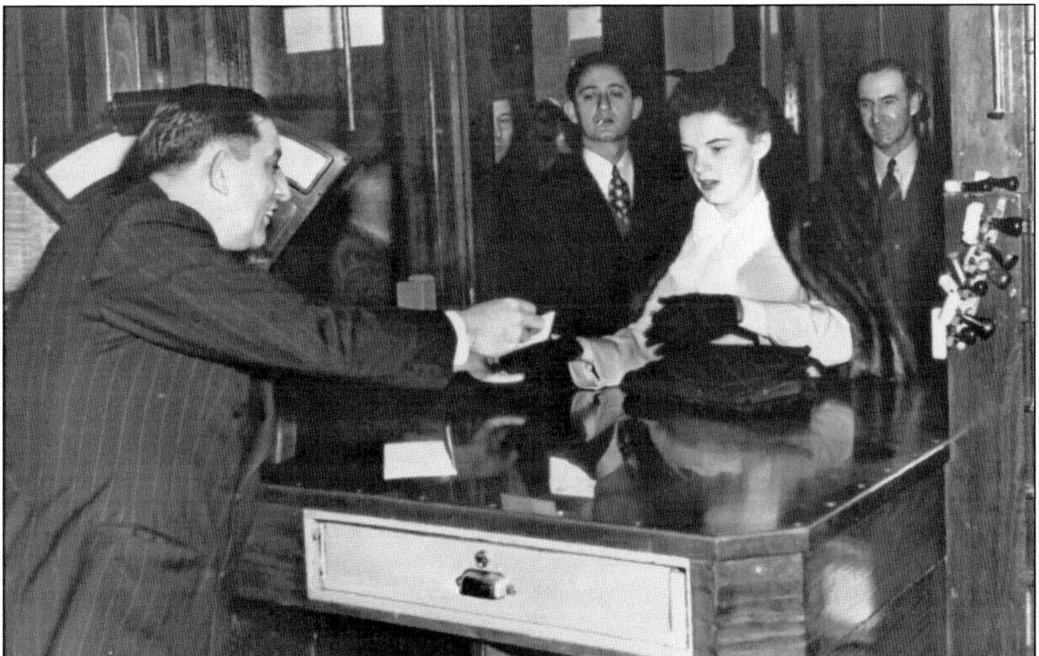

Judy Garland came to Mineral Wells to play at the USO building, and she stayed at the Baker Hotel. Here she is purchasing a money order from postmaster D. C. Harris at the old post office, which is now the Woman's Club. The man on the right was superintendent of schools W. A. Ross. The USO brought many entertainers to Mineral Wells to play for the soldiers at Camp Wolters. (Courtesy of Boyce Ditto Library, Weaver Collection.)

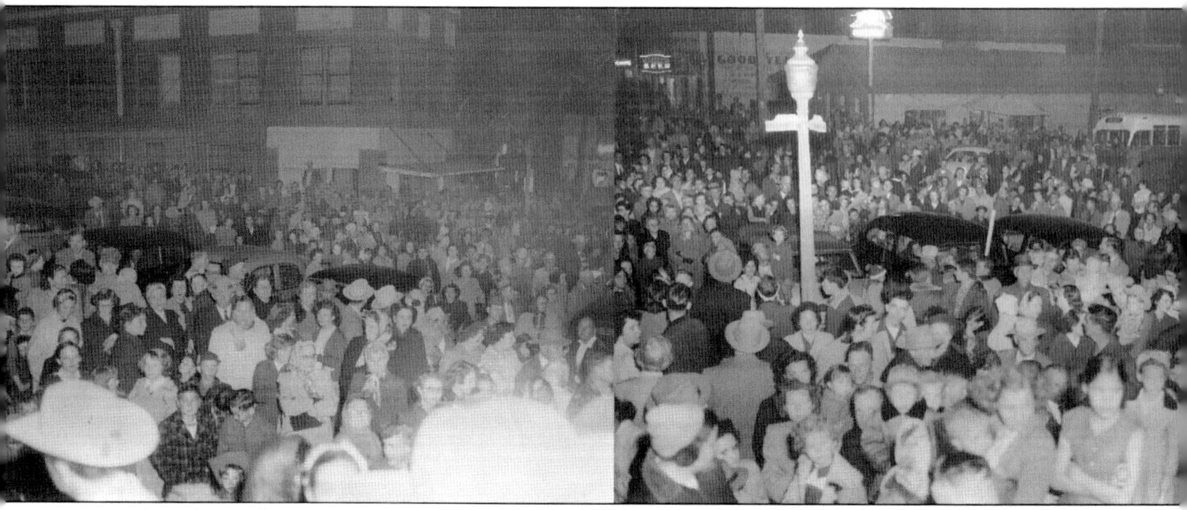

Taken from the front of the old Mineral Wells Post Office, this photograph looks both to the south and the west. Many rallies and town gatherings were held on the post office steps. This was the place where announcements, such as a declaration of war, were made. This photograph was taken during the time when Fort Wolters was Wolters Air Force Base in the mid-1950s. (Courtesy of Lou Hayes Warren.)

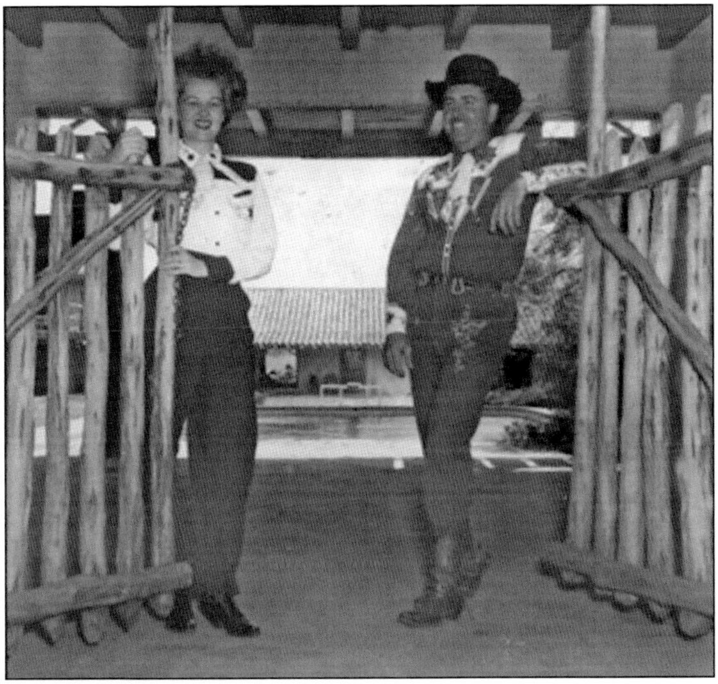

The Seybold Guest Ranch was built in the early 1940s by Elmer Seybold, who was given a blank check by his oilman father. "I found the prettiest spot in one of the most beautiful counties in Texas," he would boast to visitors. Elmer, a nationally known sharpshooter, horseman, master blacksmith, and gunsmith, and his wife, Dorothee, an international fashion model, hosted many distinguished guests, including celebrities like John Wayne, Bette Davis, and Pres. Ronald Reagan and Nancy Reagan. (Courtesy of Double J Hacienda and Art Ranch.)

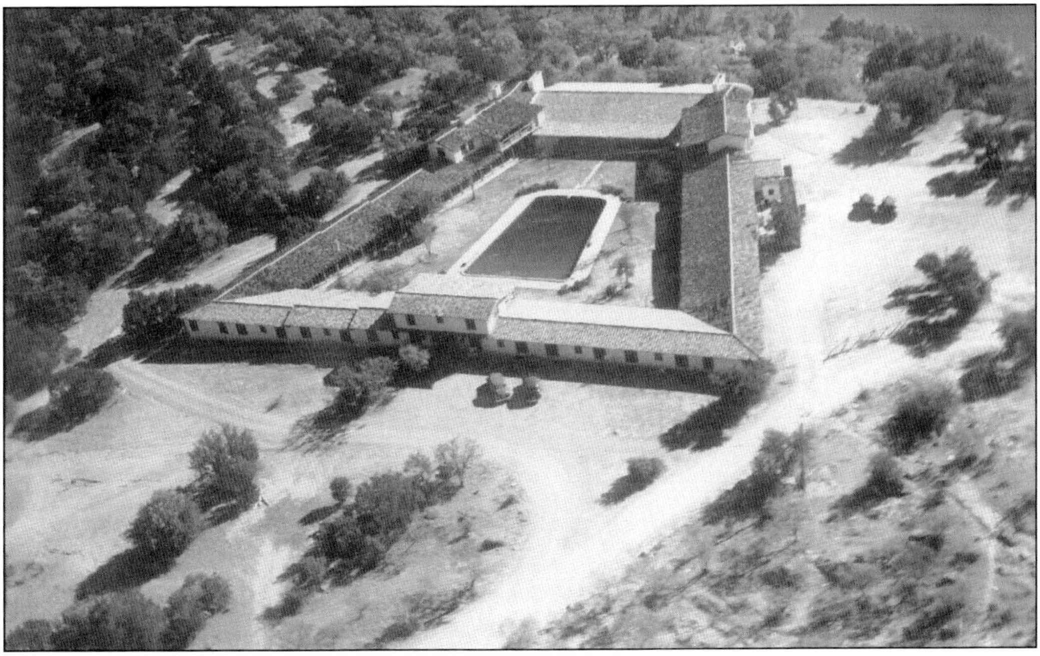

The Seybold Guest Ranch was located west of Mineral Wells on the Brazos River. It is now the Double J Hacienda and Art Ranch owned and operated by Jimmy and Jane Baldwin. The land along the Brazos River has a rich history, with legendary stories of nomadic Comanches, tenacious cattle-driving cowboys, and healing mineral waters. Quanah Parker, the last Comanche chief, roamed these hills as legendary cowboys Charles Goodnight and Oliver Loving blazed the Goodnight-Loving Trail, transporting cattle from South Texas to New Mexico. (Courtesy of Lou Hayes Warren.)

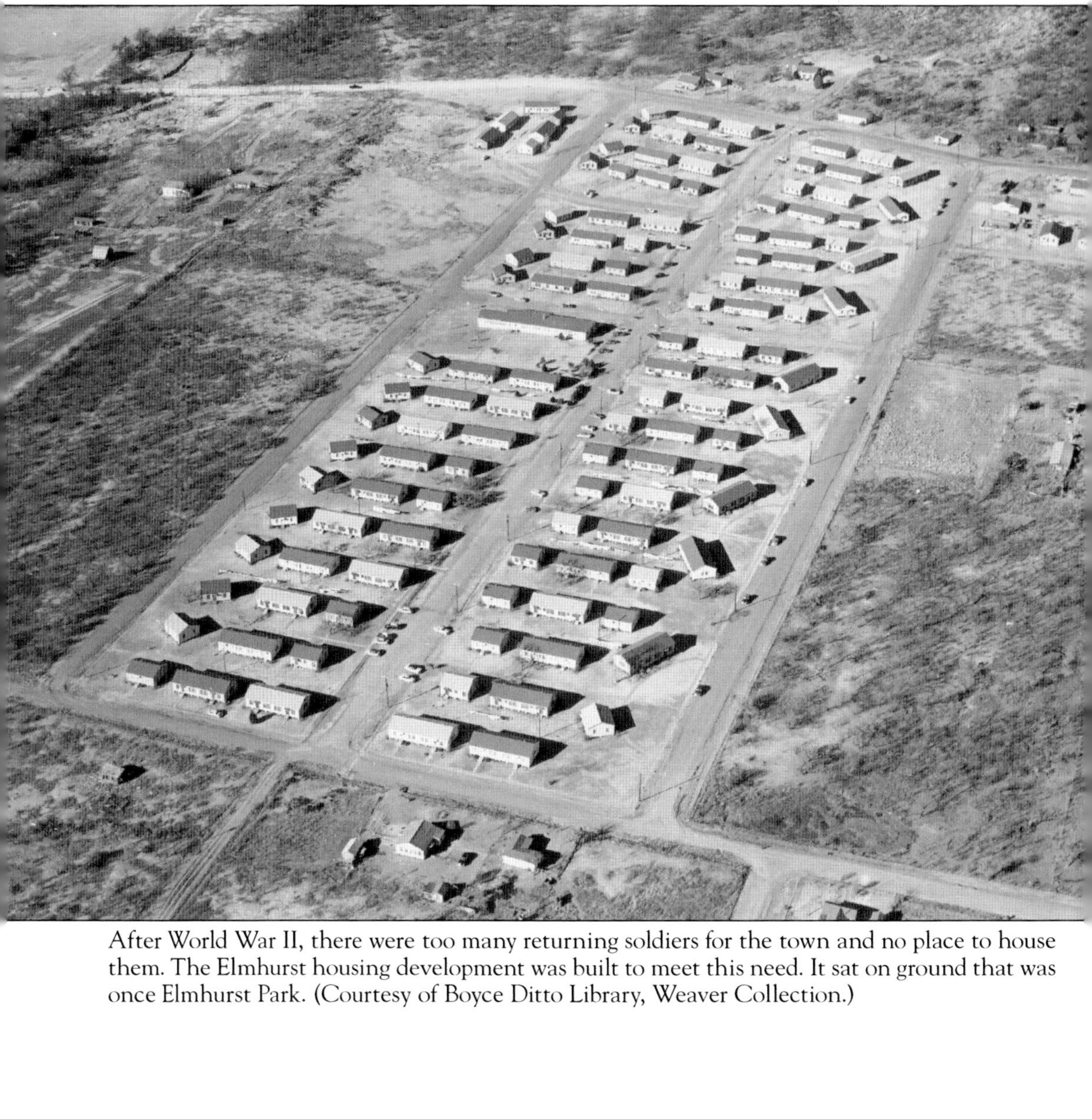

After World War II, there were too many returning soldiers for the town and no place to house them. The Elmhurst housing development was built to meet this need. It sat on ground that was once Elmhurst Park. (Courtesy of Boyce Ditto Library, Weaver Collection.)

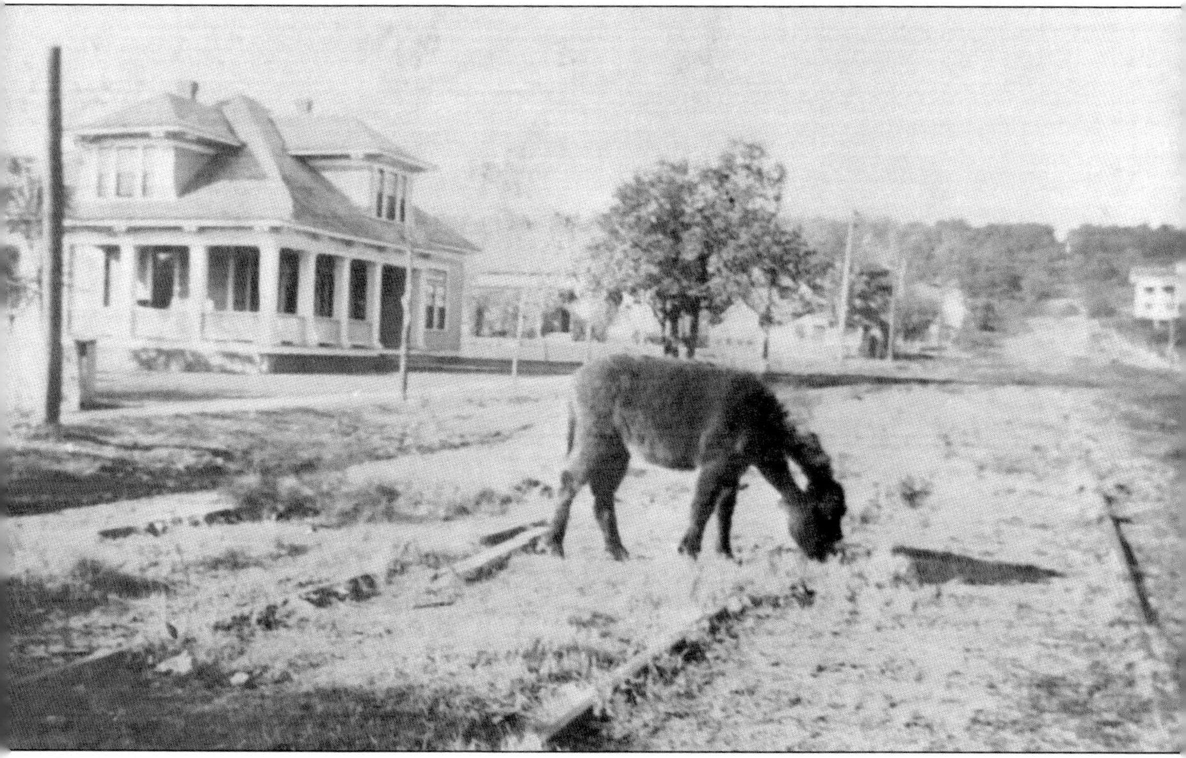

The donkey is still around today and remains an important symbol of the area. The Mineral Wells High School annual is even called the *Burro*. This donkey is shown on old dinky car tracks on Northwest Sixth Street leading to the top of West Mountain. The house up the hill on the right is the McCutcheon house, where St. Luke's Episcopal Church began. (Courtesy of Boyce Ditto Library, Weaver Collection.)

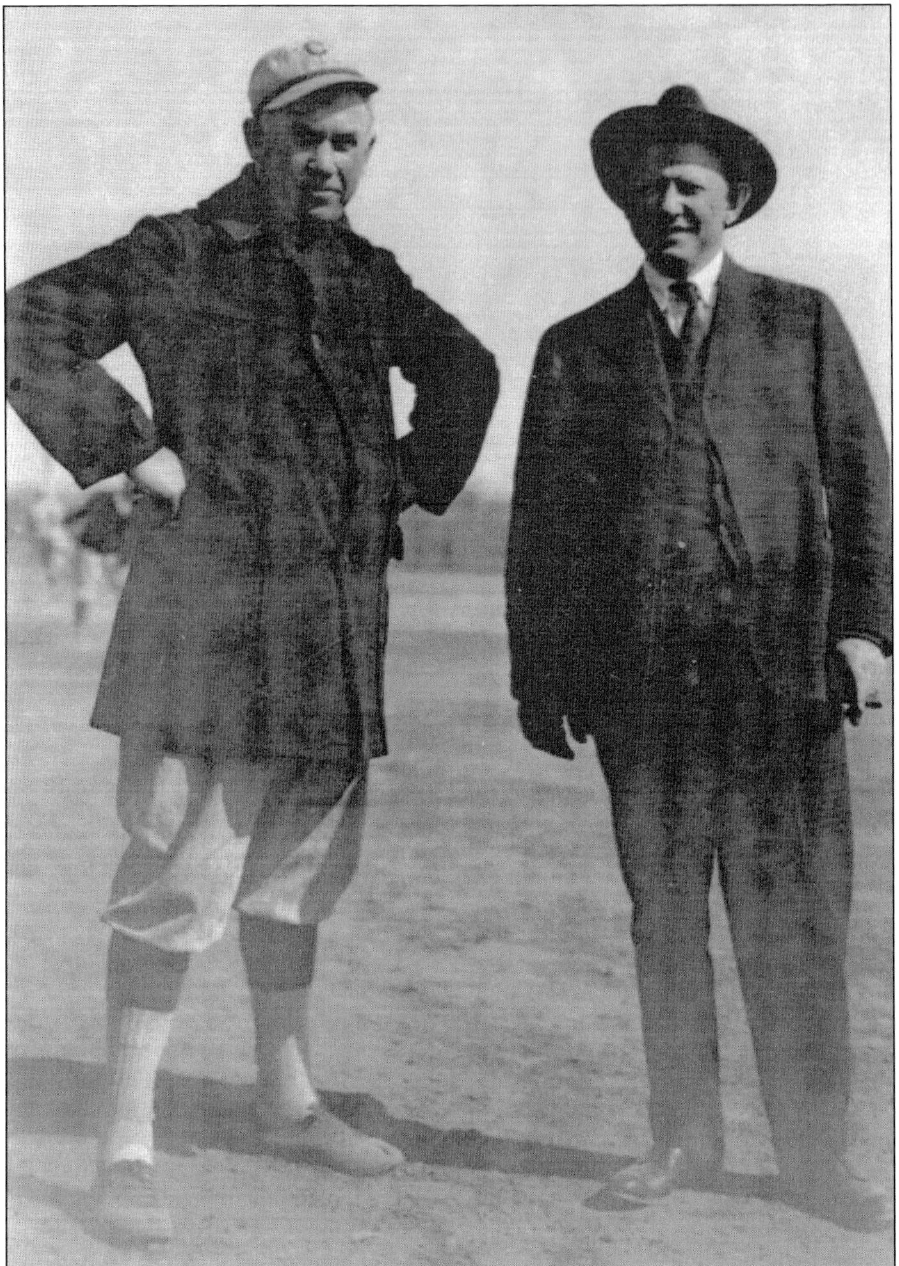

Ike Sablosky came from Russia to Philadelphia in 1890. He and his wife, Fanny Jaffee, later moved to Mineral Wells for health reasons. Ike became involved in the fur-and-hide business and once described the northwest part of Palo Pinto County as a "possum kingdom"—hence why the first flood-control lake on the Brazos River was named Possum Kingdom Lake. Sablosky sponsored a local baseball team, and after he moved to Dallas, he bought a Texas League franchise when it became available. It became the first professional baseball team in Dallas. Sablosky pioneered the founding of city farm teams and acted as umpire and coach. He is shown, on the right, with Pat (last name unknown). His team, known as the White Sox, held spring training in Mineral Wells in 1911 and again from 1915 to 1917. (Courtesy of Boyce Ditto Library, Weaver Collection.)

John Newton Hayes and his future wife, Blanche McCutcheon, pose near the welcome sign on East Mountain above the Baker Hotel and the old First Methodist Church in the summer of 1939. (Courtesy of Lou Hayes Warren.)

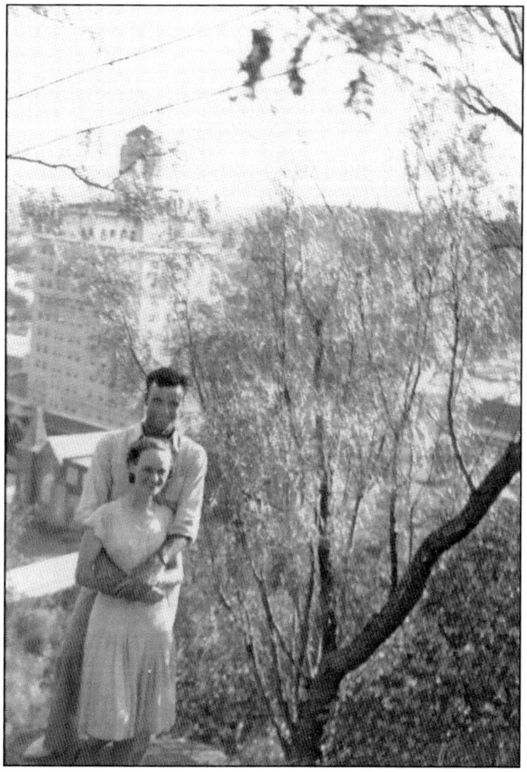

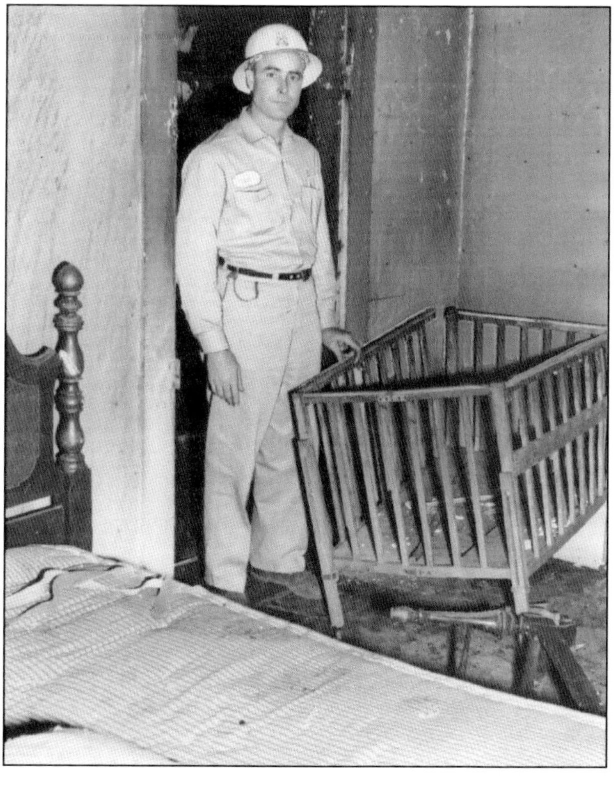

John Newton Hayes, 45, was an employee of Texas Power and Light and a volunteer assistant fire chief on March 9, 1959, when he rescued Jimmy Don Ansay, 15 months, from his burning home in Mineral Wells. Hayes entered the home three times before successfully finding and saving the boy's life. On February 26, 1960, Hayes was awarded the Carnegie Hero Fund Commission award for heroism for saving a life at the risk of his own. (Courtesy of Lou Hayes Warren.)

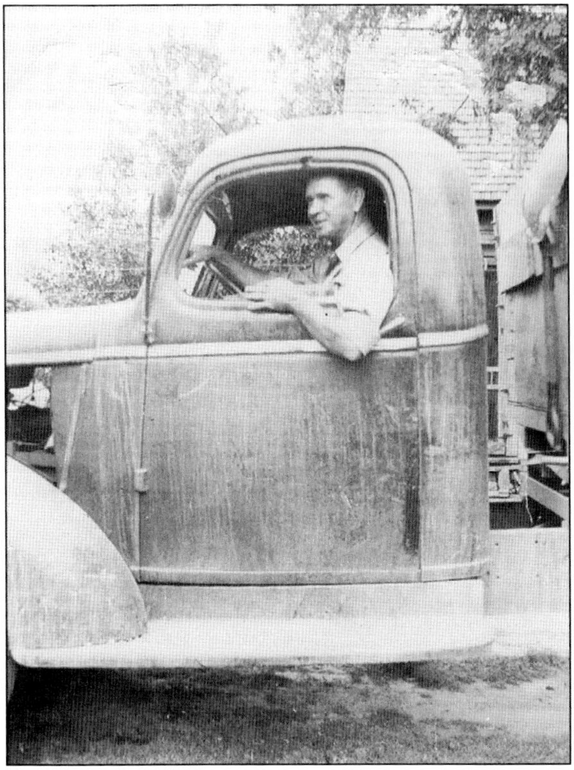

James D. "Doc" Gailey was born in Parker County in 1898 and died in Mineral Wells in 1976. He was a trucking contractor who married Edna Puckett Gailey in 1919. All of his grandchildren were graduates of Mineral Wells High School. (Courtesy of Judith Richards Shubert.)

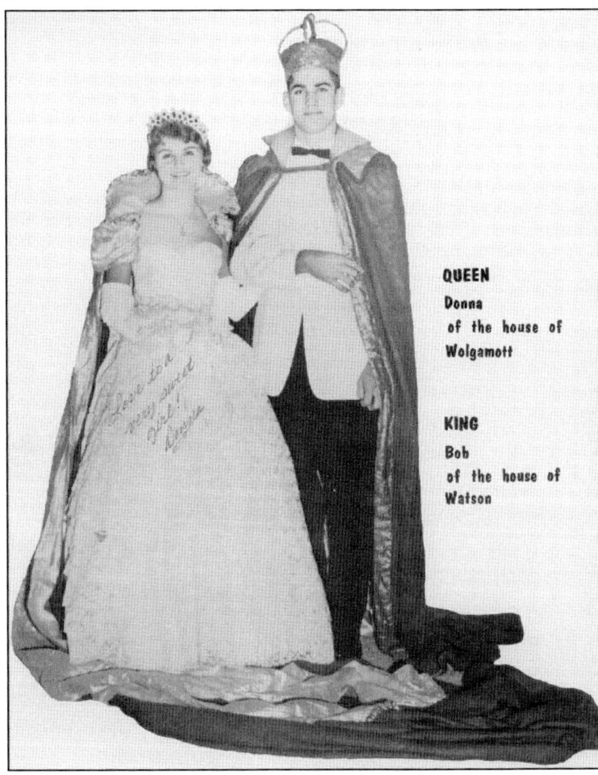

For many years, Mineral Wells High School has crowned a king and queen at its yearly coronation. In 1960, the queen was Donna Wolgamott, whose father worked for Southern Airways. Bob Watson, who later became a local attorney, was the king. (Courtesy of Sue Seibert.)

Four

Petroleum, Brick, and the Economy 1910–Present

Around 1910, oil was discovered in Palo Pinto County, and because of this discovery, Mineral Wells' economy was not solely based on tourism and its health-giving water resources.

The first test oil well in Palo Pinto County was drilled in 1901, but a boom did not occur until 1915, when the field near the town of Palo Pinto, 12 miles west of Mineral Wells, was opened and became "one of the most productive oil fields in the world," according to one historian.

Upham Oil and Gas Company was and is one of the leaders in petroleum exploration and production in the area. In the late 1800s, there were only five drilling rigs in the world, and David Upham owned one of them in Pennsylvania. Upham came to Texas looking for oil and gas in Palo Pinto County in 1914, when heard about the Ranger Field—one of the largest oil fields that had ever been discovered in the United States. He drilled his first gas well here in 1917. A few years later, his son Chester R. Upham came to Mineral Wells and purchased the Consumer's Gas and Fuel Company, a natural gas production, transmission, and distribution company serving Mineral Wells. In 1925, the Uphams extended service to rural communities in Palo Pinto County, and in 1926, the company name was changed to the Brazos River Gas Company, serving 15 communities. In 1950, the name was changed to Upham Gas Company.

In 1949, Perry Equipment Company built its headquarters in Mineral Wells, with Dunman Perry Jr. as president in 1951. This company was the first to bring innovative bypass lube-oil filtration systems to the Texas petroleum industry.

Clay pipes, aircraft systems, plastics, electronic products, brick, feeds, and cloth, including a silk factory where silk worms were grown, are some of the many other industries that have been established in Mineral Wells.

Throughout its history, Mineral Wells has been influential in both state and national politics. Tom Creighton, Democrat, was a state senator for many years and was quite influential and well regarded around the state. Chester R. Upham was the state Republican chairman and was extremely influential in strengthening the party in the State of Texas. Dunman Perry was also influential in the Republican party. Through the Upham and Perry leadership, Mineral Wells and Palo Pinto County have become almost entirely a conservative, Republican stronghold. Chester's daughter Barbara Upham now leads the party.

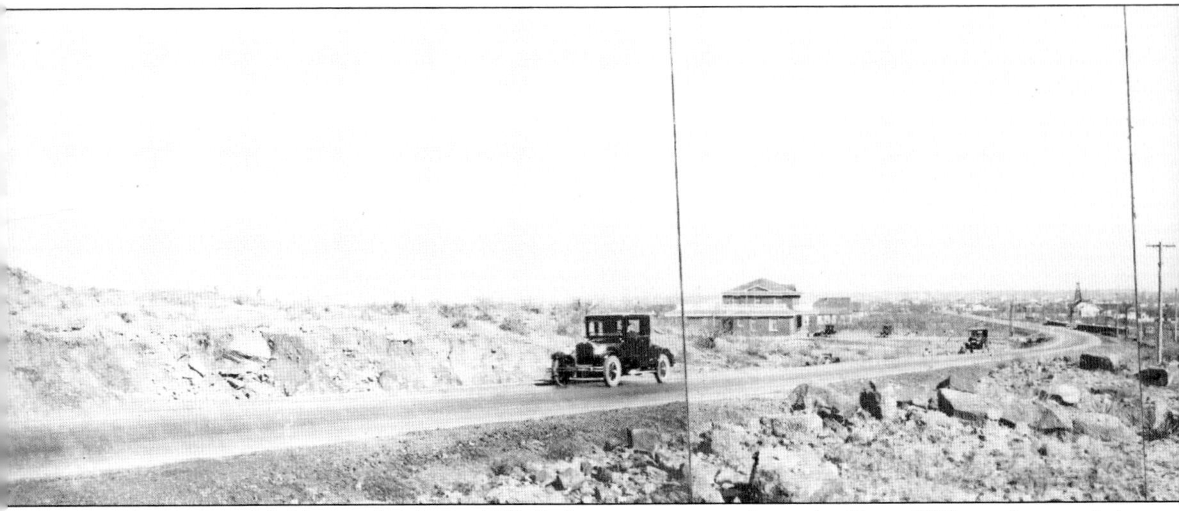

This early oil field outside Mineral Wells faces west, away from the Pinto Hills and toward the desert that is pure West Texas. The photograph was originally in the possession of M. A. Howell, who was the county surveyor, and it was probably taken around 1915. This was one of the area's

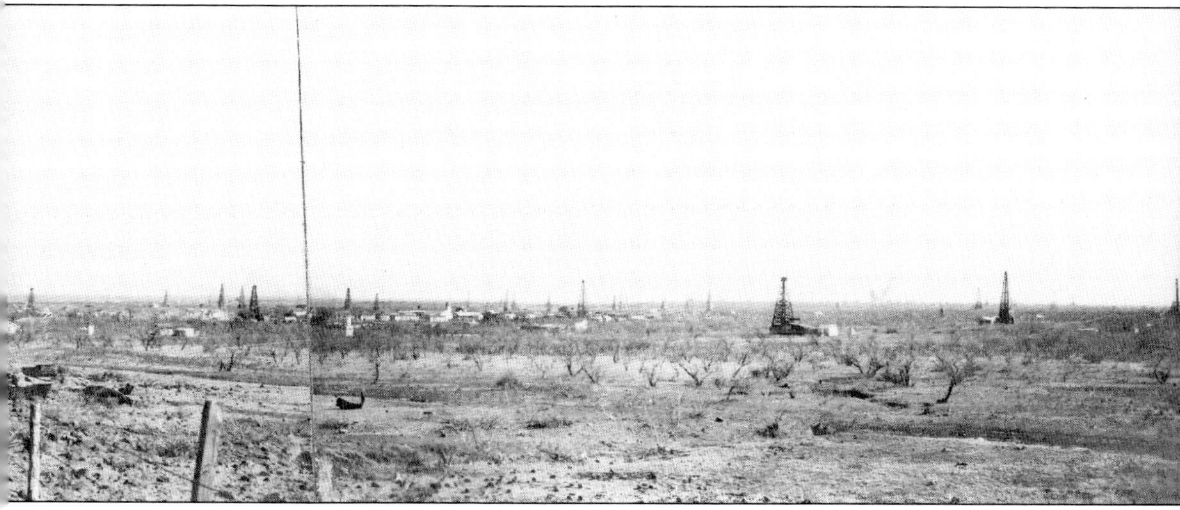

largest oil-producing fields, but only for a very short time. By 1922, it had tapered off, resulting in not only a lack of oil production, but also a decline in county population. (Courtesy of Boyce Ditto Library, Weaver Collection.)

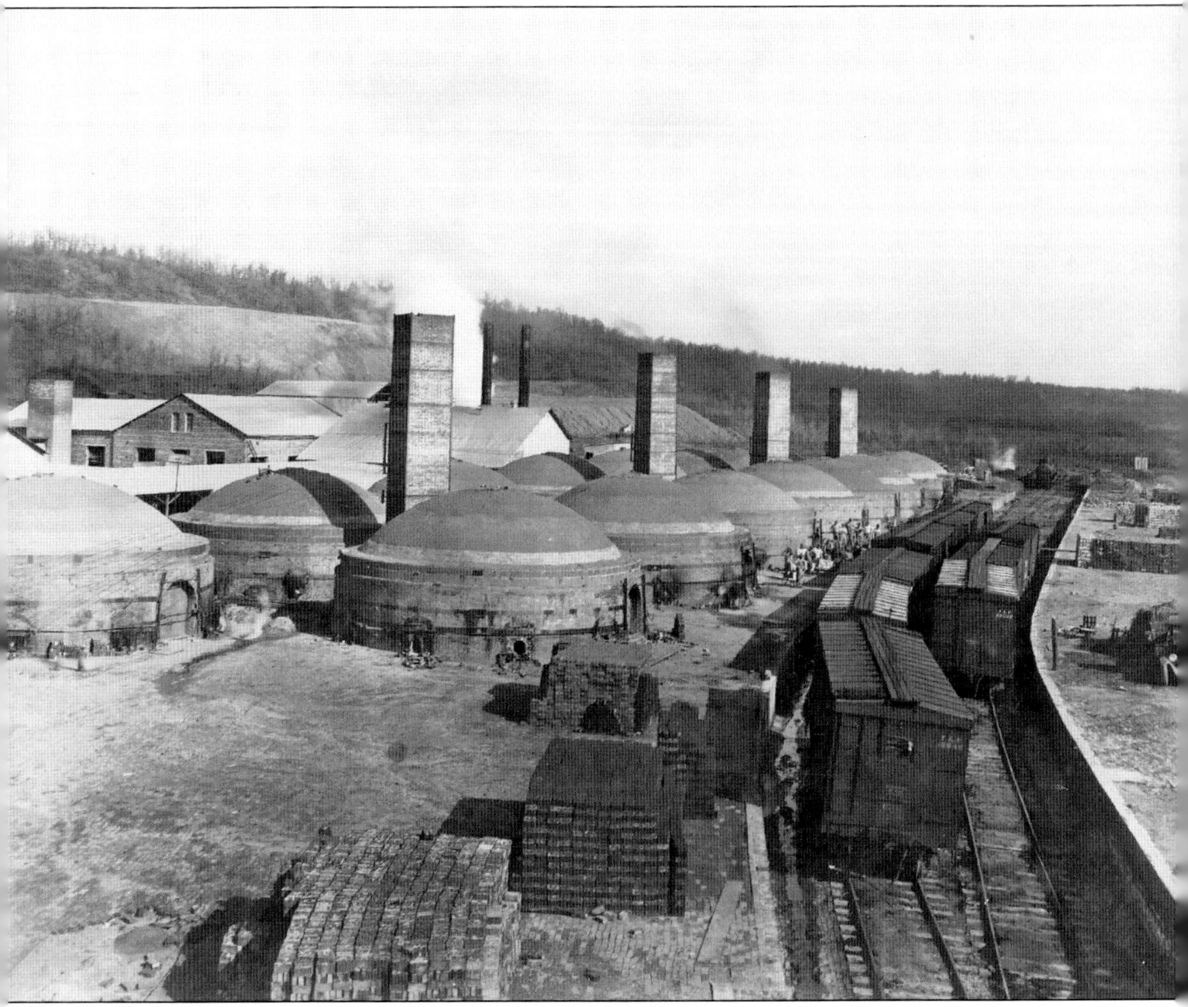

Rejected fine coal from the area's coal mines furnished heat to fire clay and bake it into brick. This brick factory is still in production on the eastern edge of Mineral Wells. Area bricks were used to build the seawall at Galveston after the disastrous hurricane of 1900 and to pave the highway from Mineral Wells to Fort Worth as well as many of the streets in that city. (Courtesy of Boyce Ditto Library, Weaver Collection.)

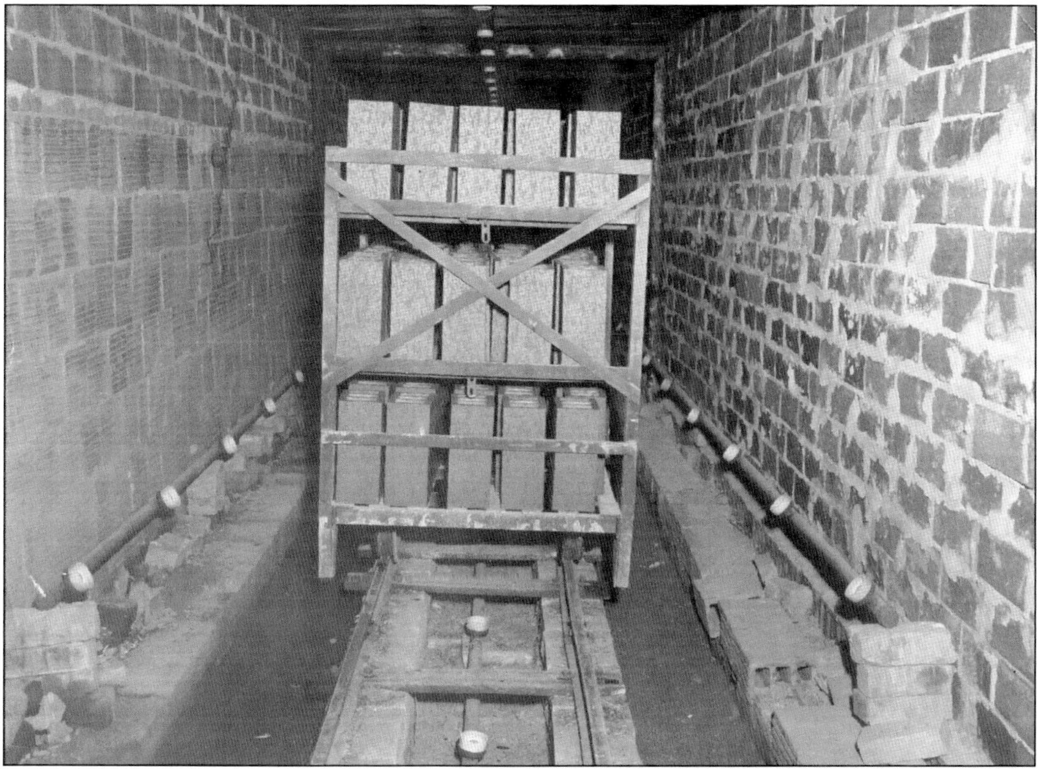

This trolley moved brick through a horizontal shaft kiln in Mineral Wells. (Courtesy of Lou Hayes Warren.)

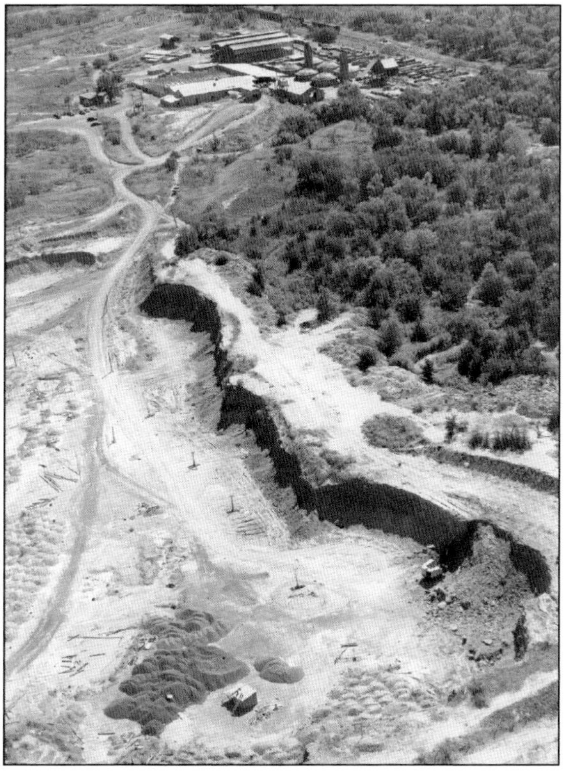

The abundant clay in and around Mineral Wells was recognized around the beginning of the 20th century as a source of raw material for brick manufacturing. The mining of clay minerals from Pennsylvanian Age shale deposits is seen in this quarry. At the top of the photograph is one of the five brick plants located in Mineral Wells. (Courtesy of Lou Hayes Warren.)

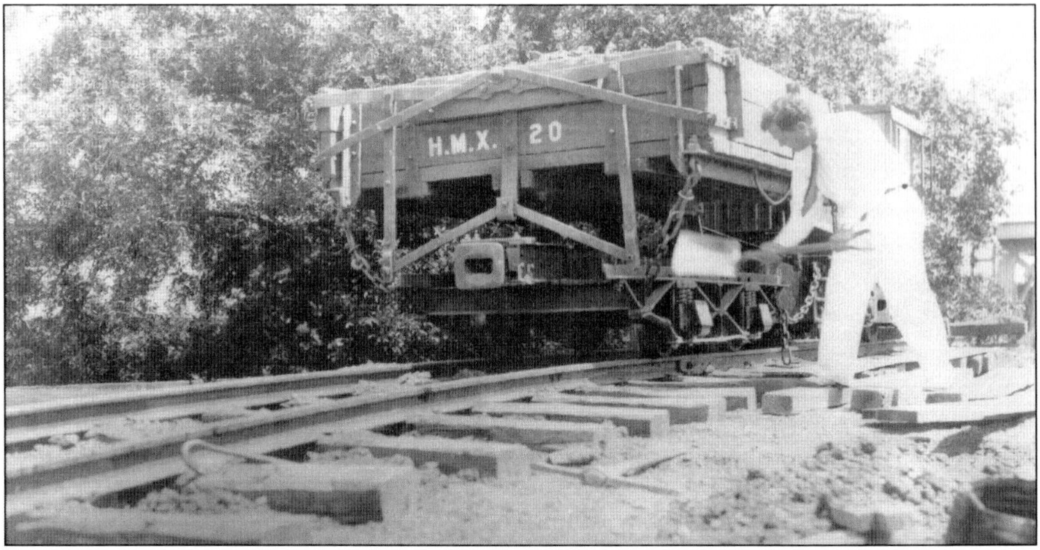

Identified as the "first car of shale," this railroad car has been labeled as "H.M.X. 20" on the rear. This picture commemorates the opening of Mineral Wells' fledgling brick-manufacturing industry, as the gentleman wearing a tie and wielding a shovel suggests a celebration of sorts. His attire is typical of summertime dress in the 1930s. (Courtesy of Boyce Ditto Library, Weaver Collection.)

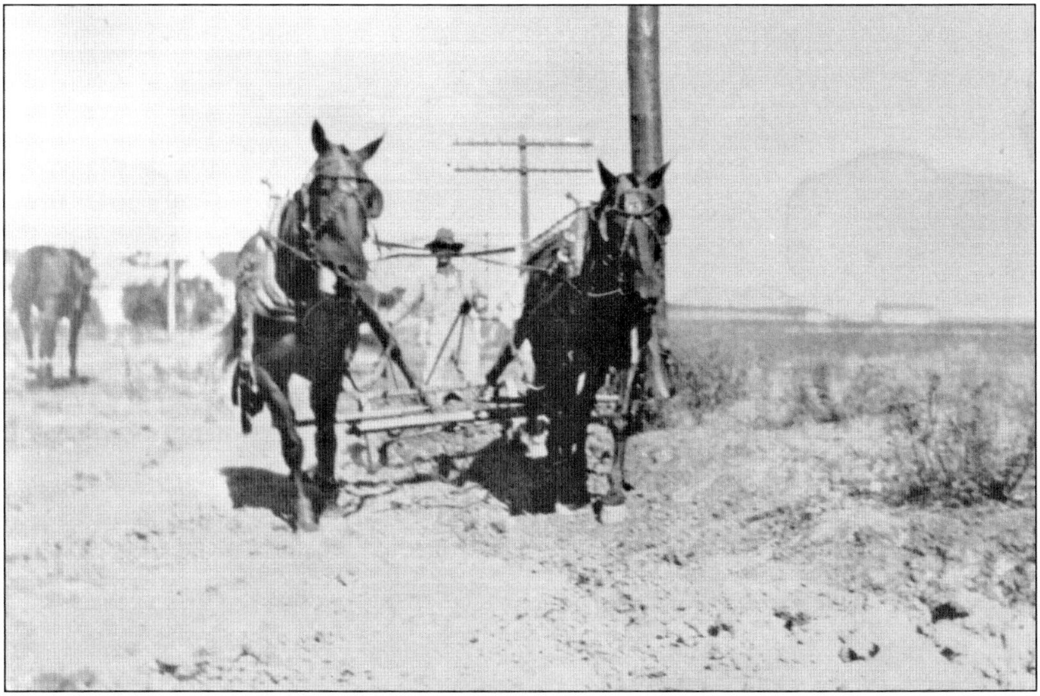

As noted on the back of this photograph, shown here is the preparation for paving the brick highway from Mineral Wells to Millsap. The note refers to the name D. M. Shrum, but does not indicate whether he is the person in the photograph. The brick highway to Millsap was part of the nation's first transcontinental highway, the Bankhead Highway, from mile zero in Washington, D.C., to San Diego, California. It was built through Mineral Wells in about 1921. (Courtesy of Boyce Ditto Library, Weaver Collection.)

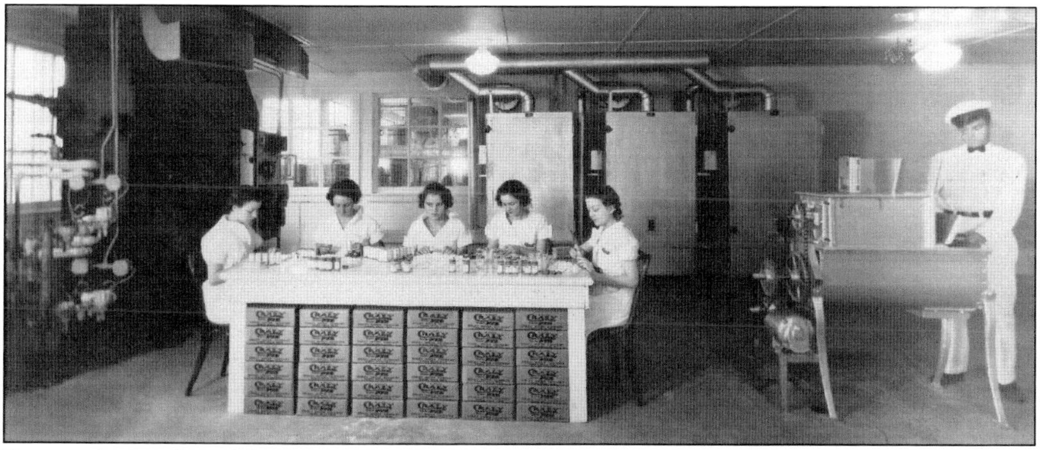

During the heyday of the Mineral Wells health industry, products were developed to satisfy the public's search for good health. One of these products was made by infusing carbon dioxide into mineral water under pressure to create a sparkling water drink called "Crazy Fiz." The women in this photograph taken inside the Crazy Water Crystal plant are packaging Crazy Fiz for distribution. The back of the picture is labeled "Crazy Fiz 1930s." (Courtesy of Boyce Ditto Library, Weaver Collection.)

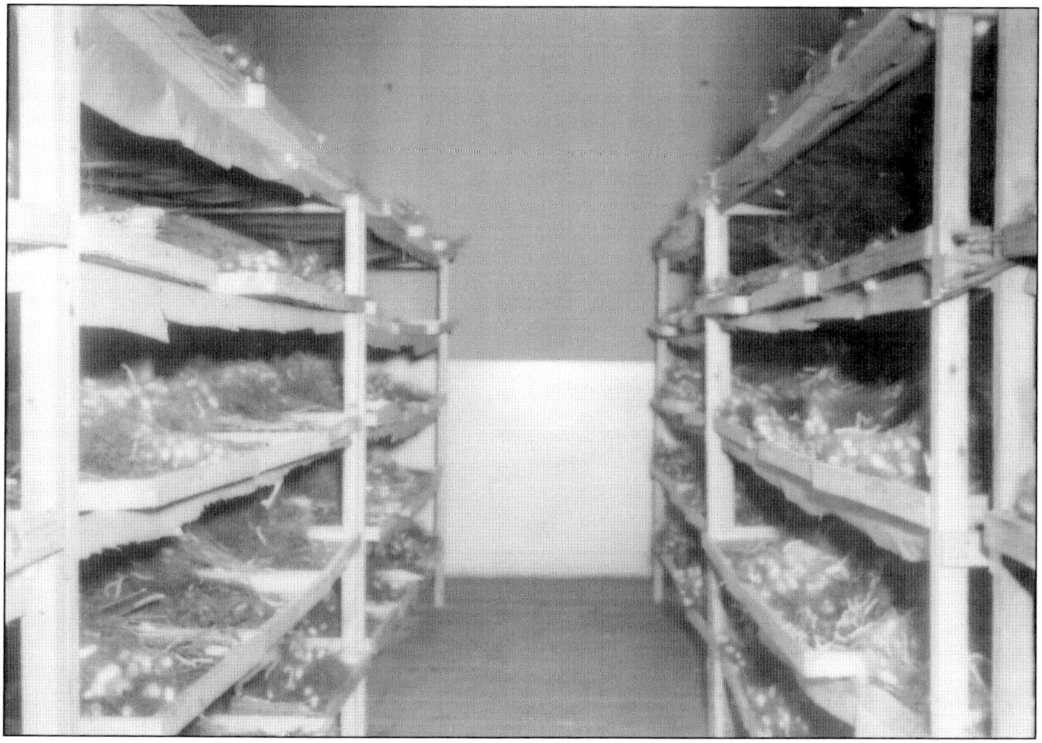

Silk worms were grown in Mineral Wells in this Kidwell Heights building in the 1930s. This building later became a school and presently houses the Knights of Pythias and the Pythian Sisters. Mulberry trees were planted all over town, particularly in the Sturdivant area and in northern Mineral Wells, to feed the silk worms. There was a silk factory in town, which later converted to nylon production. The factory made parachutes, among other things. (Courtesy of Lou Hayes Warren.)

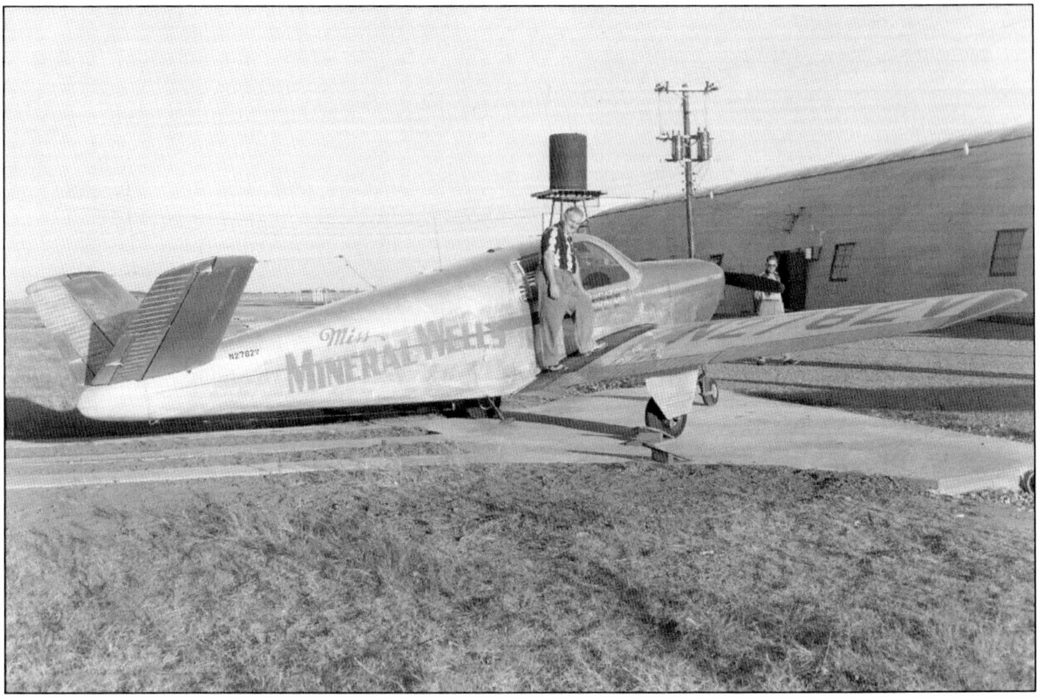

Flying all across the country, D. H. Mitchell (standing on the wing of his plane) of Mitchell Industries—later Edo-Aire Mitchell and now Century Flight Systems—advertised his autopilot while at the same time promoting Mineral Wells on his airplane *Miss Mineral Wells*. The company still manufactures autopilots and flight control systems. Century Flight Systems is housed in the building in the photograph below. (Above, courtesy of Lou Hayes Warren; below, courtesy of Lottie Williams Eubanks, Century Flight Systems.)

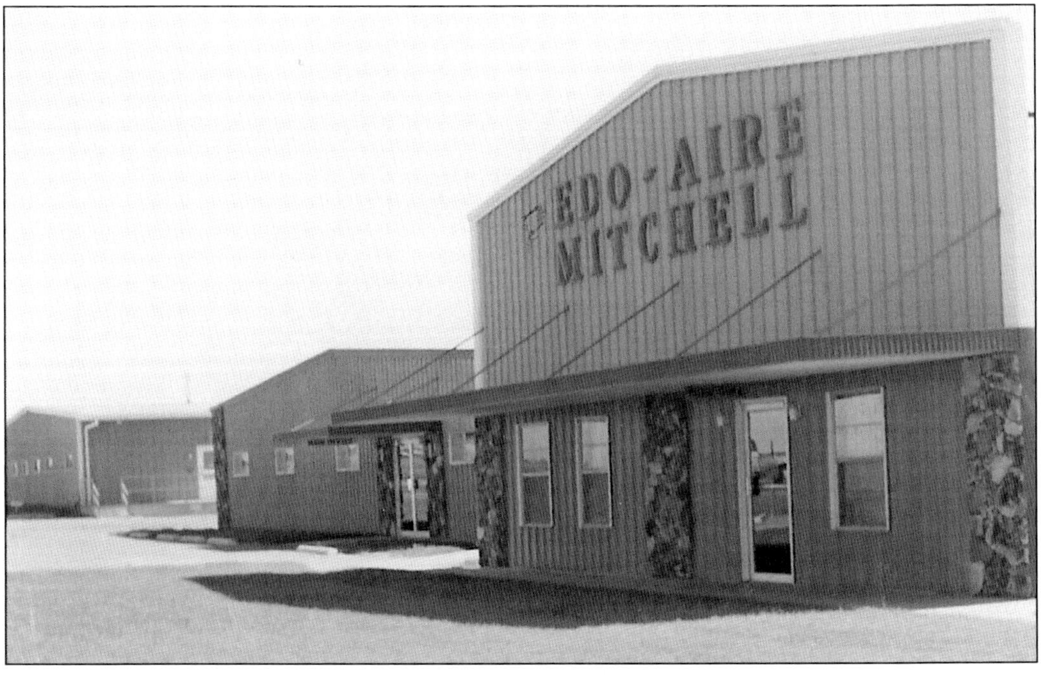

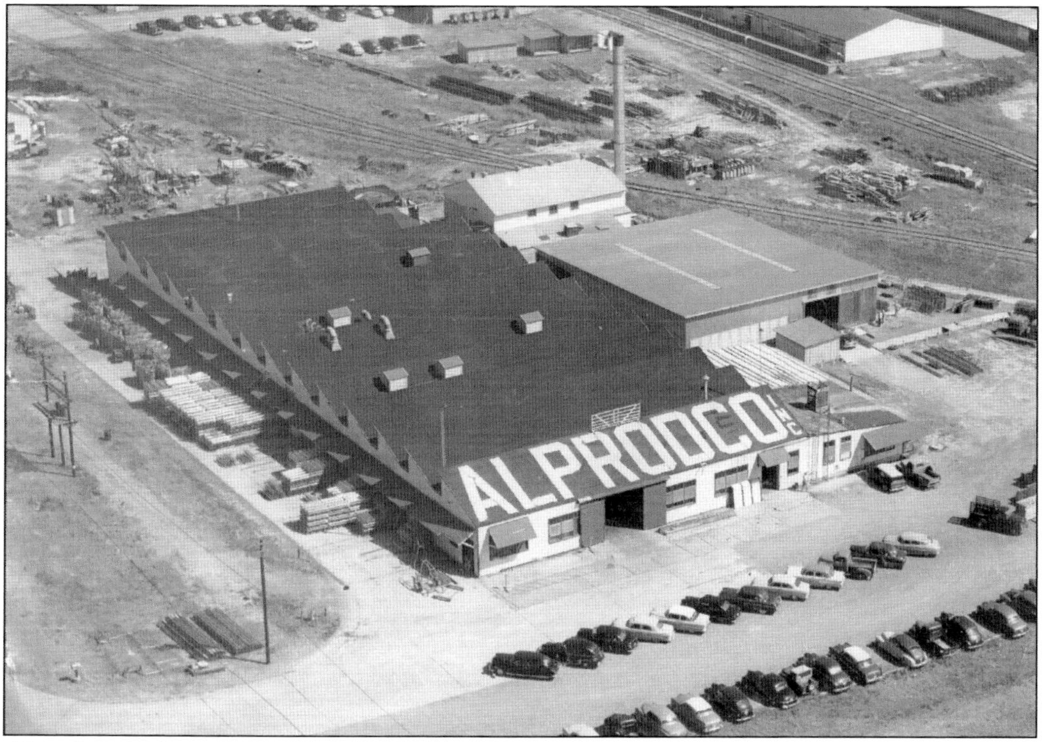

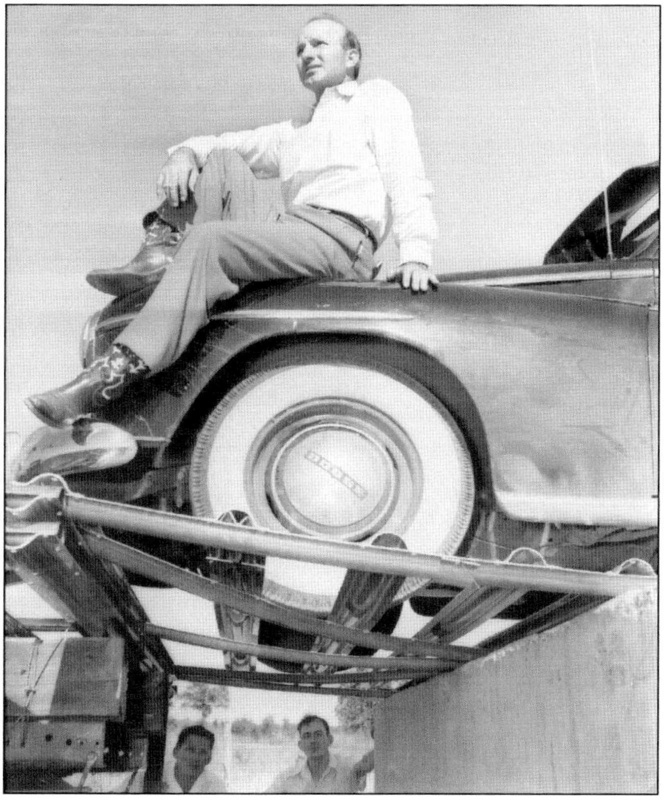

Alprodco, Carl Kessler's manufacturing business, exists today as Antenna Products. Born in 1919 in Indiana, Kessler (bottom left in photograph at right) joined the U.S. Army Air Corps in 1940 and became a flight instructor. After the war, Kessler married Sybal Wolfe of Wolfe Nursery in Stephenville. After starting a business building gates from surplus aluminum slats from B-24 Liberators, they moved to Mineral Wells, where Kessler purchased a building near Fort Wolters for his manufacturing business. Kessler designed the Distant Early Warning Line radar system to detect Soviet bombers during the Cold War and held at least half a dozen patents. Kessler also designed First Christian Church and built the steeple. (Both, courtesy of Lou Hayes Warren.)

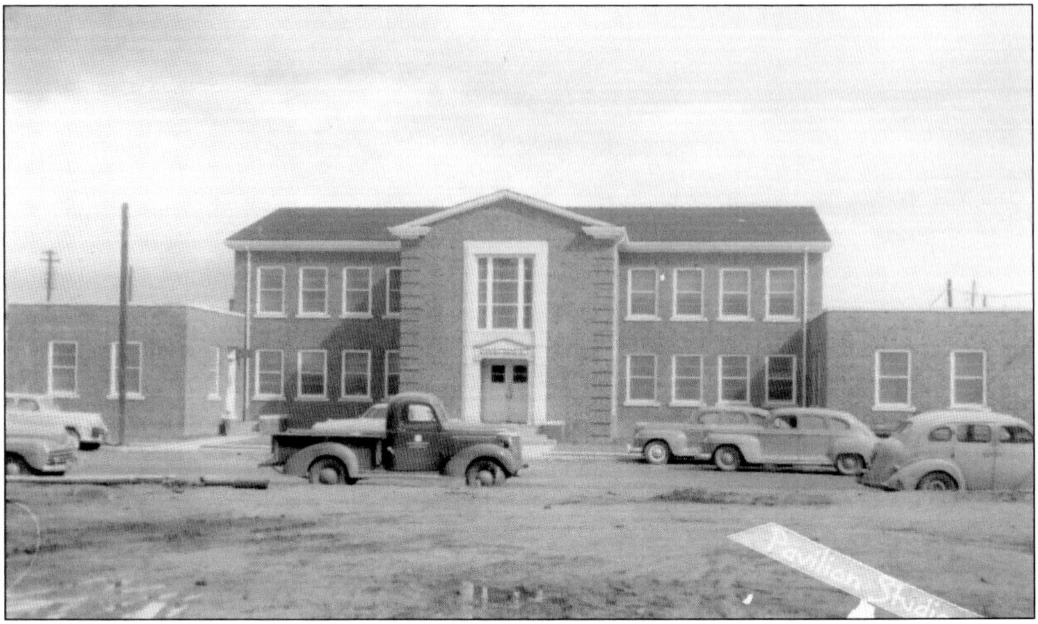

Mineral Well's current city hall, police station, fire station, and jail was originally built as a public health facility treating people with tuberculosis and venereal disease. (Courtesy of Lou Hayes Warren.)

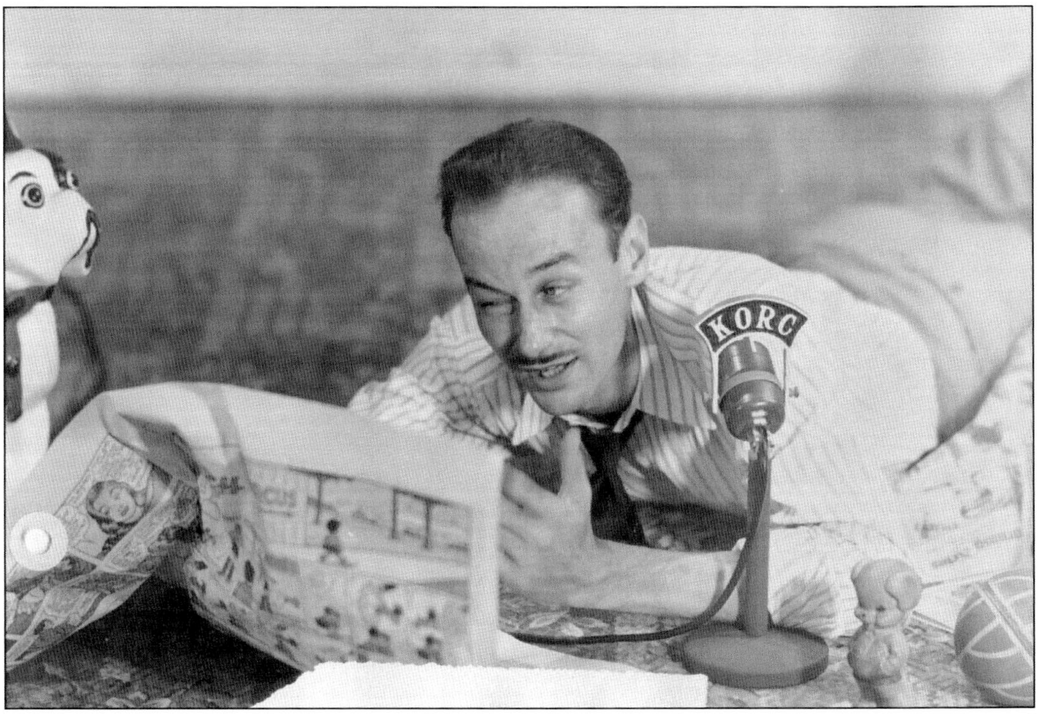

KORC was the local radio station for Mineral Wells. Maj. Achllies "Corky" Corcanges owned and operated the radio station. He also owned the Sport Shop, a women's clothing store, in the bottom of the Baker Hotel. Corcanges is pictured here reading the "Sunday funnies" to his listening audience. (Courtesy of Lou Hayes Warren.)

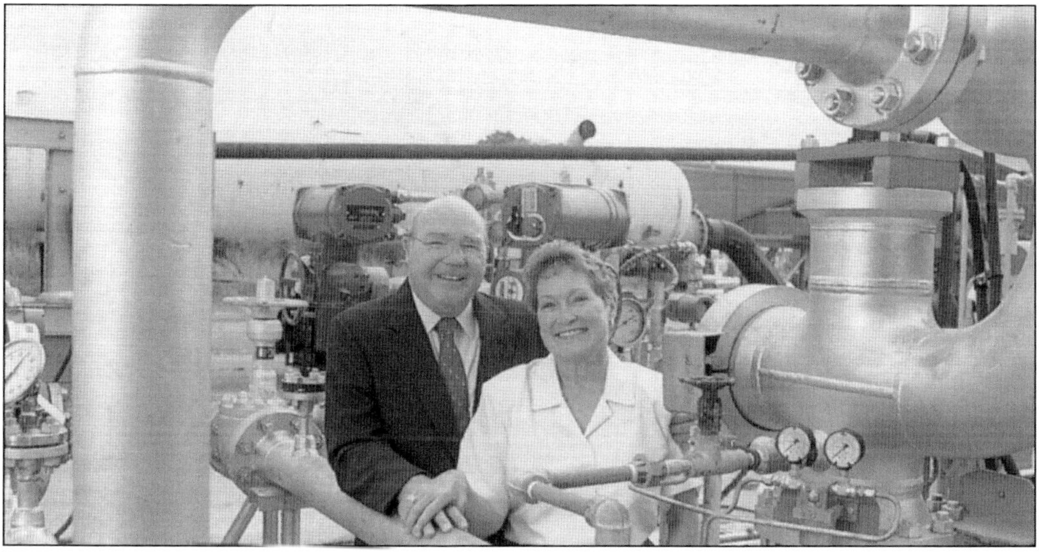

Dunman Perry Jr., grandson of Mineral Wells city father Cicero Smith and Peco chairman and chief executive officer, and his wife, Doris, facilities manager and secretary of the board, are shown viewing a crude oil metering system on its way to Venezuela. (Courtesy of Doris Perry McConnell.)

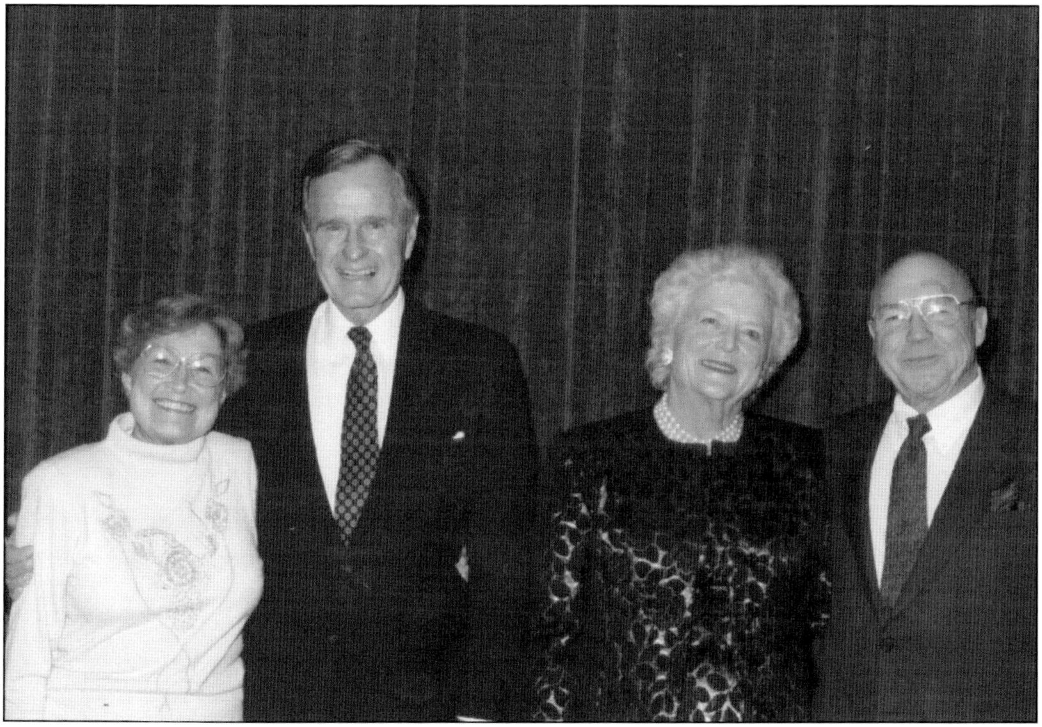

Here Doris and Dunman Perry Jr. pose with President and First Lady George and Barbara Bush. The Perrys were very active in the politics of the Republican Party. (Courtesy of Doris Perry McConnell.)

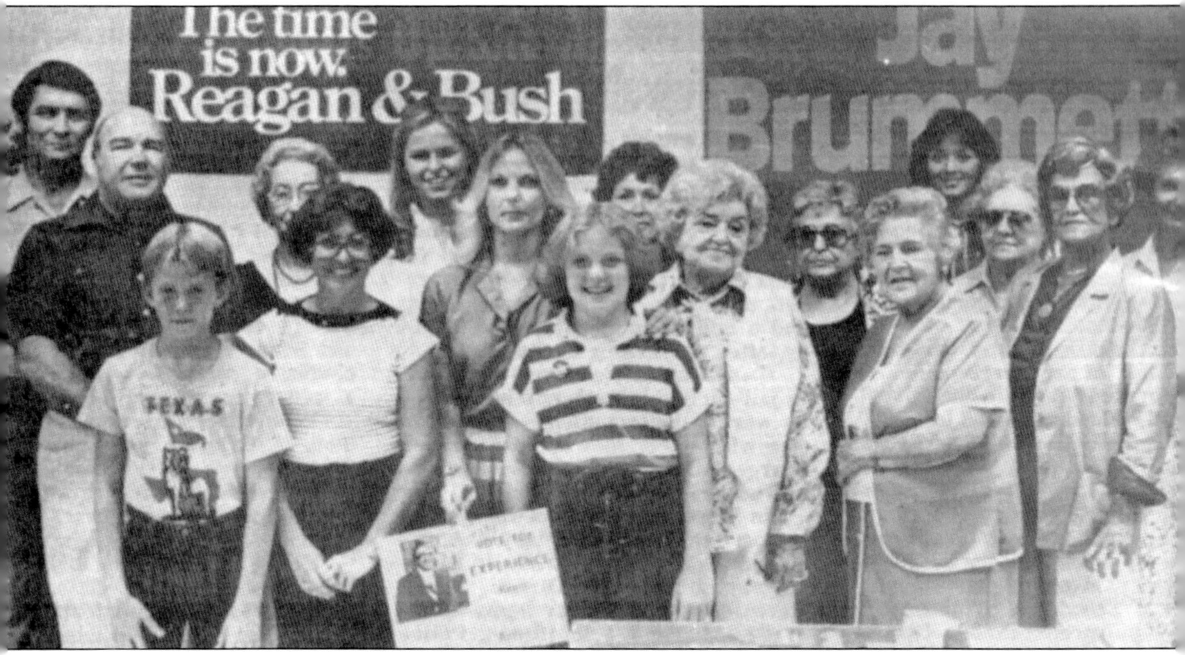

Local Republicans gathered for the grand opening of their 1978 campaign headquarters in the mall of the Brazos Shopping Center in Mineral Wells. At far left is Bill Rivers, who was the county campaign chairman for Ronald Reagan and district attorney Wayne Hughes. Next to Rivers is Republican county chairman Dunman Perry Jr., and holding the placard near the center is Kay Flynt, county chairman for district 22 state senatorial candidate Jerry Brummett. Virginia Upham, Lori Upham, Bea Harris, Nancy Busby, and Doris Perry are also among the group pictured here. (Courtesy of Doris Perry McConnell.)

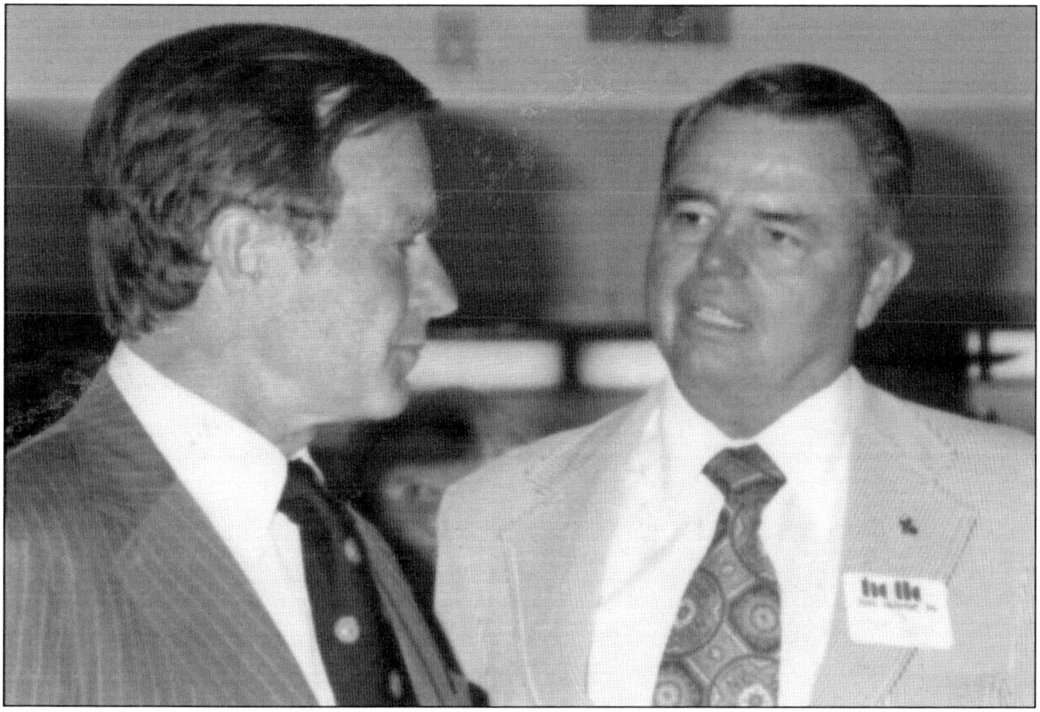

Chester R. Upham (right), founder and owner of Upham Oil and Gas, is having a discussion with presidential candidate George Bush. Upham was the Texas State Republican Chairman from 1979 to 1983. (Courtesy of Doris Perry McConnell.)

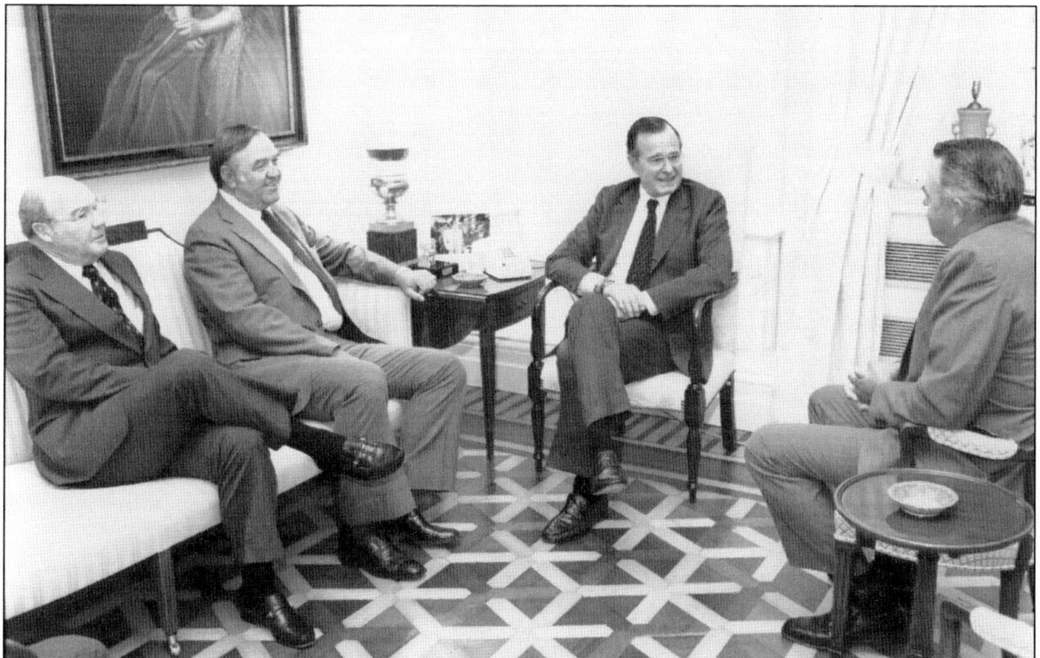

At the White House, Dunman Perry Jr. (far left) and Chester R. Upham (right) speak with Pres. George Bush (center). (Courtesy of Doris Perry McConnell.)

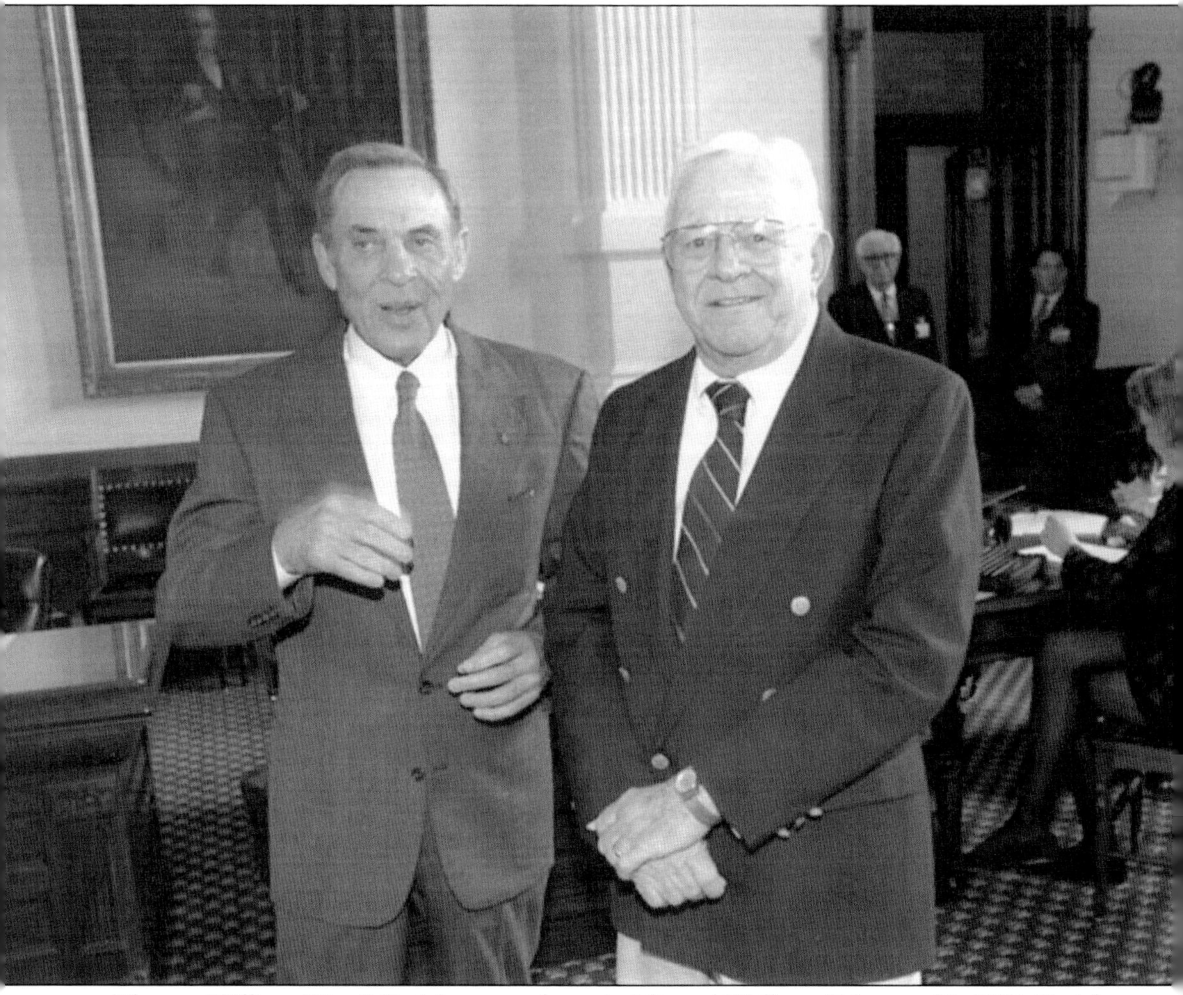

Thomas William "Tom" Creighton was born in Mineral Wells on February 26, 1927. Creighton was a local lawyer who served in the U.S. Navy in World War II. He was a Democratic member of the Texas State Senate from 1961 to 1981. This photograph was taken in January 1997 when Creighton (right) and his wife, Mary, took a student to Austin to be an honorary page of the state senate for the day. The senate surprised Creighton by recognizing him on the floor, and his good friend Lt. Gov. Bob Bullock joined him in the photograph. (Courtesy of Mary Creighton.)

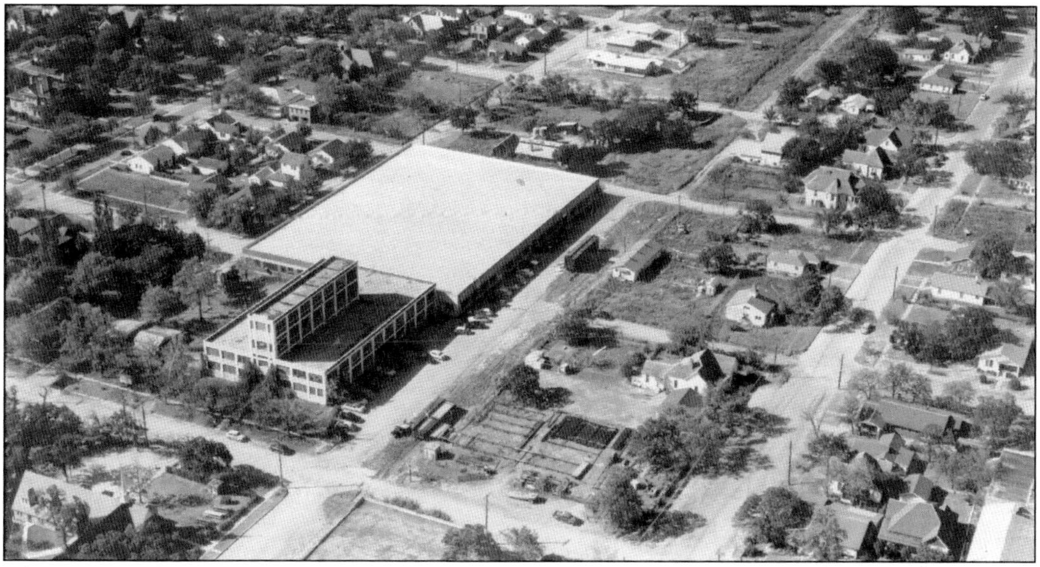

The Texas Packaging Box Factory, formerly the Crazy Water Crystal plant, is located northwest of the Crazy Water Hotel. The Crazy Water Company built the plant in 1919 to extract minerals from its water, box the crystals, and sell them nationwide as Crazy Water Crystals. Part of the crystal enterprise included a box factory. Following an action by the Food and Drug Administration in the late 1930s, crystal operations were reduced and the box operation was diversified. (Courtesy of Lou Hayes Warren.)

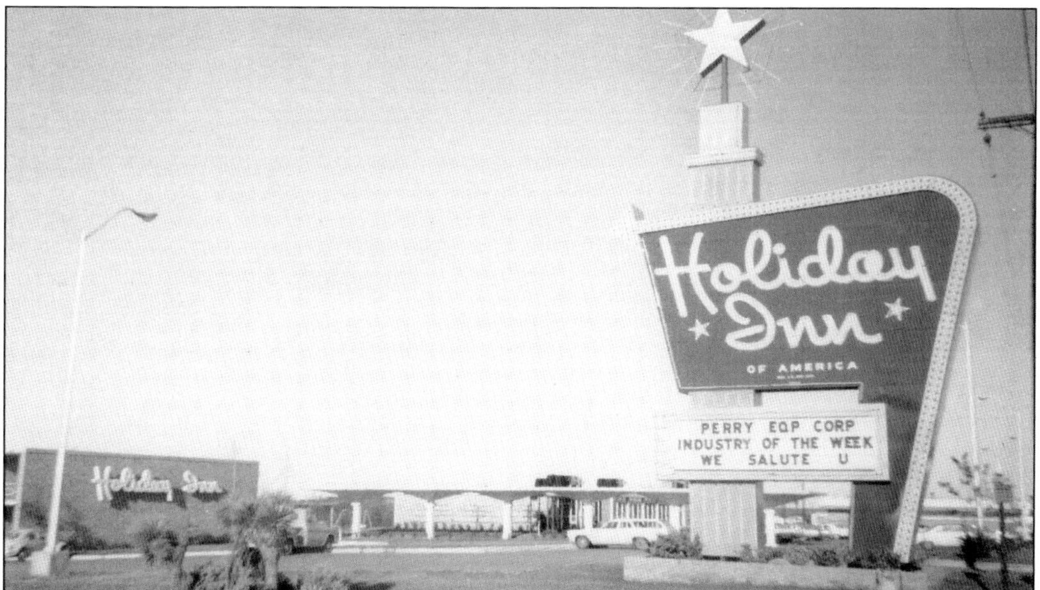

The Pratt Hotel Corporation (PHC) traces its roots to 1967, when brothers Jack, Edward, and William Pratt purchased their first Holiday Inn franchise in Mineral Wells, Texas. Over the years, the PHC became the nation's third-largest developer of Holiday Inn franchises, opening about 40 hotel and resort properties in the United States and abroad. There was a local tradition at this Holiday Inn: When a soldier received his helicopter pilot wings at Fort Wolters, he was thrown into the Holiday Inn swimming pool. (Courtesy of Lou Hayes Warren.)

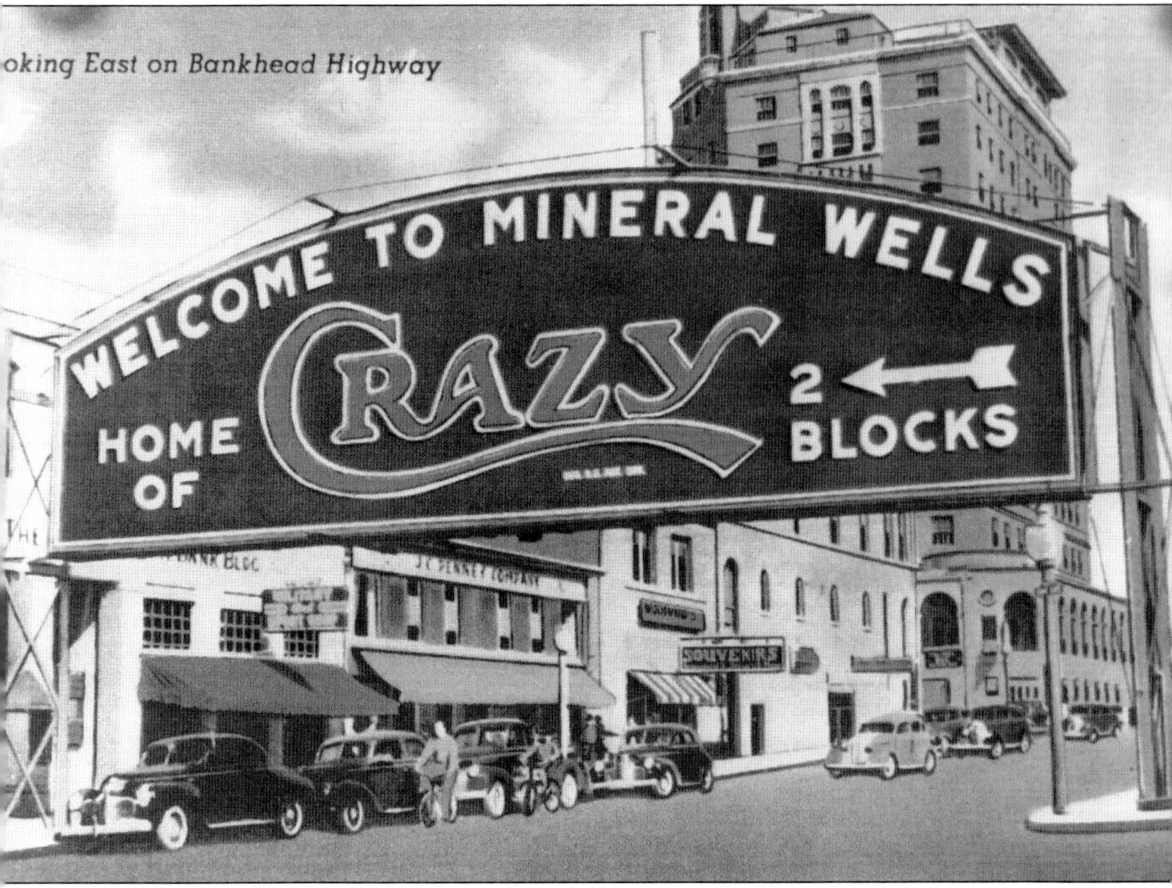

The "Crazy" sign was constructed in 1933 in the center of Mineral Wells and spanned Hubbard Street (Highway 180) at its intersection with Oak Avenue. It was quite a landmark, as it was one of only two signs allowed by the Texas Department of Transportation to cross a highway maintained by the state. The sign was torn down on December 24, 1958. The urgency of its removal during the Christmas season was not explained, nor was it ever quite understood by the general public. It was sold for scrap some time later. (Courtesy of Boyce Ditto Library, Weaver Collection.)

Five

Military Presence
Indian Wars–Present

Since before the town of Mineral Wells was established, there was a military presence in the area, mainly because of the Native American depredations. Fort Richardson in Jacksboro was opened in 1867, followed by Fort Griffin near Albany in 1874, to establish control over the Indians and the lawlessness of area citizens.

In 1921, the 56th Cavalry Brigade of the Texas National Guard was organized and used the Rock Creek–Mineral Wells areas as field-training grounds. A grant for construction of the Texas National Guard training camp was given to Brig. Gen. Jacob F. Wolters, commanding officer of the brigade. The city commissioners purchased 50 acres of land next to Mineral Wells Lake for location of the headquarters. Citizens of Mineral Wells, led by Mayor John Miller, joined together and leased 2,300 acres surrounding the original 50 acres. The population of the city at that time was 7,500.

Troop F, 124th Cavalry, of the Texas National Guard, along with a band and medical detachment, was moved to Mineral Wells in 1923. During its time of service, Troop F performed service along the Rio Grande River from Brownsville to Fort Bliss and, during World War II, in Burma, where it was assigned to clear the enemy from the route of the Burma Road.

On October 13, 1940, the U.S. Department of Defense announced that Mineral Wells had been selected for location of an Infantry Replacement Training Center (IRTC) large enough to house 17,000 men. Additional acreage was leased totaling 7,500 acres, and the first trainees arrived on March 1, 1941. Training began on March 24, and the first rifle was fired on the 100-yard firing range. Brig. Gen. William H. Simpson arrived on April 5, along with his executive officer, Col. Fay W. Grabson. At this time there were 15 infantry battalions either in operation or awaiting trainees. During the war years, Camp Wolters was noted as being the nation's largest IRTC, which housed 30,000 soldiers at its peak.

The most decorated soldier in World War II, Audie Murphy, was trained here, as was fellow Congressional Medal of Honor recipient Lt. Jack Knight.

From 1942 to 1945, a German prisoner of war camp with about 300 prisoners was located in the center of the camp. It was surrounded by a high mesh fence with sentry towers at intervals around the compound.

In February 1951, the camp was reactivated and redesignated as Wolters Air Force Base. Its mission was to house the newly formed Aviation Engineer Force, which was established in April 1951. Special Category Army Reassigned with the Air Force (SCARWAF) personnel were trained here until 1956, when the SCARWAF function reverted to army control.

On April 27, 1957, the first class graduated from U.S. Army Primary Helicopter School at Camp Wolters, and on June 1, 1963, Camp Wolters was redesignated as Fort Wolters, a permanent military installation. In March 1966, the post was designated as the U.S. Army Primary Helicopter Center. In 1973, the helicopter school transferred to the U.S. Army Aviation School at Fort Rucker in Alabama, and Fort Wolters was closed permanently.

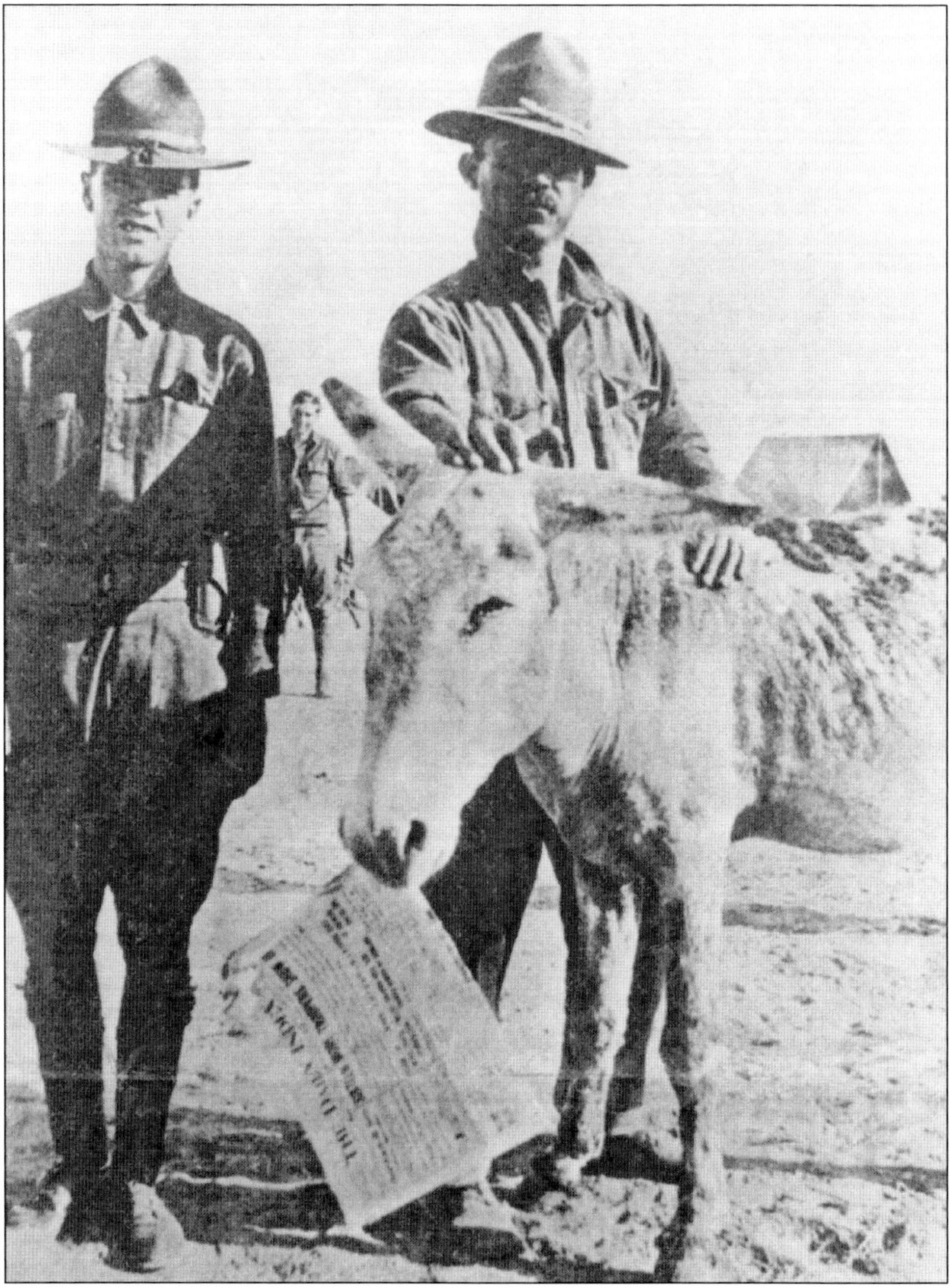

Company 1 of the 4th Texas Infantry patrolled the Mexican border. The company's home base was in Mineral Wells. Later it was called into federal service and designated as Company B, 144th Infantry, 36th Division, with combat duty in France on the Meuse-Argonne Campaign and the Argonne Forest. In this picture is the company's pet donkey, about to consume a copy of the *Daily Index*. On the left is Bill Cameron, and Spencer Heath is at the right. This picture was taken in Marathon, Texas, in 1916. Bill Cameron was employed in various capacities by the Mineral Wells newspaper for many years. At the time of his death in 1976, he was its business manager. (Courtesy of Boyce Ditto Library, Weaver Collection.)

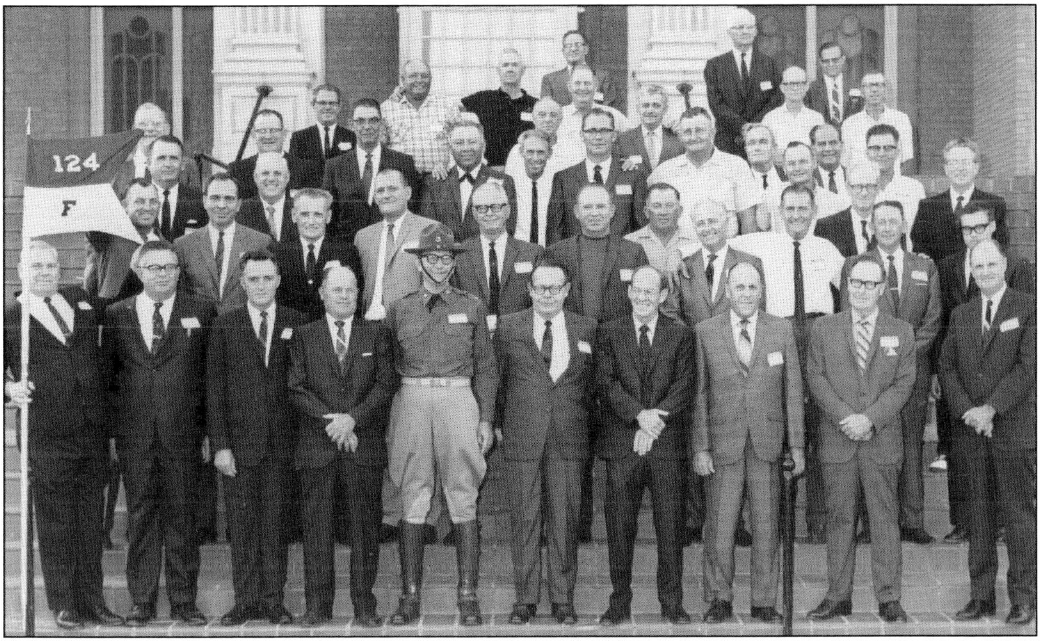

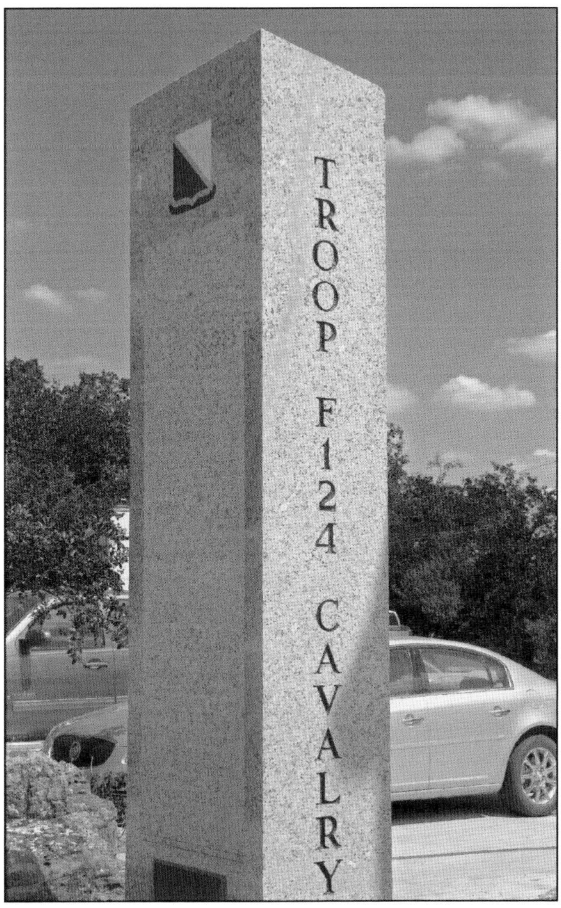

The image above of Troop F, 124th Cavalry, was taken on the steps of the Baker Hotel at one of its annual meetings in the 1960s. Identified on the back of the photograph are, from left to right, (first row) J. Harrington, P. Henson, M. Yell, J. Scott, L. Holt, J. Cooper, W. McQueary, W. Holt, and G. Rankin; (second row) F. Crow, J. Warner, T. Owens, L. Knight, A. Lee, R. Huddleston, H. Warren, C. Baker, L. Hudspeth, T. Newton, and T. J. Newton; (third row) G. Hines, E. Warren, O. Keller, N. Yates, J. Kincaid, R. Bell, H. Rochelle, D. McMinn, G. Lee, and T. Blanton; (fourth row) J. Harrington, V. Poe, N. Stockstill, A. Hudspeth, H. Blanton, N. Kimbrough, and W. Bell; (fifth row) C. Kirby, J. Harrison, O. Martin, S. Whatley, J. Dews, and Dr. J. Huey. Troop F served with distinction in the China-Burma-India (CBI) Theater of World War II. England's Lord Mountbatten, commander of the CBI Theater, dedicated a monument to Troop F in Mineral Wells on October 14, 1972. The monument still stands on the south side of the 500 block of Southeast First Street. (Above, courtesy of Boyce Ditto Library, Weaver Collection; right, photograph by Raf Seibert.)

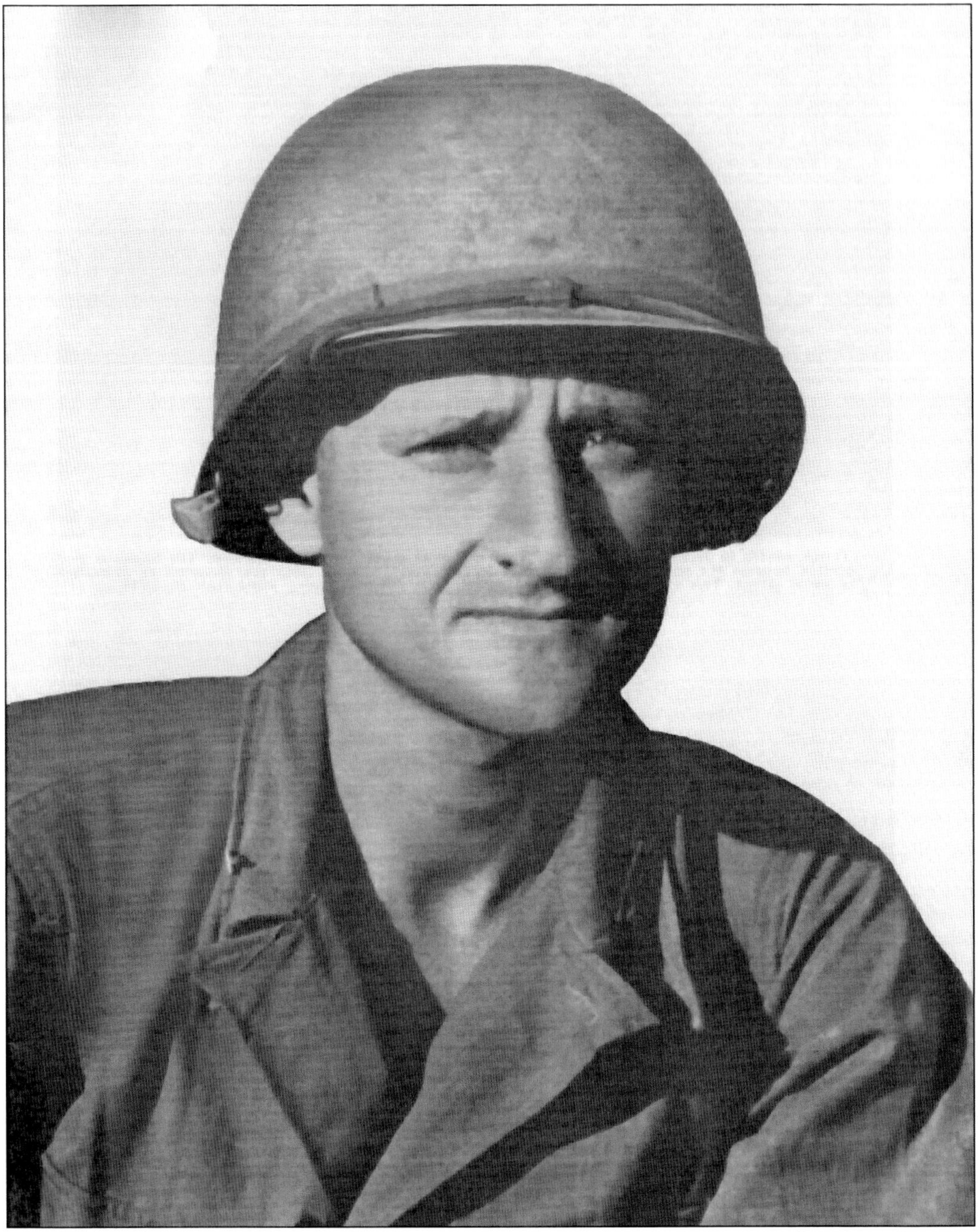

During World War II, American fighting men earned 432 Medals of Honor. In the China-Burma-India Theater, however, only one Medal of Honor was awarded to a ground combatant. That medal was awarded posthumously to the commander of Troop F, 1st Lt. Jack Llewellyn Knight, who was a member of the Mars Task Force, a long-range penetration unit that is part of the heritage and lineage of army special-operations forces. He was buried at the Holders Chapel Cemetery in Cool, Texas. (Courtesy of A. Silva.)

In 1925, Gen. Jacob F. Wolters was instrumental in the acquisition of a 50-acre tract of land, later to be named Camp Wolters in his honor, near Mineral Wells as a training area for his brigade. Later his brigade was recognized as the best cavalry unit in the National Guard by the U.S. War Department. He retired on November 1, 1934, after 43 years of service to his state and nation. Below is the gate to Camp Wolters during the World War II era when it was the largest Infantry Replacement Training Center. (Right, courtesy of Texas Military Forces Museum, Camp Mabry, Austin, Texas; below, courtesy of Boyce Ditto Library, Casper Collection.)

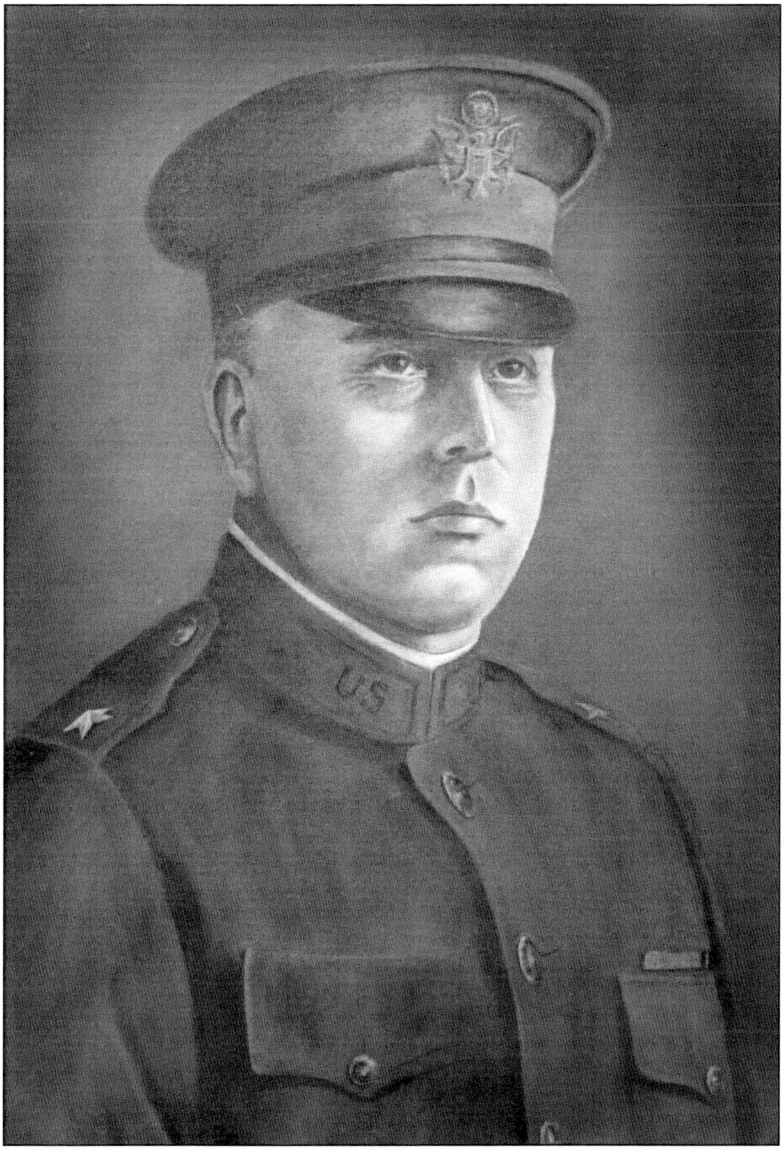

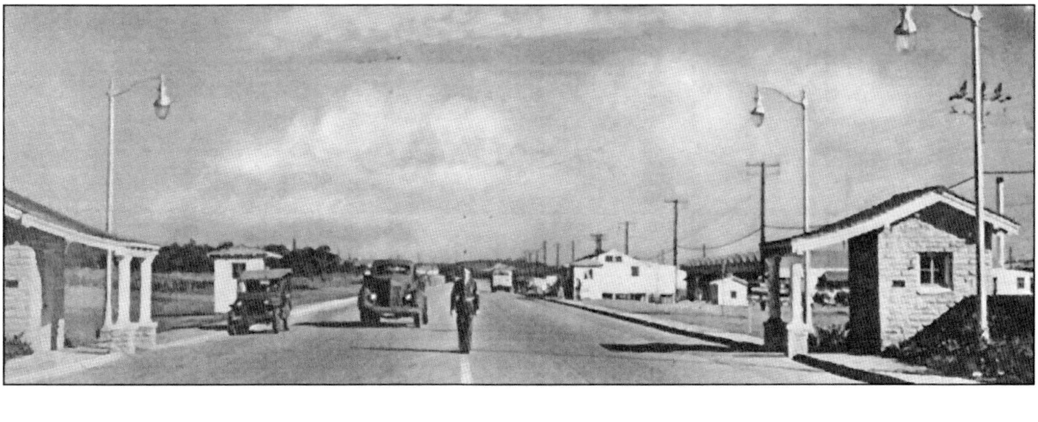

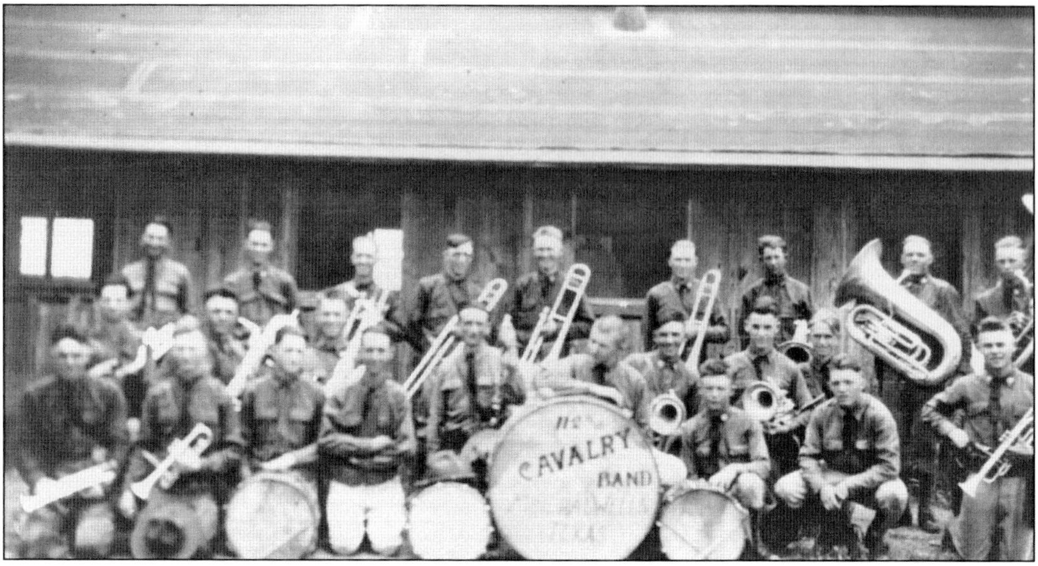

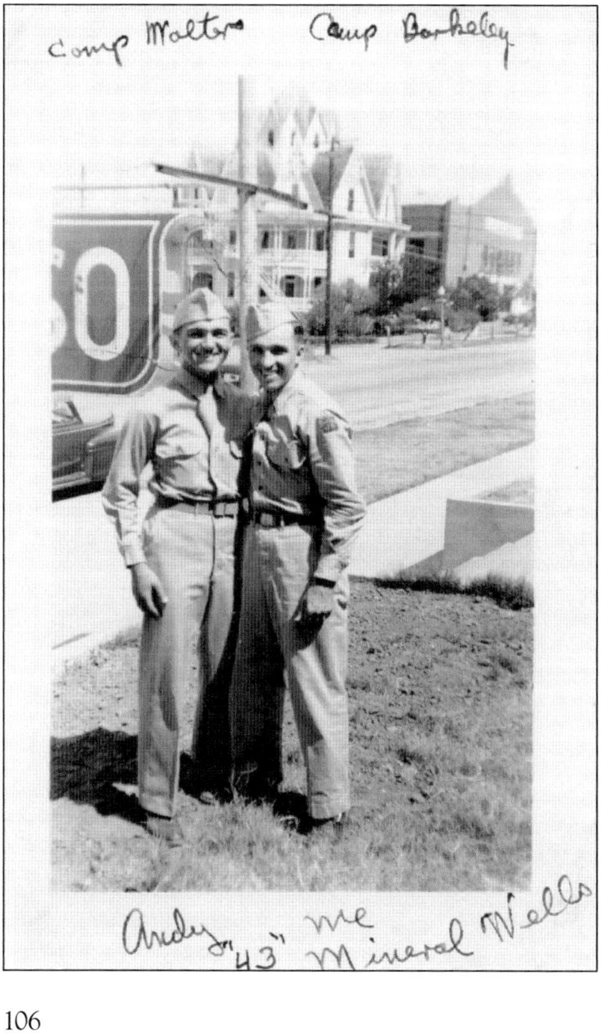

The 112th Cavalry Band was stationed at Camp Wolters, along with Troop F, 124th Cavalry. (Courtesy of Boyce Ditto Library, Casper Collection.)

The soldier on the left is Andrew Pocalyko (now 87 in 2011), and the soldier on the right is his older brother, Michael Pocalyko (1917–2007). They are standing in front of the Mineral Wells USO on North Oak Street. The Hexagon House Hotel is in the background. Andrew earned the Combat Infantry Badge in the 97th Infantry in Europe and later served in the Asian Theater in the occupation of Japan before returning to the United States, where he graduated from Yale on the GI Bill. He then went on to a distinguished career as a metallurgical engineer at DuPont. These are but two of the thousands of soldiers who were stationed in Mineral Wells in World War II. (Courtesy of Andrew Pocalyko.)

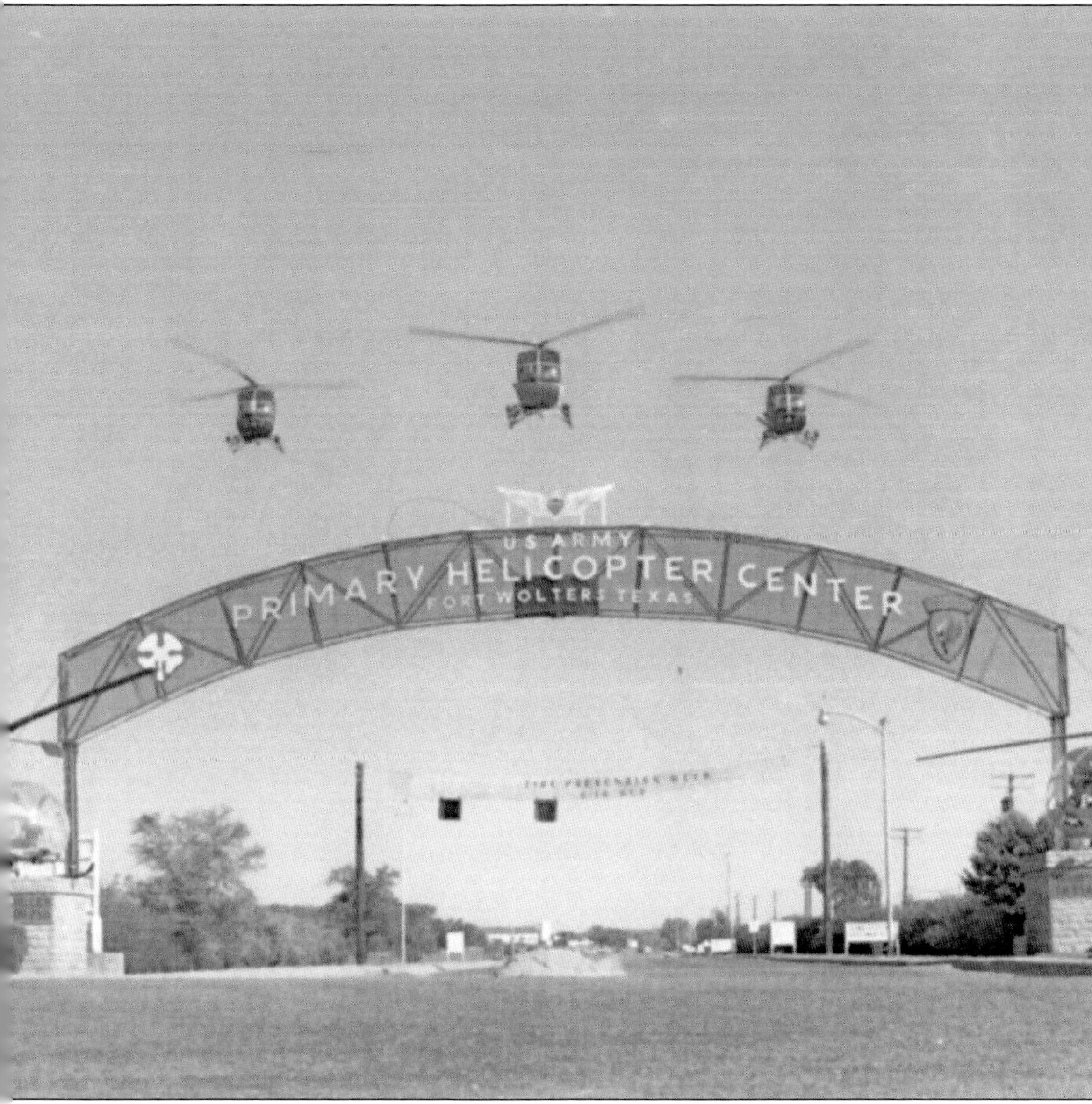

This is the gate to Fort Wolters, the Primary Helicopter Training Center for the U.S. Army during the Vietnam War. (Courtesy of Boyce Ditto Library, Casper Collection.)

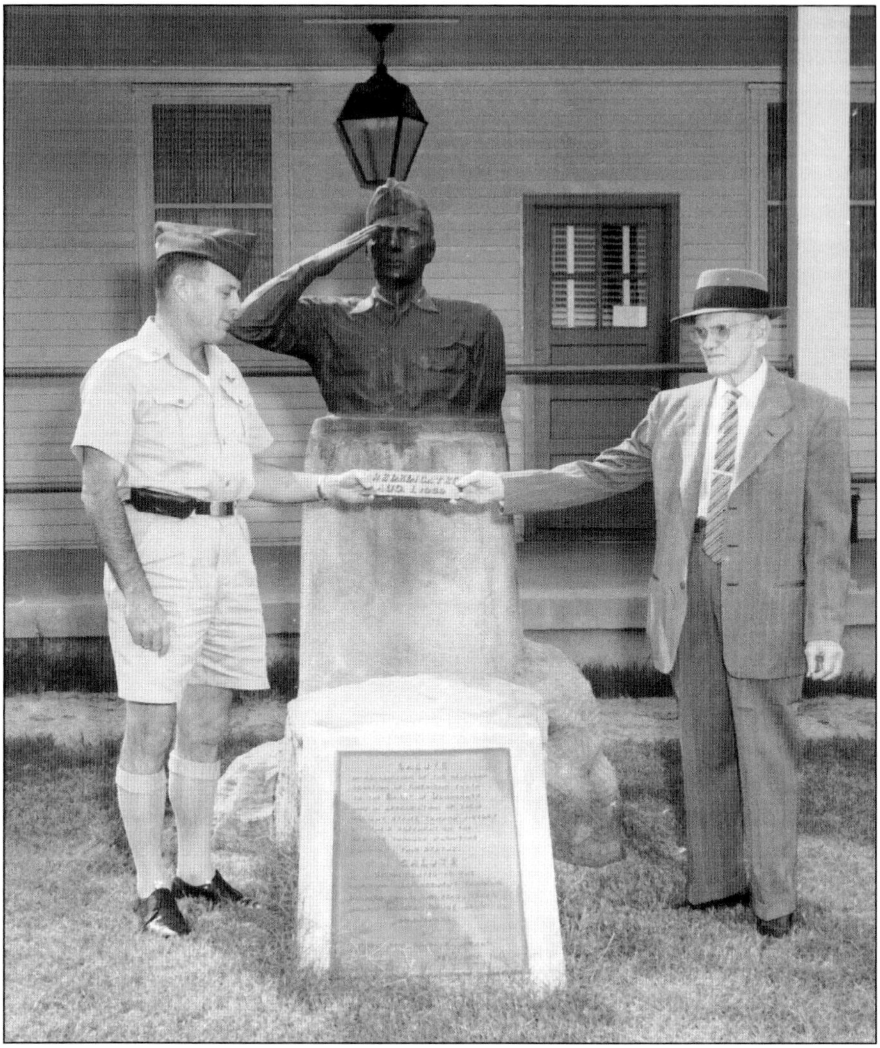

In the summer of 1941—five months before the Pearl Harbor attack that officially brought the U.S. into World War II—a lanky, farm boy draftee named Glenn C. Amon, the first selected by his Holton, Kansas, draft board, found himself at Camp Wolters in Mineral Wells. Amon's command presence was noted by his superiors. He was quickly promoted to first sergeant of the 60th Training Battalion and remained stationed at the camp for the duration, until 1946. Maj. Gen. Bruce Magruder, commanding officer at Camp Wolters, learned that T.Sgt. Simon G. Michael, of Cleveland and New York, was a nationally famous sculptor in civilian life and that he was attached to Amon's battalion. As a morale booster, Magruder ordered the sculptor to make a statue of a soldier as a dedication to the sacrifices being made by American youth in the war effort. In their spare time away from training duties, Amon and Sgt. Eugene Fruhwirth were ordered to pose as the model for the renowned sculptor. Two or three plaster molds of the finished clay sculpture were made before it was cast in iron in 1943 at the Bateman Foundry and Machine Company, located at 113 Southwest Seventh Street and owned by W. W. Bateman. Sculpted from the waist up, *Salute* is the life-size cast-iron statue of a uniformed soldier offering a formalized hand salute. It rests outside VFW Post No. 2399, but unfortunately is now missing one hand. A plaster copy is at American Legion Post No. 75. (Courtesy of Boyce Ditto Library, Casper Collection.)

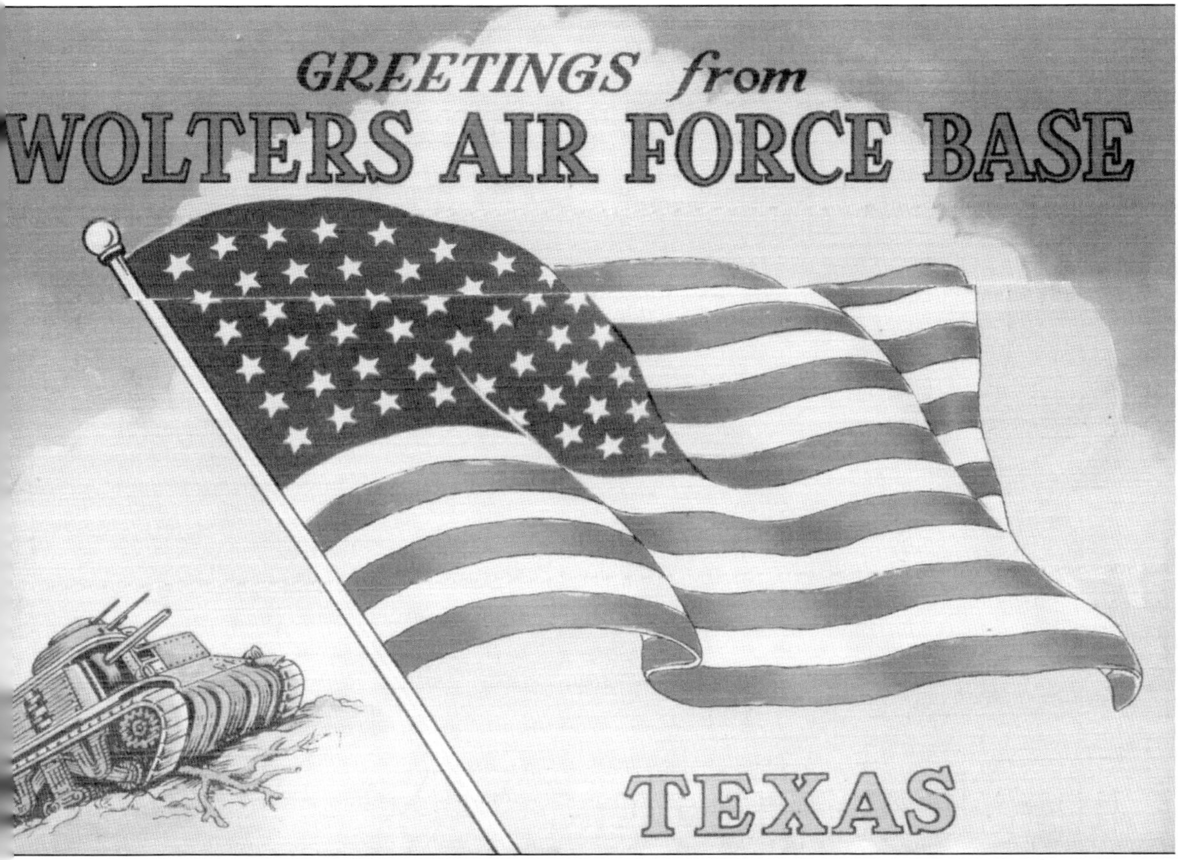

Camp Wolters was a U.S. Air Force Base from 1951 to 1956. It was an engineer aviation unit for demolitions and base defense. (Courtesy of Lou Hayes Warren.)

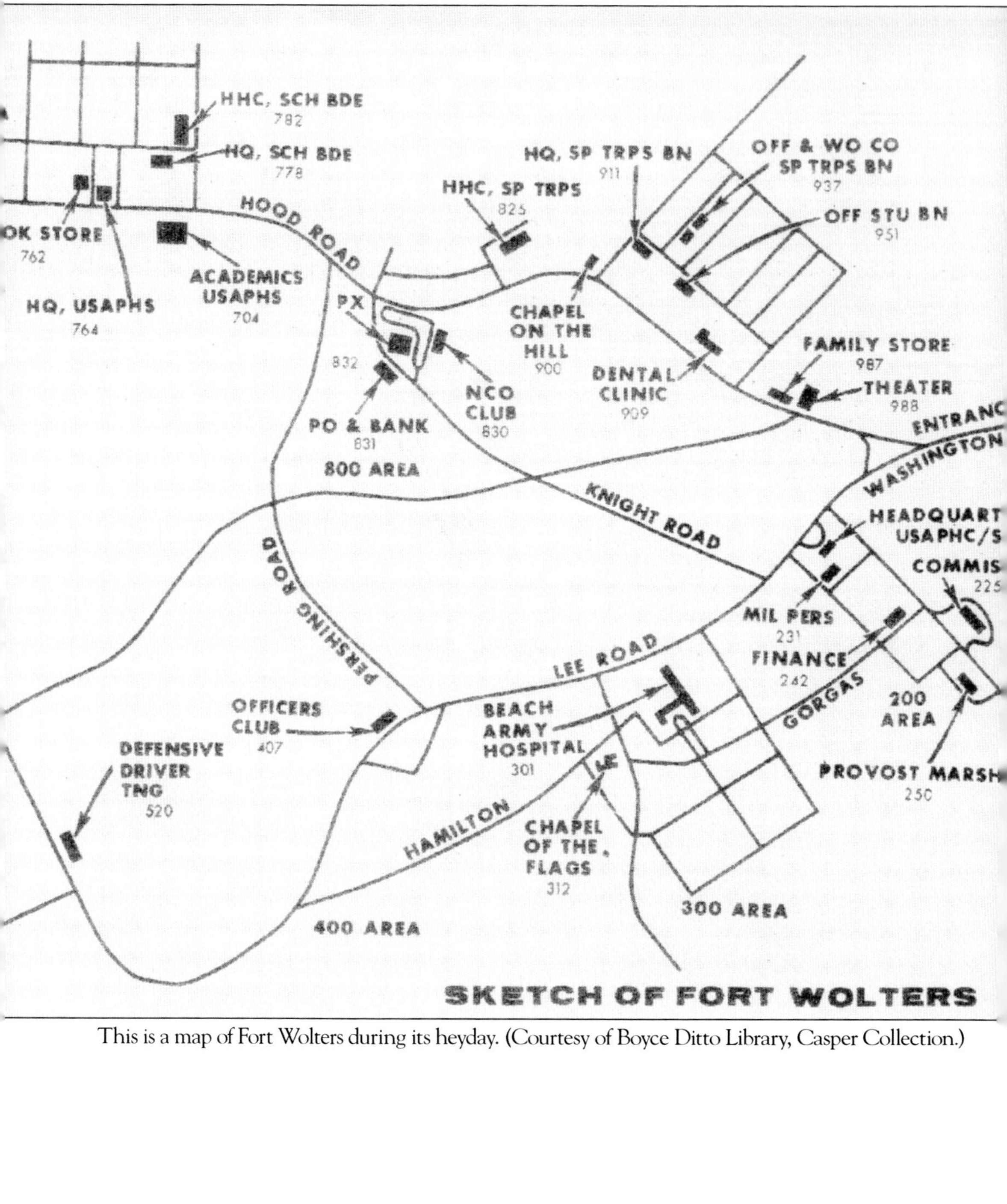

This is a map of Fort Wolters during its heyday. (Courtesy of Boyce Ditto Library, Casper Collection.)

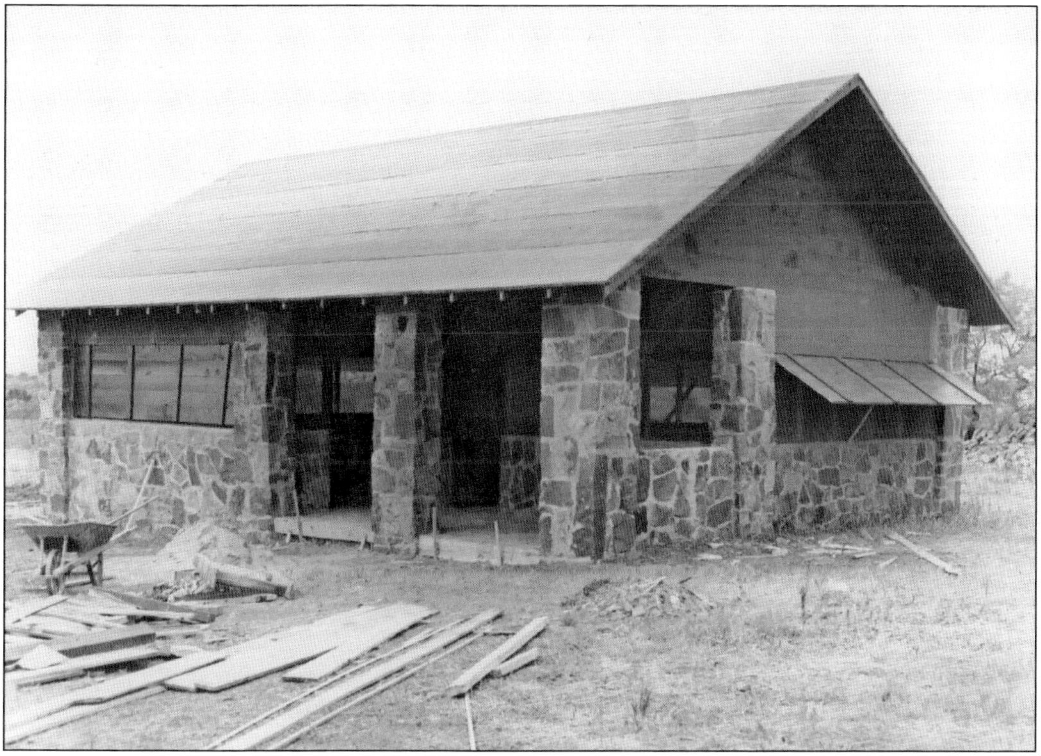

The prisoner of war (POW) quarters were built to house German POWs during World War II. The only building left of old Camp Wolters is shown in the photograph below. It was the German officers' quarters in the POW section of Camp Wolters. (Above, courtesy of Lou Hayes Warren; below, photograph by Raf Seibert.)

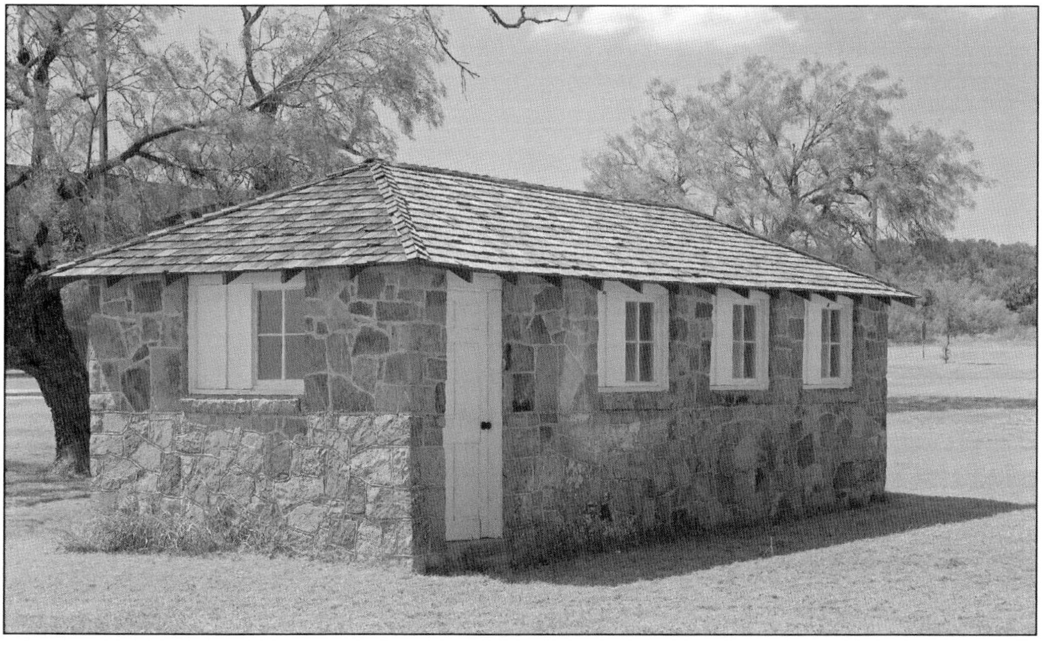

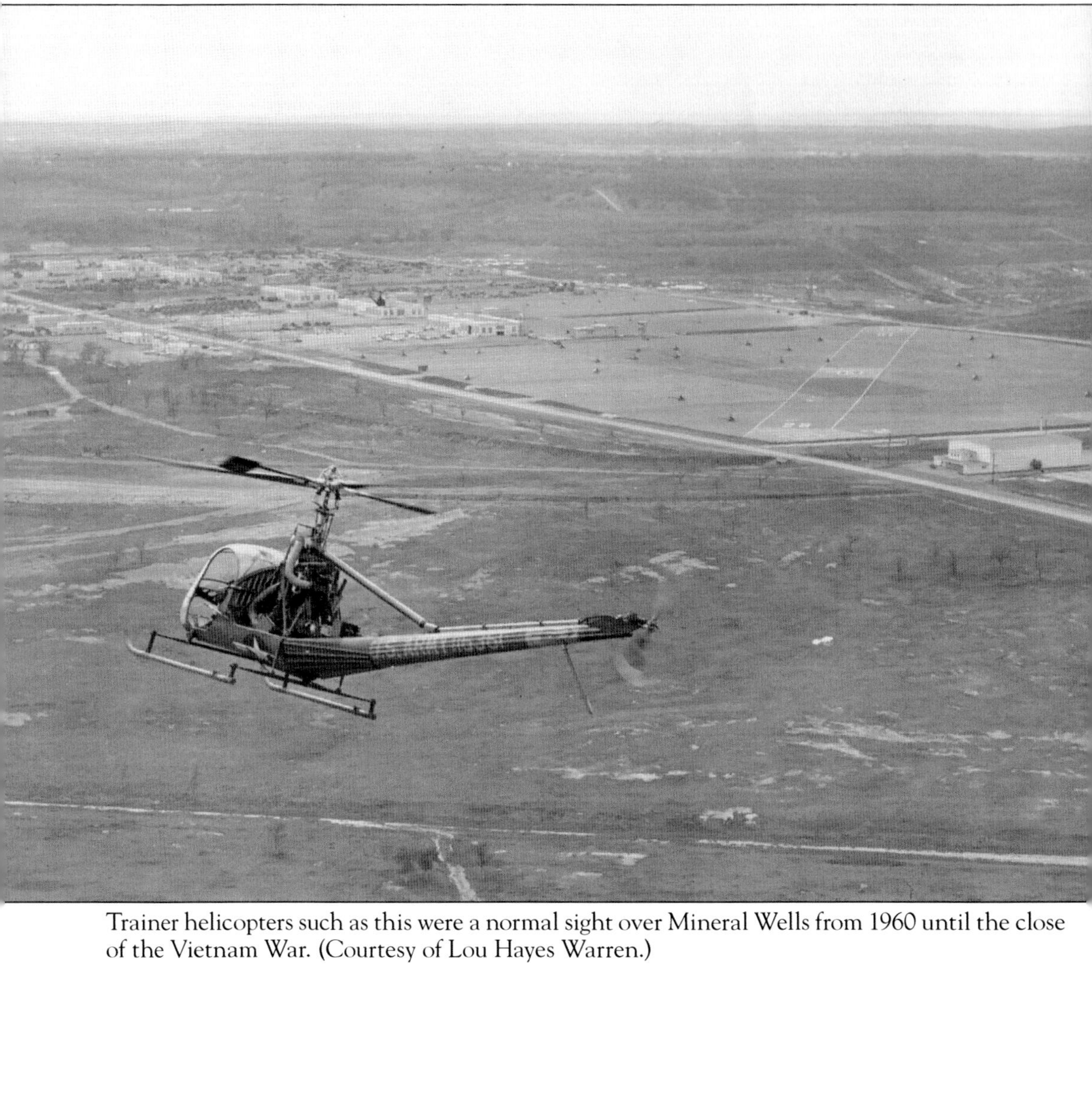

Trainer helicopters such as this were a normal sight over Mineral Wells from 1960 until the close of the Vietnam War. (Courtesy of Lou Hayes Warren.)

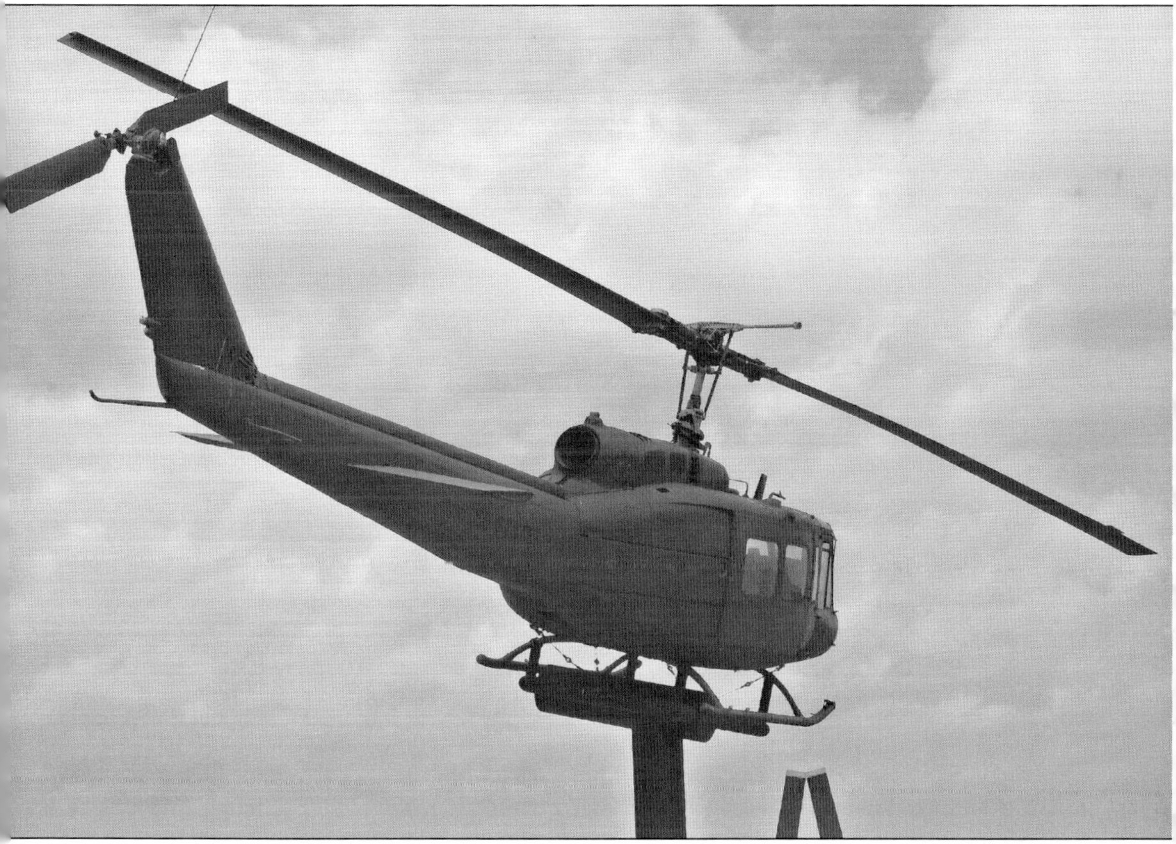

The Bell UH-1 Iroquois is a military helicopter powered by a single turboshaft engine, with a two-bladed main rotor and tail rotor. This was the type of helicopter, the "Huey," that most of the Fort Wolters trainees flew in Vietnam. It can be seen at the National Vietnam War Museum just east of the city of Mineral Wells on Highway 180. The museum was incorporated in 1999, and its goal is to present an unbiased and balanced view of the events of the Vietnam Era. (Photograph by Raf Seibert.)

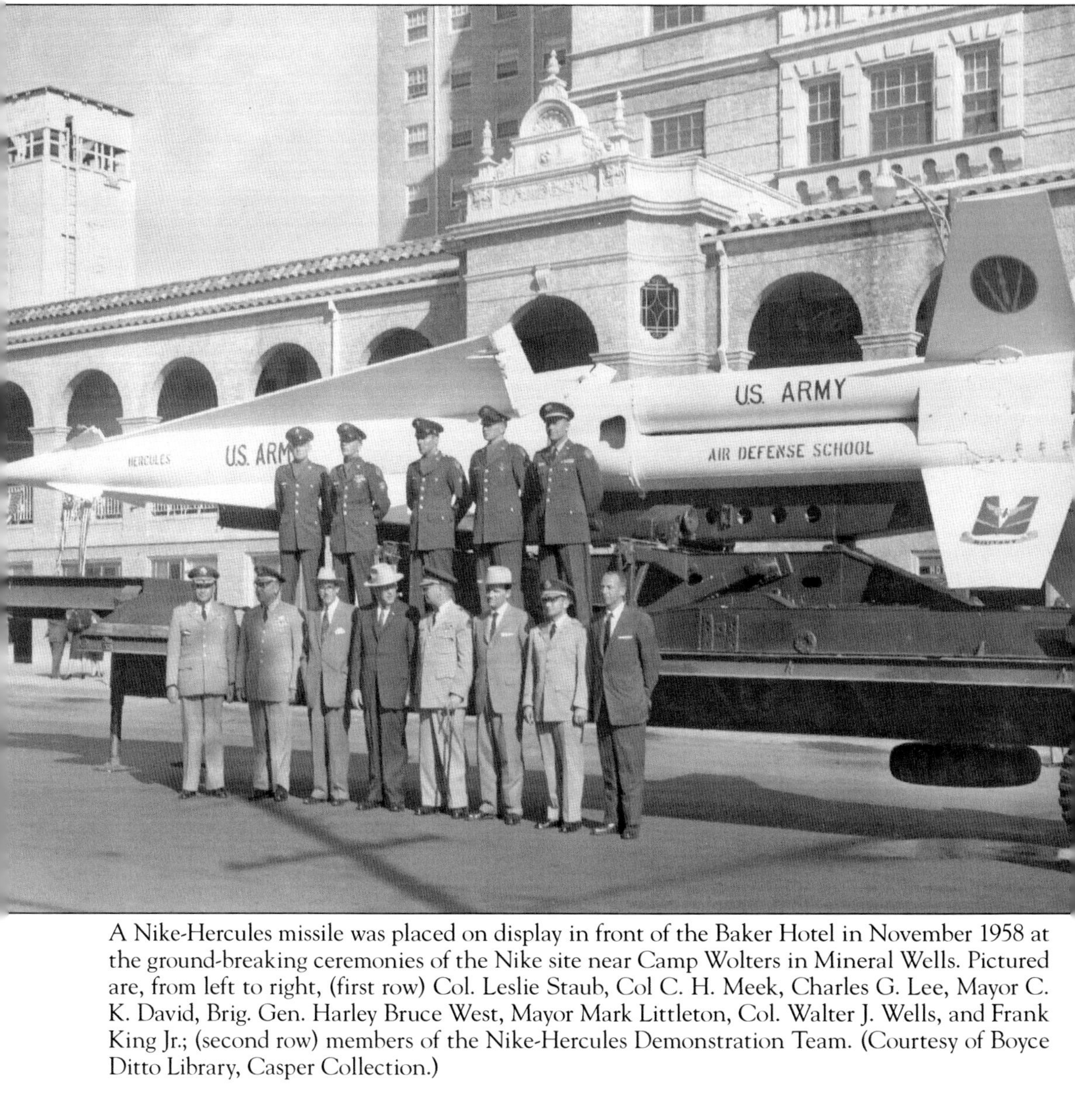

A Nike-Hercules missile was placed on display in front of the Baker Hotel in November 1958 at the ground-breaking ceremonies of the Nike site near Camp Wolters in Mineral Wells. Pictured are, from left to right, (first row) Col. Leslie Staub, Col C. H. Meek, Charles G. Lee, Mayor C. K. David, Brig. Gen. Harley Bruce West, Mayor Mark Littleton, Col. Walter J. Wells, and Frank King Jr.; (second row) members of the Nike-Hercules Demonstration Team. (Courtesy of Boyce Ditto Library, Casper Collection.)

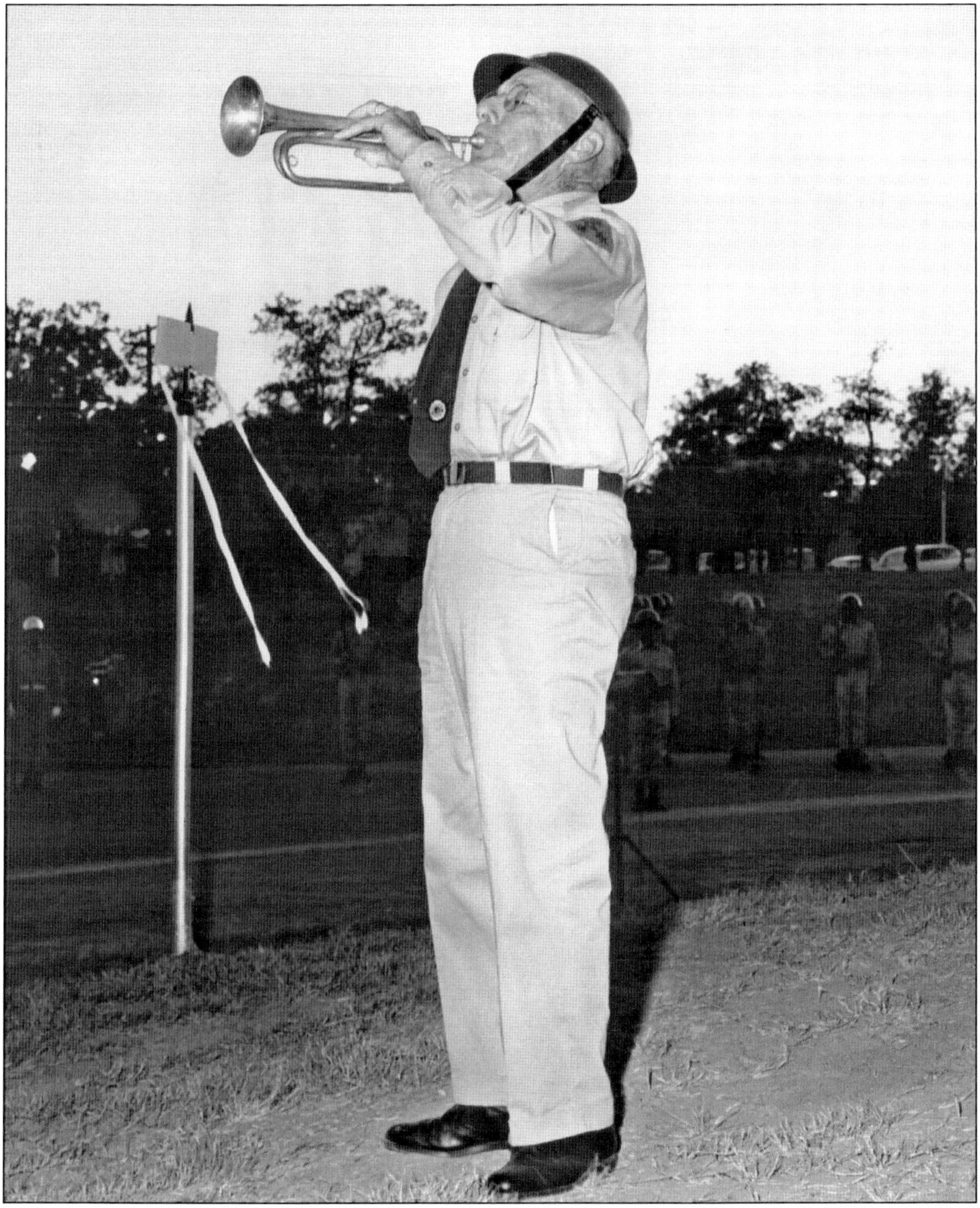

Harley Edwards of Denison, Texas, was Gen. John J. Pershing's bugler at the Headquarters in France during World War I. Here he "blows" Taps at Camp Wolters for the Pershing centennial celebration on September 13, 1960. (Courtesy of Boyce Ditto Library, Casper Collection.)

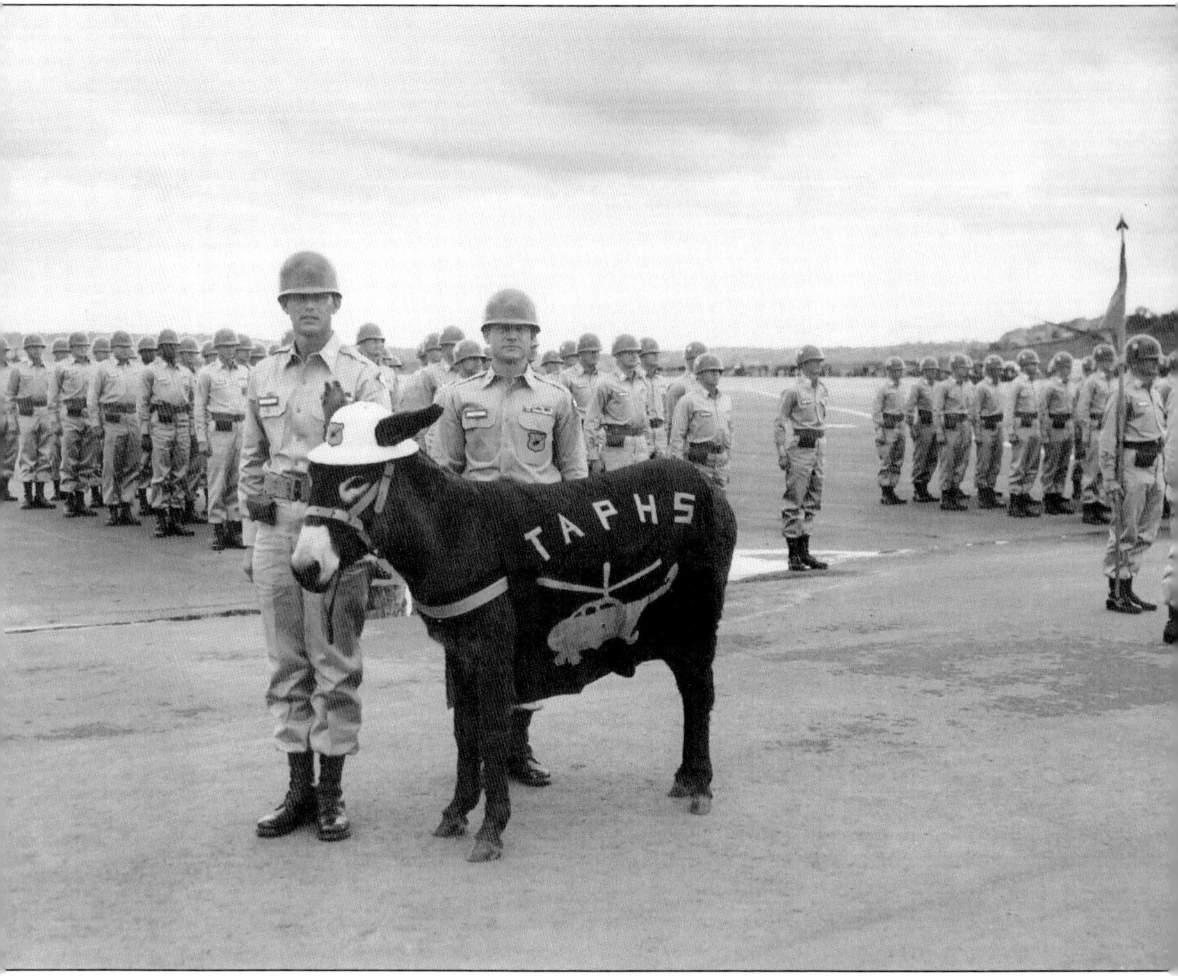

On April 27, 1957, Mrs. Mealy Mouth, mascot of the Texas Army Primary Helicopter School at Camp Wolters Texas, displayed the emblem of the school before massed troops during the first graduation ceremony. Later, Mrs. Mealy Mouth had a daughter, who was named Miss Mushy Mouth. Donkeys have clearly been a tradition in Mineral Wells almost since the beginning. (Courtesy of Boyce Ditto Library, Casper Collection.)

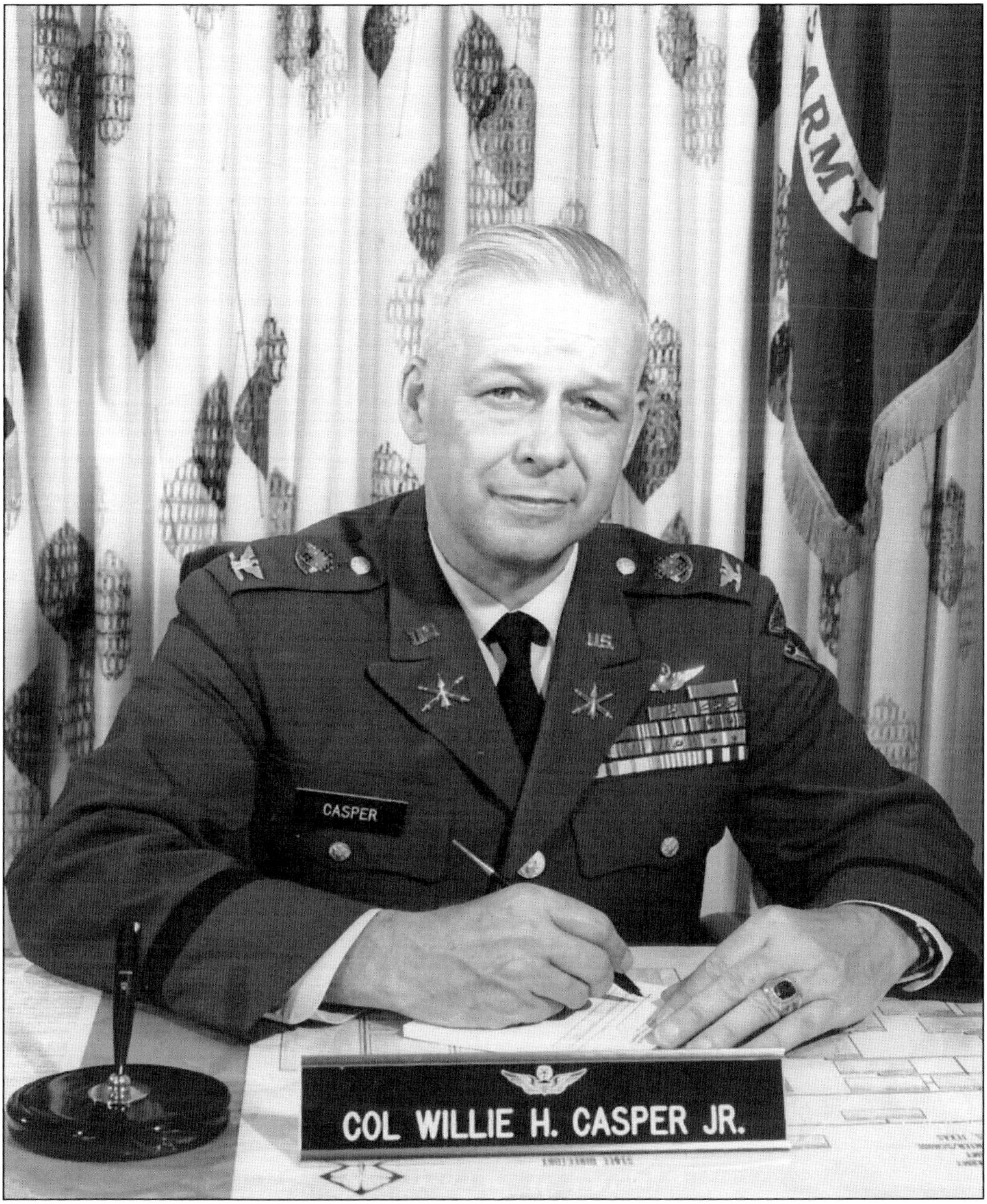

Col. Willie H. Casper Jr. came to Fort Walters on February 25, 1966, from Vietnam, where he was deputy chief of staff to the U. S. Army Support Command and secretary to the general staff of the U.S. Army. He retired after 24 years of active service on May 27, 1971, with full military honors. Casper made his home in Mineral Wells after his retirement and became a great civic asset to the community. (Courtesy of Boyce Ditto Library, Casper Collection.)

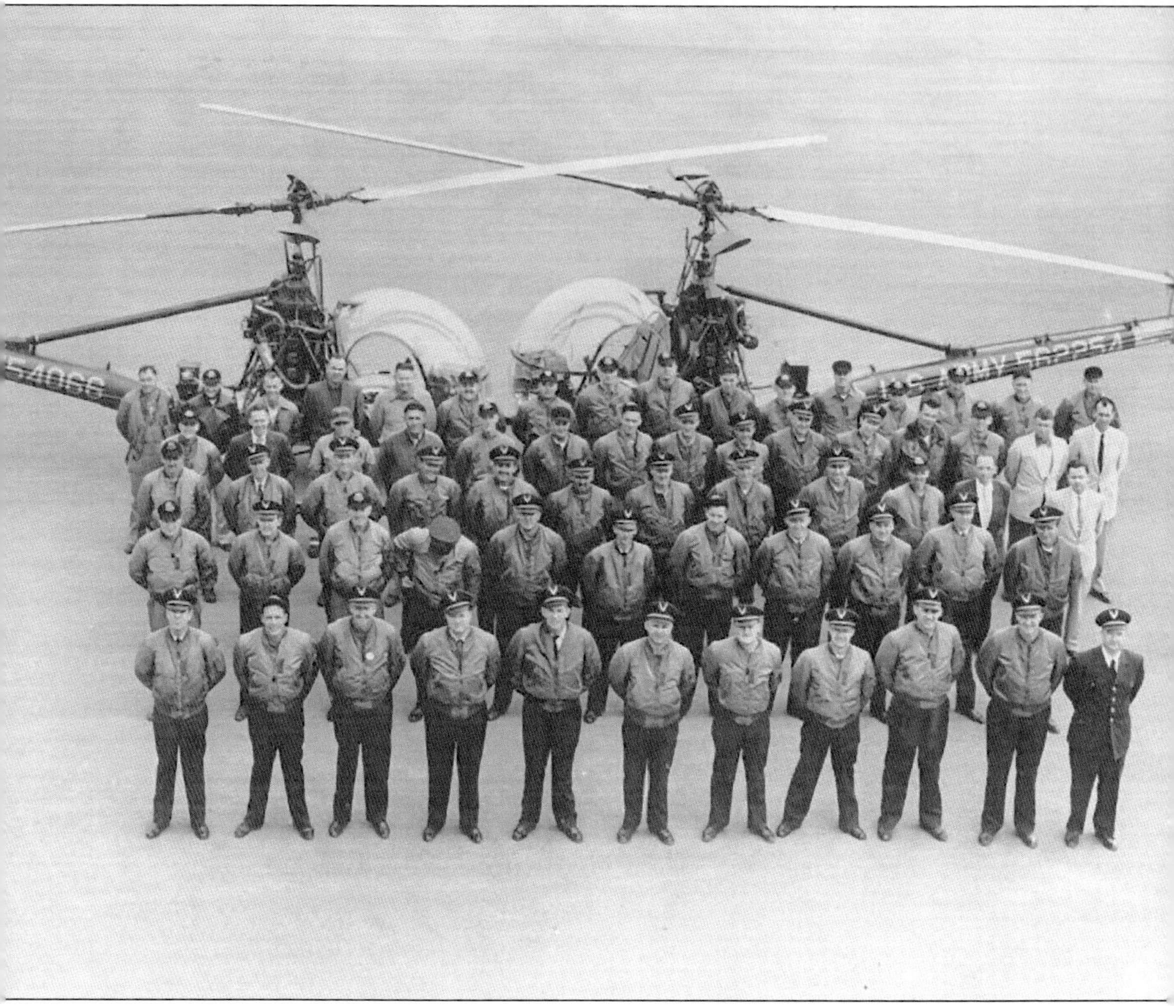

In 1963, Camp Wolters was renamed Fort Wolters permanently and served as the home for primary helicopter training during the Vietnam War. New Fort Wolters saw some 40,000 students from 30 countries go through the 20-week program conducted by the Southern Airways Company. In 1957, this was the Southern Airways Company personnel, including flight instructors, test pilots, and personnel instructors. (Courtesy of Boyce Ditto Library, Casper Collection.)

Six

The Fall and Rise of Mineral Wells 1973–Present

Mineral Wells rose as a health resort and spa town almost from the time it was founded in 1877. It is hard to believe how quickly word got out about its healing waters with curative powers. By the start of the 20th century, hotels, bathhouses, and water pavilions were everywhere. Casinos, horse racing, water, and donkey rides brought tourists—not just for their health, but for entertainment. In 1929, the *pièce de résistance*, the Baker Hotel, opened, and thousands of celebrities and regular folk flocked to Mineral Wells to take the water cure and be pampered by the hotel's staff and the town residents.

In April 1941, Mineral Wells grew even larger and more important as the U.S. Army opened Camp Wolters under the command of Brig. Gen. William H. Simpson. Camp Wolters became the largest induction center during World War II, with thousands of soldiers stationed there on their way to both theaters of operation.

Then in 1951, Mineral Wells felt its first fall when Camp Wolters was decommissioned and became Wolters Air Force Base. But in 1956, Camp Wolters came back stronger than ever as the primary helicopter training base during the Vietnam War, and in 1963, it became a permanent fort.

Throughout all these ups and downs, Mineral Wells remained a hub of tourist activity. In 1973, however, shortly before Fort Wolters closed for the last time, the Baker Hotel closed its doors, and the tourist industry failed.

Another rise was on the horizon when an oil and gas boom in the area began to take place in the late 1970s, but this was short lived and collapsed in 1983.

After that, Mineral Wells became fallow ground for both tourism and the petroleum industry as many oil field service companies closed and motels and restaurants failed, but the Barnett Shale became a practical source of gas around 2000, putting Mineral Wells back on the map.

At the same time, the tourist industry began expanding, new motels were built, and area attractions were developed. The hope of the town is that the Baker Hotel will rise as a phoenix from its ashes and perhaps become a destination as it was a century before. Moving toward that goal, Mineral Wells is progressing as a modern Texas town, and it still celebrates its heritage each year with the Crazy Water Festival on the second Saturday in October.

The landscape of Mineral Wells looking south from Union Hill Cemetery Road shows the beauty of the Pinto Hills, with the Baker Hotel standing prominently in the center of the photograph and West Mountain to the left. This is the view tourists fall in love with. It is the beauty through which

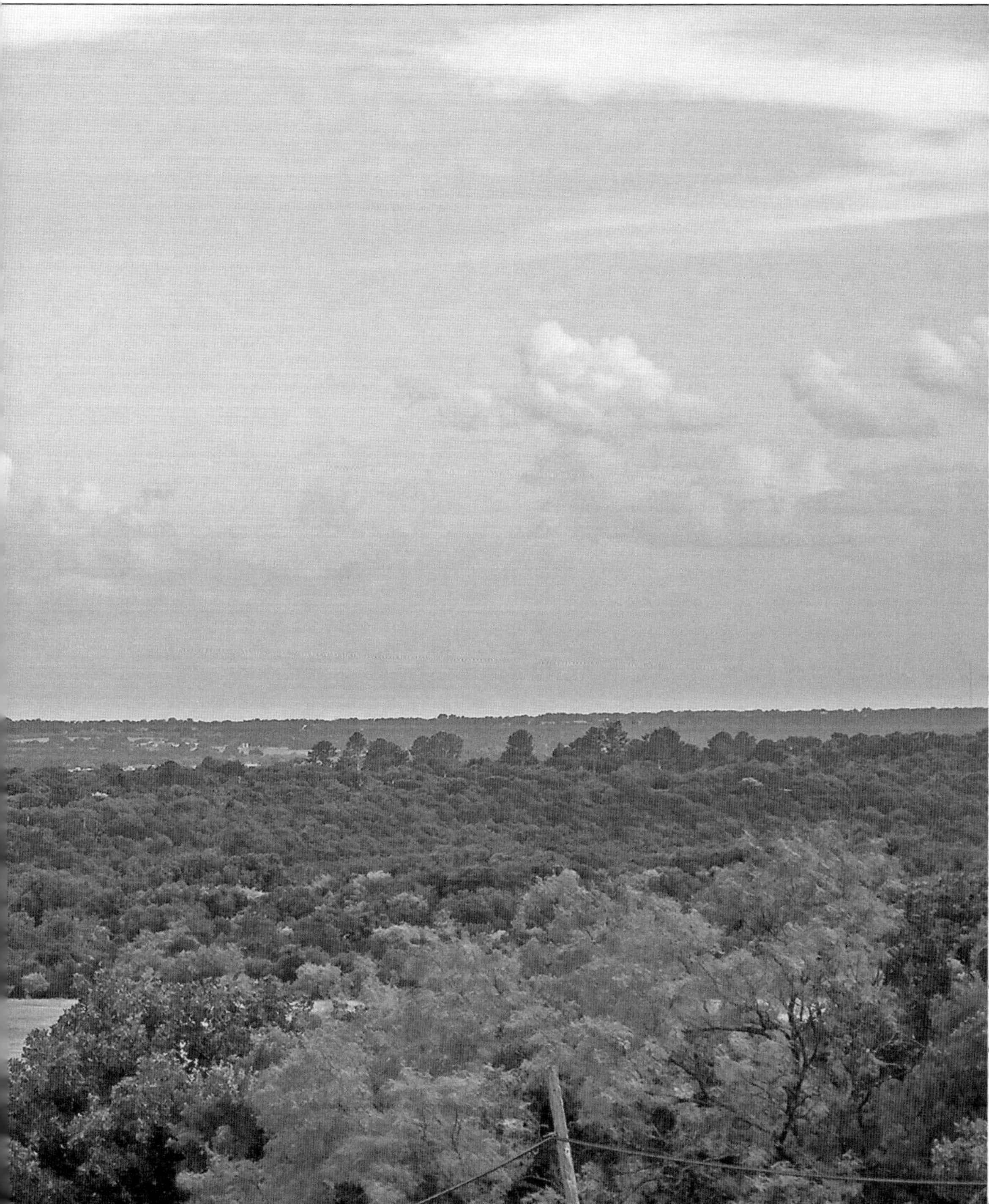

bicyclists and motorcyclists revel in as they ride along the roads of the area. This picturesque setting is typical Mineral Wells and the North Texas Hill Country. (Photograph by Raf Seibert.)

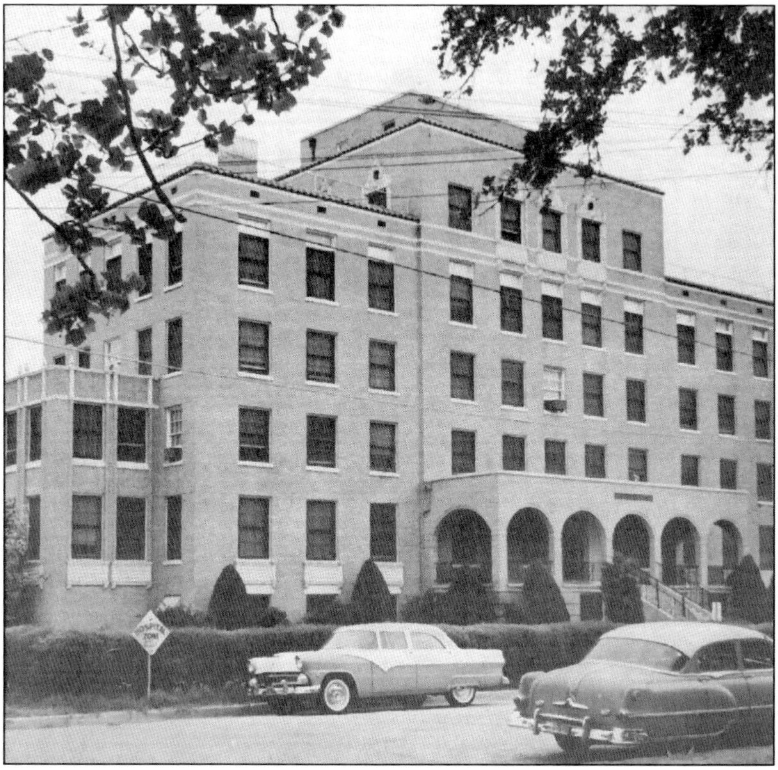

The Mineral Wells Clinic was built in 1927. In 1931, the Holy Sisters of Nazareth purchased the 46-bed facility for $135,000 and moved into the top floor of the building to live with and minister to the patients of the Nazareth Hospital. The hospital was closed in the mid-1960s. (Courtesy of Lou Hayes Warren.)

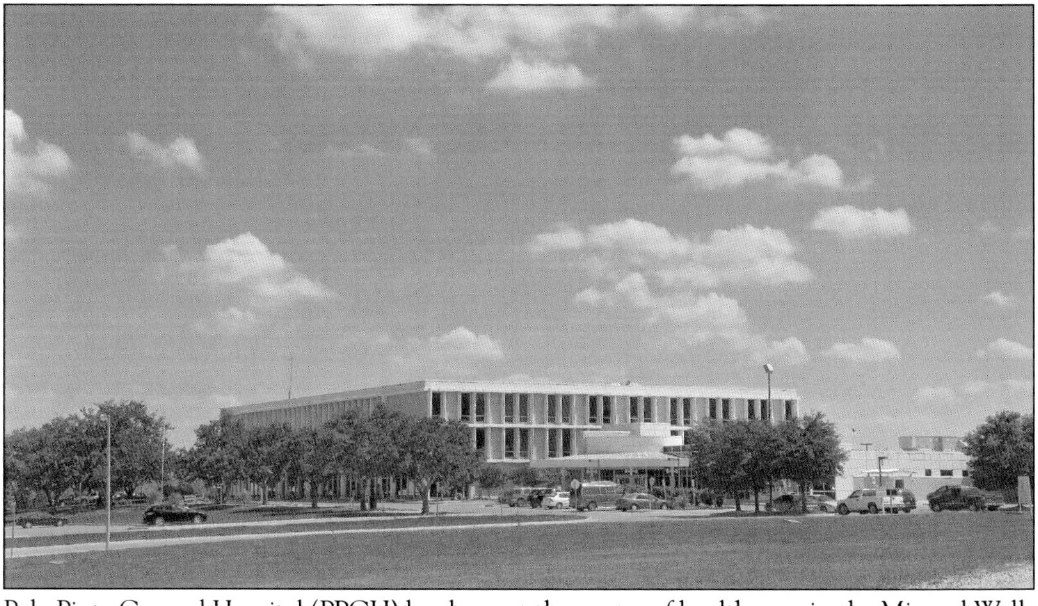

Palo Pinto General Hospital (PPGH) has been at the center of health care in the Mineral Wells area and Palo Pinto County since it opened in 1970. Inspired and supported by the community, PPGH's mission is to promote optimal health care for the entire community by providing customer-centered, quality service. The 99-bed hospital's list of services is diverse and ever-growing, including a fitness and rehabilitation center, radiology services, day surgery, emergency room, mobile clinic, and rural health clinics. (Photograph by Raf Seibert.)

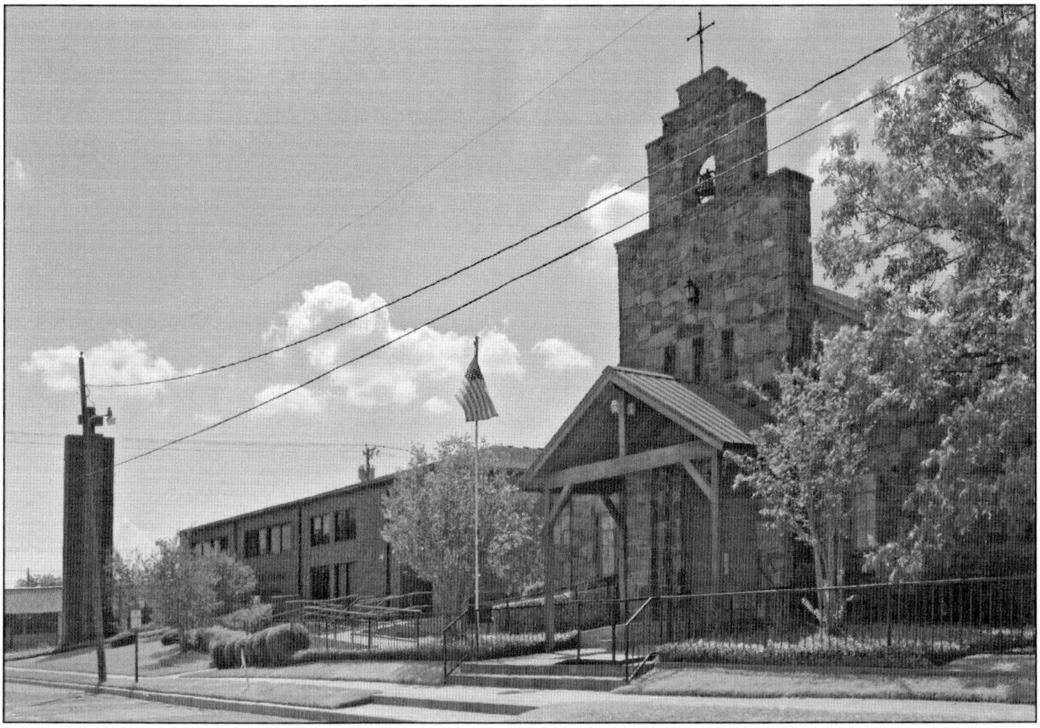

In the early 1900s, a Roman Catholic priest from St. Stephen's parish in Weatherford came by train each Sunday to hold services in the home of the Busey family. Around 1906, funds were raised for the construction of a small frame church, halfway up West Mountain on Northwest Third Street. At this time, Rev. P. J. Cussick from St. Stephen's Catholic Church in Weatherford began to serve the new mission church in Mineral Wells. In 1952, Bishop Thomas K. Gorman placed the Weatherford and Mineral Wells churches under the care of the Society of the Catholic Apostate, commonly known as the Pallotine Fathers. In February 1960, Fr. John Nagle was appointed as the first pastor of Our Lady of Lourdes Church. Here is both the old (right) and the new (left) church. (Photograph by Raf Seibert.)

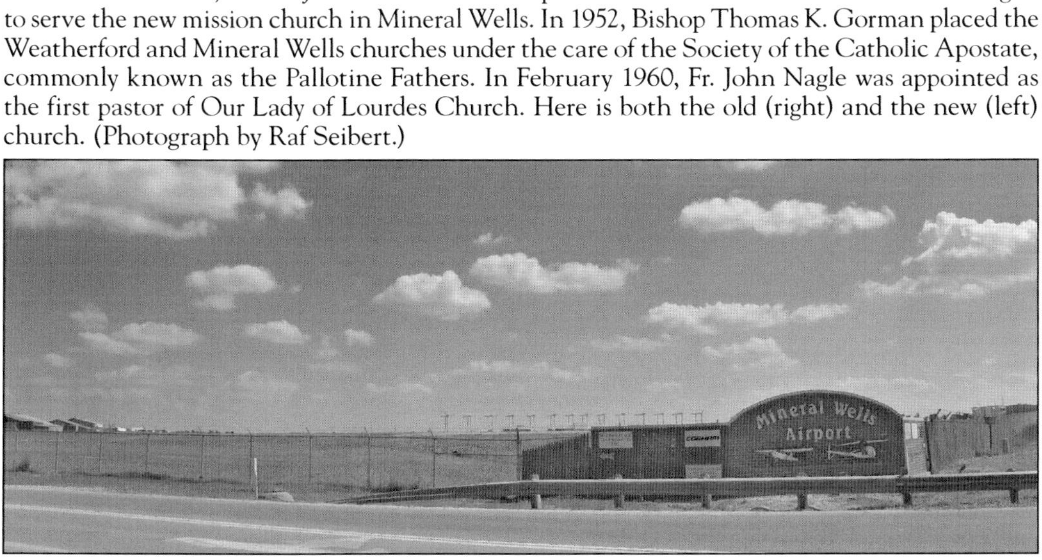

Mineral Wells Municipal Airport is a full-service, fixed-base operator that is conveniently located just outside the Dallas–Fort Worth International Airport terminal control area. The airport's Avgas is competitively priced, and it offers volume discounts for Jet A. The Mineral Wells Municipal Airport received the Airport of the Year award from the Texas Department of Transportation. (Photograph by Raf Seibert.)

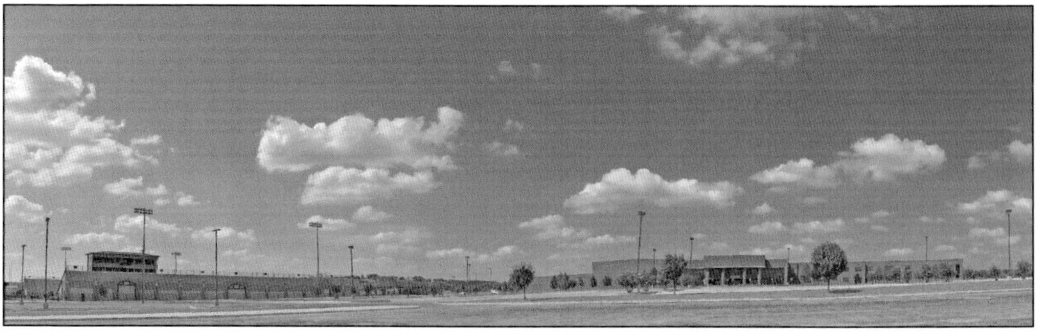

The new Mineral Wells High School opened in the fall of 2000. It is the newest of the public school buildings in Mineral Wells. A multipurpose complex for extracurricular activities, with a football stadium that seats up to 7,000, was completed in the fall of 2007. (Photograph by Raf Seibert.)

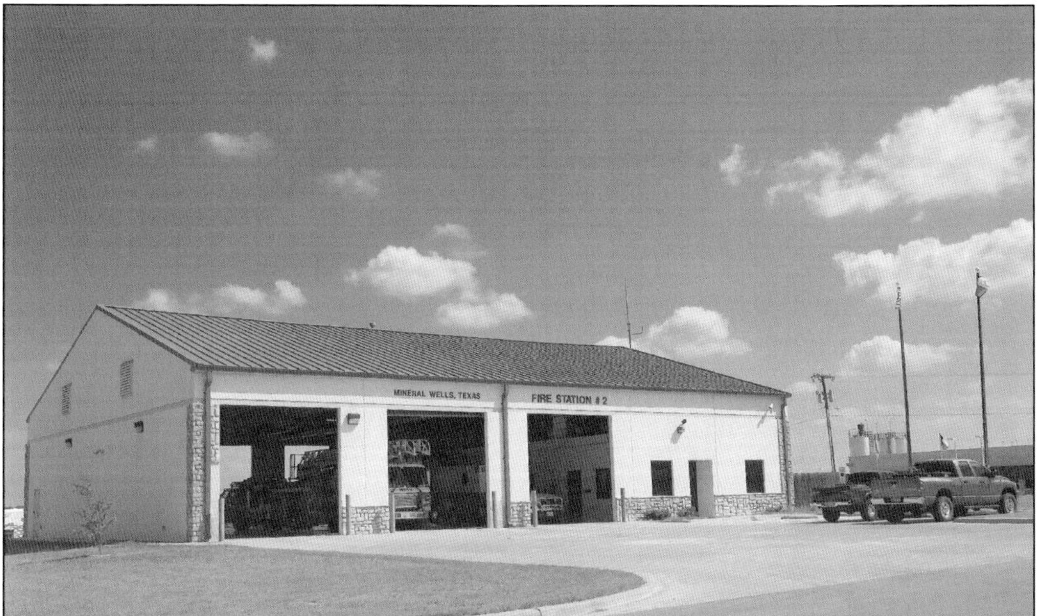

This new fire station on the east side of Mineral Wells shows how the town is growing and providing new facilities for its citizens. The town provides fire and EMS service within city limits and in certain areas of Palo Pinto County, along with fire suppression and rescue services, emergency medical calls, and fire prevention programs. (Photograph by Raf Seibert.)

This rock, on the north side of the Highway 180 between Weatherford and Mineral Wells, is the first welcome to Mineral Wells from the east. For more than 30 years, this rock has been painted over and over by residents as they welcome, congratulate, admire, or remind the citizens of things that are happening in Mineral Wells. (Photograph by Raf Seibert.)

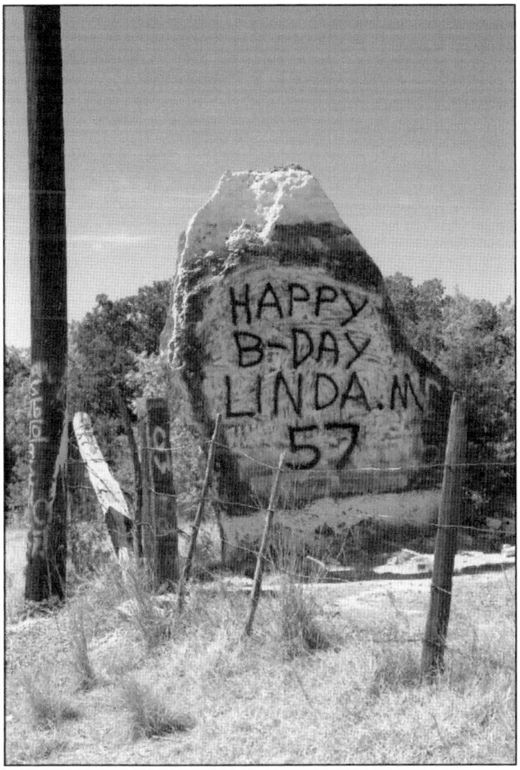

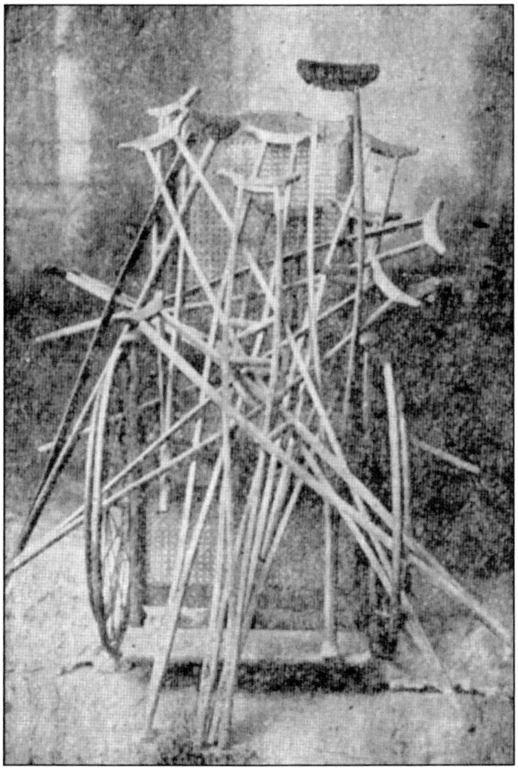

These crutches are reminders of the history of the town that was founded on water. Mineral Wells cannot promise a cure for a person's health, but it can promise a visit through time and a glorious trip through the beautiful hills of the North Texas Hill Country. (Courtesy of Lou Hayes Warren.)

BIBLIOGRAPHY

Clarke, Mary Whatley. *The Palo Pinto Story*. Fort Worth, TX: Manney, 1956.

Fowler, Gene. *Crazy Water: The Story of Mineral Wells and Other Texas Health Resorts*. Fort Worth, TX: TCU Press, 1991.

Gibson, Barbara Belding. *Painted Pole*. Austin, TX: Eakin Press, 2001.

Marshall, Doyle. *A Cry Unheard*. Aledo, TX: Annetta Valley Farm Press, 1990.

Palo Pinto Historical Association. *History of Palo Pinto County*. Dallas, TX: Taylor, 1978.

Palo Pinto Historical Association. *Painted Post Past—Palo Pinto County History 1857*. Dallas, TX: 2007.

Weaver, A. F. *Time Was in Mineral Wells*. Mineral Wells, TX: A. F. Weaver, 1975.

INDEX

Baker Hotel, 4, 29, 30, 71, 75–77, 83, 94, 103, 114, 119, 120
Baker, T. B., 75
Barber, G. P., 38
Birdwell, Mat, 40
Bush, George, 95, 97
Casper, Willie, 6, 117
Crazy Water Hotel, 8, 26, 63
Creighton, Thomas William "Tom," 8, 85, 98
Dismuke, Ed, 38, 39, 41, 43, 44
Camp/Fort Wolters, 8, 49, 60, 72, 77, 78, 93, 99, 101, 105–111, 113–119
Ditto, Boyce, 73
East Mountain, 2, 6, 12, 17, 21, 27, 31, 32, 38, 50, 51, 53, 62, 71, 72, 74, 83
Famous Water Company, 2, 39, 43–45
Gailey, James D. "Doc," 84
Galbraith, David G., 27
Gallagher, Pat, 6, 37
Green, G. C., 28
Green, T. J., 40
Griffith, D. W., 72
Harris, D. C., 54, 77, 96
Hayes, George Thomas, 29
Hayes, John Newton, 83
Hexagon House Hotel, 8, 27, 33, 47, 49, 61, 67, 106
Holmgreen, George, 72
Kessler, Carl, 93
Knight, Jack, 101, 104
Laverty, Jim, 28
Lynch, Armanda, 15, 18, 19, 25, 33
Lynch, James Alvis, 7, 8, 15, 17–21, 28, 33, 39
McCutcheon, Blanche, 83
McCutcheon, W. S., 69, 81
Milling, H. H., 70
Millsap Valley, 7, 15, 19, 30, 33
Mitchell, D. H., 92
Murray, Z. Z., 74
Pennsylvanian Period, 7–10, 12, 13, 85, 89
Perry, Dunman Jr., 85, 95–97
Pierce, Arizona, 17
Pratt Hotel Corporation, 99
Prisoner of War, 111
Richards, Frank, 30, 54
Sablosky, Ike, 82
Savage, Sam, 7, 8, 15–17
Seybold, Elmer, 79
Smith, Cicero, 6, 38, 39, 41, 45, 46, 95
Troop F, 8, 101, 103, 104, 106
Upham, Chester, 8, 39, 41, 85, 97
Wallace, William A. A. "Bigfoot," 7, 15
Welcome Sign, 71, 72
West Mountain, 12, 39, 41, 63, 72, 81, 120, 123
Wolters, Jacob F., 101, 105

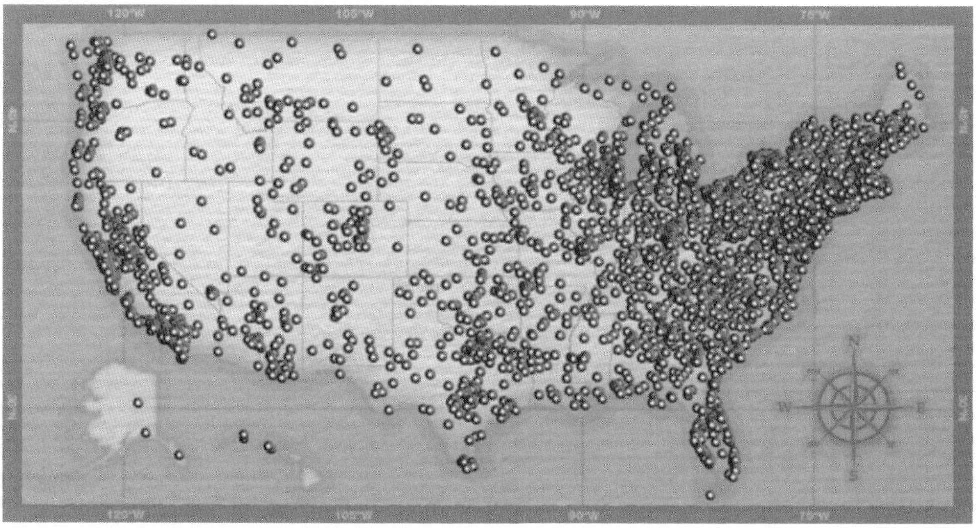